"The Freibergs have written the Manifesto every leader wants their people to embrace! This book has the power to change your life and transform your company. Read it, practice it, and hand it to everyone who has an impact on your business. These Seven Choices provide an ultrafresh approach to creating a culture of commitment and accountability!"

—Marcus Buckingham, author of *Go Put Your Strengths to Work*

"The Freibergs have hit another home run with *BOOM!* People are our most important resource—our competitive advantage. Every leader asks, 'How can we motivate our people?' Kevin and Jackie get to the heart of what it takes to create engaged and results-oriented team members—one choice at a time."

—Jay Welker, Executive VP, Head of Private Client Services, Wells Fargo

"The Freibergs' principles have been key in helping us make our corporate promise to customers, 'With Us It's Personal,' a reality. We are convinced that only engaged associates at store level can deliver this promise. This book inspires individuals to engage by realizing the value of their life at work, the freedom of personal choices, and the power to make a difference every day. It's a companywide must read!"

—Mary Sammons, CEO, Rite-Aid

"In their prior literary hits, *Nuts* and *Guts*, the Freibergs provided breakthrough leadership insights for students of corporate culture. In *BOOM!* Jackie and Kevin have cracked the code for surviving, thriving, and engaging in the new world of work. Their Seven Choices are timely and important."

—Steve Harrison, President, Chairman, Lee, Hecht, Harrison

"This book is inspiring and challenging, it brings to life the freedom in personal choice, the value of finding more life at work, and the significance of making a difference. The Freibergs place the power of personal and professional success in the right hands—YOURS."

—Mike Murphy, President and CEO, Sharp Healthcare

"In the fast-paced realities of the global economy—when faced with instability, changing requirements, and uncertainty—action is required to make a difference. Every leader wants to recruit and motivate results-oriented people. The Freibergs hit the target on what it takes to lead and inspire a culture of engaged and resilient people who work hard to blow the doors off business-as-usual."

—Lt. Col. Eric C. Hastings, Director, Marine Corps Recruiter School

"You can't change your boss, your employees, or the team, but you can change yourself. If you're serious about becoming more engaged, and making a difference, read the Freibergs' Manifesto for a new lease on what it takes to achieve lasting success at work. At the end of the day, YOU are the difference."

—Marilyn Carlson Nelson, Chairman and CEO, Carlson Companies

"This is the Freibergs' best book yet. It empowers you to enjoy your life at work and make the most of turning a job into a career. It's the prescription for more successful employees, better companies, and happier customers."

—Don Peppers and Martha Rogers, PhD, coauthors of *Return on Customer* and the *One to One* series of books on managing customer value

"Every leader wants the secret recipe for motivating people. The Freibergs get to the heart of what it takes to create engaged and results-oriented employees— CHOICES—one at a time. A must-read for anyone who wants to know what it takes to be fully engaged at work."

—Richard Floersch, Executive VP, Worldwide HR, McDonald's Corporation

"The Freibergs have done it again with their newest Manifesto for blowing the doors off business-as-usual. The message here is all about realizing the value of engagement, understanding the impact of personal choices, and unleashing the passion to wake up and make a difference every day. If you've ever wondered what it takes to achieve lasting success at work, this book is for you."

—Tom Reddin, CEO, LendingTree

"I love this book. I absolutely love it! *BOOM!* is a no-nonsense, kick-in-the-seat-of-the-pants, wake-up-and-smell-the-coffee declaration of the one thing that matters most to the quality of our daily lives—our personal choices. Choice is the glue that binds us to our actions, and it unleashes our internal drive to do what's necessary to make things happen. In their Manifesto, Jackie and Kevin Freiberg dedicate themselves to supporting us in making the choices we must make to fully use our gifts and talents. They entertain, educate, and inspire with compelling stories, straight talk, and practical examples. I implore you to choose to read this book and choose to put it to use. That choice will be richly rewarded."

—Jim Kouzes, coauthor of the best-selling
The Leadership Challenge and *A Leader's Legacy*

"If you are unhappy with your job and with your work environment, there are basically three choices: fix it, change it, or leave it. Whatever decision you take, it is your personal decision. The Freibergs remind us in their book, *BOOM!*, that we have to take personal responsibility for every situation we are in, and, no matter how difficult the situation, the way out always starts with understanding that the first step has to come from yourself and not from others. Taking responsibility, engaging yourself, and getting involved not only will help you to be more satisfied at work, it also will help to live a more rewarding private life."

—Marcel Kiessling, President, Heidelberg Americas, Inc.

"Are you here to serve or be served? If you've often wondered about why they won't let you do the remarkable, the Freibergs have some powerful answers."

—Seth Godin, author, *The Dip*

"Life is incredibly short, and the Freibergs challenge each and every one of us to make sure that our lives count in everything we do. It's a phenomenal piece of writing that begs the question, 'what are you doing to take personal responsibility for your life and success at work?' And it reminds us that the only limitations we have are those that we place upon ourselves. It's a must-read!"

—Hugh "Goldie" Gouldthorpe, Senior Vice President,
"Head Cheerleader," Owens & Minor

"This book inspires and challenges everyone to step up and engage. It's about realizing the value of life at work, the freedom to make personal choices, the power to make a difference every day. A must-read for anyone who wants to know what it takes to be fully engaged at work. 'Engagement is a choice. I choose to be fully engaged!'"

—Barry Crystal, VP Retail Division, Sony of Canada Ltd.

"This book is a must-read for all who work in retail stores where the quality of the interaction between the employee and the customer can either build the brand or damage it. The Freibergs' Manifesto will show you how to become fully engaged and make a difference in the lives of your customers by delivering great experiences, every day."

—Lester Nazareth, National Customer
Experience Manager, Sony of Canada Ltd.

"If you improve the process by which you make a choice, you will exponentially increase your wealth and influence. The greatest accomplishments you've ever had can be traced to a great choice you made at a critical time. This book will give you the process to leverage the power of choice into success. In this breezy but helpful book, the Freibergs deliver with easy-to-act-on ideas and their spirited and irreverent voice. Make the choice to read it, and put yourself on course."

—Tim Sanders, author, *Love Is the Killer App:
How to Win Business and Influence Friends*

"In a world of downsizing and outsourcing, workplace bullying, and companies and managers that don't tell the truth, it is easy to get discouraged and cynical. *BOOM!* reminds us that none of us have to be victims and that each of us, by how we approach our work and our colleagues, can choose to live a fully engaged, joyful, and productive life. In a book filled with inspiring stories, the Freiberg's challenge us to change our world by changing how we think."

—Jeffrey Pfeffer, Professor, Stanford Business School, and author of
The Human Equation: Building Profits by Putting People First

"Drs. Kevin and Jackie Freibergs' book is meant to shake up people, most of whom go about their jobs in a very pedantic way. It makes you think and almost forces you to reevaluate how you live your life both in official and personal spheres. It offers clear direction peppered with interesting examples for bringing passion to work and being engaged. It not only makes you feel good but is also highly productive for business leaders, who in their own interest must find ways to engage the people within their organization as well as around the world."

—Ravi Kant, Managing Director, Tata Motors Ltd., India

"This book puts the spotlight on the most significant aspect of leadership—the choices we make, including the choice of ownership. Ownership for action and ownership for the results of those actions. The approach is palpable and not theoretical—an authentic distillation of the 'choice' manifesto."

—Vinita Bali, Managing Director,
Britannia Industries Ltd., Bangalore, India

"The Freibergs' unique ideas and concepts always refresh us with the truth about life and management. *BOOM!* is filled with profound choices to make the world around us a better place, through personal and corporate leadership. A must-read!"

—Kouichi Sumino, Chairman and CEO,
Autobacs Seven Co., Ltd., Japan

"It's about time someone wrote a book about every workplace I've ever seen! 'Dead People Working' so accurately describes the syndrome, but the Manifesto even more precisely describes the remedies. As one who's tried to practice servant leadership for many years, I was reenergized and refocused by reading the entertaining trials, tribulations, and successes others have had on their journeys through work and life. This is a must-read for the newest entry-level employee to the sagest of CEOs!"

—Jeff Bowman, Fire Chief, Retired, Cities of Anaheim, San Diego, Oceanside

"Engagement with our ChiliHead employees and the 1 million customers that we serve every day is what will determine the success of our brand. Our restaurant leaders know that the curtain goes up every day at 11 a.m. and we don't have the luxury of a 'dress rehearsal'. *BOOM!* is a call to action for anyone who wants to make a difference as a leader."

—Todd Diener, President, Chili's Grill & Bar

"The Freibergs have delivered a message that will catapult individuals, companies, and America's global competitive culture to perhaps unprecedented levels of success and fulfillment. It invites—no, it demands—individuals to become the CEO of 'Me, Inc.' It's about making individual choices and seizing the opportunity to personally lead ourselves and our companies to breakthrough levels of performance. Every individual who wants to put their signature on their performance will absolutely love what they learn from this book. It's one of the very few I would put on the must-read list for those committed to leaving it all on the field."

—Allen M. Fredrickson, MCE, President/CEO, Signature Performance

BOOM!

7 CHOICES FOR BLOWING THE DOORS OFF BUSINESS-AS-USUAL

KEVIN AND JACKIE FREIBERG

THOMAS NELSON
Since 1798

NASHVILLE   DALLAS   MEXICO CITY   RIO DE JANEIRO   BEIJING

Published in Nashville, Tennessee, by Thomas Nelson. Thomas Nelson is a trademark of Thomas Nelson, Inc.

Thomas Nelson, Inc. titles may be purchased in bulk for educational, business, fund-raising, or sales promotional use. For information, please e-mail SpecialMarkets@ThomasNelson.com.

Library of Congress Cataloging-in-Publication Data

Freiberg, Kevin, 1958–

    BOOM! : seven choices for blowing the doors off business-as-usual / by Kevin and Jackie Freiberg.
       p. cm.
    Includes bibliographical references (p. 276) and index.
    ISBN 978-1-5955-5116-0
    ISBN 978-1-5955-5134-4 (IE)
    1. Success in business–Psychological aspects. 2. Employee motivation. I. Freiberg, Jackie, 1963– II. Title.
    HF5386.F772 2007
    650.1–dc22

                                  2007026464

Printed in the United States of America

08 09 10 11 12 13 RRD 10 9 8 7 6

To Herb Kelleher and Colleen Barrett,
two of the world's most beloved leaders; gutsy freedom fighters
who inspired the greatest success story in the history of commercial
aviation. You have been *indespensable* to the global airline industry,
indespensable to the people of Southwest Airlines,
and *indespensable* to us as mentors and friends.

Thank you for showing us
how to blow the doors off business-as-usual!

CONTENTS

INTRODUCTION

YOU ARE DESIGNED TO CHOOSE . . . DEFINED BY CHOICE

The freedom to choose may be the most powerful attribute and precious resource you have in your life. It shapes who you become, how you express yourself, the success you achieve, and your influence in the world. You are a product of your choices, not your conditions. Your choices will determine whether you become a person who is truly indispensable or one who is hardly missed.

CHOICE #1

BE A PLAYER, NOT A BYSTANDER

Extraordinary Happens When Ordinary People Do Whatever It Takes

In the game of life, there are players and those who shrink from their God-given abilities. Players charge onto the field with passion, energy, and a desire to win—sometimes they get their hands dirty, their faces sweaty, and their bodies bloody and bruised by giving their all to the game. Blowing the doors off business-as-usual and coming to work fully alive starts with understanding what makes a "player" a player.

CONTENTS

We wrote the book you are now holding in your hands because first and foremost, we (the authors) needed to read it. Do we get overly critical of people? Do we play the blame game? Do we fail to accept responsibility for our "bonehead" moves? Do we overemphasize the problem instead of being part of the solution? Do we fall prey to the victim mentality? Do we close our hearts off to other people and close our minds off to new opportunities? Do we exhibit the symptoms of dead people working?

The answer to all of these questions and many more—embarrassingly—is an emphatic YES! If you are human, we suspect that you wrestle with some of the same issues.

If you want to blow the doors off business-as-usual, stop doing the things that derail you from being a force for positive change in the lives of others, and do the things that will make you come alive at work, this book is for you. We want you to have the courage to think BIG and act BOLD. We want you to be an integral part of creating a place where impassioned people come to work fully engaged, knowing they are going to be part of something special. We want you to play a significant role in creating a place where impassioned customers drive away turned-on and evangelistic about the experience you create for them. We want to help you win more decisively and be able to look back over your life with fewer regrets. We want you to make a mark in the world and know that the world has taken you seriously.

> "THE BEST DAY OF YOUR LIFE IS THE ONE IN WHICH YOU DECIDE YOUR LIFE IS YOUR OWN. NO APOLOGIES OR EXCUSES. NO ONE TO LEAN ON, RELY ON, OR BLAME. THE GIFT OF LIFE IS YOURS; IT IS AN AMAZING JOURNEY; AND YOU ALONE ARE RESPONSIBLE FOR THE QUALITY OF IT."
>
> —DAN ZADRA, FOUNDER AND CREATIVE DIRECTOR OF COMPENDIUM, INC.

From time to time as you read this book, you might get the distinct feeling that we are going for your jugular vein, but *don't be mistaken*— we are reaching for our own jugulars as well. That is because we are passionate about the principles that fill the pages of this book. We feel that if our organizations are going to BOOM for the better, then we *all* need to become more accountable and do a better job of assuming responsibility for our lives. So we do not stand above you; we sit beside you. We write as partners in your success, who are trying to practice accountability and engagement in our own lives as we encourage you to do so in yours. Our desire is to be the kind of players we've met and written about in this book.

BOOM! speaks to *you* as an individual contributor, whether you are the CEO or working on the front line. You matter, because the creation of a phenomenal culture is never unidirectional. A booming culture is about great people throughout the organization, folks who are inspired and are absolutely convinced that the culture/success of the organization is the *will of the people* as much as it is the will of the CEO. That means *your* will and *your* choices. This book also speaks to *you* as a leader who is looking for something gritty and substantive that will inspire your people to stop taking orders and start taking charge—something you can practice and teach that will yield a significant return on investment. Let this book fuel your fire.

As you read on, please resist the temptation to say, "Man, my boss needs to read this." Or, "My team needs to get this book. Or, "The XYZ team or department needs to read this!" You may be absolutely right, but you will also be doing what the central message of the book cautions against—shifting responsibility. If there is a mantra that runs throughout these pages, it is this: *"So you're not the CEO—make a difference anyway."* As you will learn, you can't change your boss, your people, or the XYZ team, but you can change yourself. If you are serious about becoming more engaged and being a difference maker, keep the mirror in front of *you*. Don't depend on others to determine your success at work; at the end of the day *you* are the difference.

> **YOU WERE PUT ON THIS EARTH FOR A PURPOSE— A PURPOSE THAT GIVES MEANING TO YOUR LIFE AND TO THE LIVES OF THOSE YOU TOUCH.**

We believe that you can indeed move a flawed organization toward excellence by becoming a pocket of excellence within it, by *choosing* to lead wherever you are planted! You were put on this earth for a purpose—a purpose that gives meaning to your life and to the lives of those you touch. Remove the obstacles, and you'll feel a sense of fulfillment and joy that—once experienced—you'll never want to let go of—making a difference is addictive.

There is a revolution underway;
it's a revolution of men and women
who refuse to be victims and who choose
to take charge of their lives at work —
a revolution that will blow the
doors off business-as-usual.

INTRODUCTION

YOU ARE DESIGNED TO CHOOSE ...
DEFINED BY CHOICE

Put fifty people in a room. Ask them to identify the movers and shakers in their organizations and what these individuals have in common. We guarantee that there will be at least one common denominator that cuts across every person—they believe in the power of ONE person to make a difference, to be a force for positive change. It's a belief that is expressed in the passion and energy they bring to work each day, as well as the small pockets of success they create wherever they go. These people are fully present and thoroughly engaged in what they are doing. They don't let unfortunate circumstances or limitations drag them down, and they don't let negative people influence how they are going to act. Their lives are simply too full and their energy far too precious to waste on self-pity or emotionally draining acts of recrimination. They set the bar of performance higher for themselves than others would for them, because no one knows their capabilities better than they do. This is why they've earned a reputation as "go to" people among their customers and coworkers, and differentiated themselves from most everyone else in the workforce.

These movers and shakers are ordinary people like you—like *us*—and we all CAN have extraordinary influence and achieve extraordinary things when we choose to be accountable and take responsibility for our lives. Fully awake, fully checked-in, fully alive, and firing on all cylinders, these players focus forward, find a solution, and get it done. Their internal code of conduct is "whatever it takes," and their vivacity—their liveliness—is absolutely contagious. Check it out!

PLAY While You Work

When we're not in San Diego, our home away from home is Sundance, Utah, the one-of-a-kind ski resort and arts community founded by Robert Redford. If you're looking for a breeding ground for passion and "aliveness" at work, check into the Sundance Ski School. Francis Ford Coppola once said, "If you love something, you'll bring so much of yourself to it that it will create your future." You would be hard-pressed to find a group of people who bring more of themselves—heart, mind, and spirit—to work than the staff at the Sundance Ski School.

Already incredibly talented skiers, no one at Sundance gives the impression that they have "arrived." Many of them jump at the chance to spend a morning fine-tuning their skills with Scott Nyman, former ski school director, and Jerry Warren, director of Mountain Operations. And who wouldn't? Nyman has trained a son who is currently on the U.S. Ski Team, and Warren is recognized among ski instructors around the world as the guru's guru. Both men are fanatical about finding new ways to effectively transfer their skills to their students. Spend an hour or two with any one of their instructors and you quickly get the feeling that they want you to fall in love—with skiing and with Sundance.

What wows us about the team at Sundance is their desire to create a uniquely customized experience for the people they are teaching. Compared to other major resorts, the facilities are small and understated yet comfortable, but the place buzzes with a spirit of hospitality that is unprecedented.

Consider our six-year-old, Dylan, who is wild at heart and loves to ski as fast as he can, straight down the hill, but is *not* very excited about turning, which just slows him down. The ski instructors got together and created some tickets that read PLEASE SLOW DOWN and TURN MORE, PLEASE for Dylan to give out to other violators on the hill. Imagine a six-year-old coming up behind you, making the sound of a police siren, pulling you over, and issuing you a ticket. Of course, good officers must "role-model" the behavior they are looking for in others, so Dylan found himself turning more as well. It was a creative and fun way to hold our son's attention and teach him at the same time. It was also the result of a cadre of instructors who weren't just going through the motions. The instructors at Sundance are alive, engaged, and passionate about doing whatever it takes to make the experience unforgettable.

One of the most seasoned of the team at Sundance is a character named Kim Francom. With shiny blond hair, deep blue eyes, and a big bushy mustache, Francom looks like he just came off the set of the epic western *Lonesome Dove*. Park yourself at the top of Sundance some morning before ski school starts and you're likely to see the fifty-two-year-old Francom just flying down the mountain, gleefully catching big

> ## "I CAN'T WAIT TO SEE HOW GOOD A DAY I CAN HAVE. YOU CAN'T HELP BUT NOT COME UP HERE WITHOUT A SMILE. AND IF YOU SEE SOMEONE WITHOUT A SMILE, GIVE 'EM YOURS."
>
> —KIM FRANCOM, SUNDANCE

air off a jump and making some of the prettiest, near-perfect turns you've ever seen. No fear, no hesitation, and no room for looking back, Francom lives life the way he skis—as an adventure. He approaches his job the same way.

What makes Kim Francom so unique? Among many things, he skis on one leg. He lost the lower half of his left leg when a rookie ski patrolman prematurely set off an avalanche above him that caused Francom to go down, wrapping his leg and just about everything else around a tree. The result: two broken femur bones, a shattered foot, a busted shoulder, and a cracked pelvis. Two years after the accident and twenty-seven surgeries later, the doctors still couldn't get the paralyzed leg to function. As Kim recalls matter-of-factly, "It was useless; it just got in the way. I asked them to amputate so I could get back to doing what I love—skiing, horseback riding, golfing, basketball, and being a hunting and fishing guide."

For many active outdoor types, this would've been the end. Life as they knew it would be over. Not for Kim Francom. He saw it as a choice: live fully and be alive, or be a victim of circumstances and let something inside of you die. Francom chose to be alive. At thirty-eight, competing against racers twenty years younger, he made the U.S. Disabled Ski Team and won the overall World Championship title in 1990. Since then Kim has helped hundreds of children and adults with physical challenges overcome adversity—he helped launch the Disabled Skiing Program at Park City, Utah, which now serves over forty-five hundred kids a year.

Impossible is a word that Kim Francom doesn't understand very well. Listen to him describe the courage of a young man—both blind and paraplegic—whom he taught to ski or the autistic child who spoke her first word when he got her on a horse, and it's hard not to be moved by the exuberance with which Francom lives life. He explained:

> When a kid climbs out of a wheelchair and goes 40 mph down a mountain on skis or takes control of a horse as they are out in the backcountry seeing an eagle or an elk for the first time in their natural environment, something extraordinary happens. All of a sudden that victory transfers into other aspects of their life. Rather than sitting on the couch, drinking beer or doing drugs and residing in a terminal state of self-pity, they develop the confidence to go back to school, get a job, and make a contribution that brings them a tremendous sense of pride.

He continued, "You become addicted to the joy on a kid's face when you watch them do something they thought would be impossible" (Interview with Kim Francom at Sundance, March 19, 2007).

The families of these children have come alive too. Parents who had no hope are now engaged and recreating with their kids. Looking out at the majestic splendor of Mount Timpanogos above Sundance, Francom says, "I can't wait to see how good a day I can have. You can't help but come up here with a smile. And if you see someone without a smile, give 'em yours."

Every one of the amazing individuals at Sundance is *engaged*. They are passionately focused on the job at hand and on the results they seek to achieve. They don't just show up for work; they give every ounce of discretionary effort they have. They don't separate work and life, because their love of their work is part of the fabric of their lives.

Imagine the possibilities if you and everyone in your organization brought the same level of passion and enthusiasm to your work as Kim Francom and the instructors at the Sundance Ski School do to theirs.

BOOM!

If you want to see Kim Francom ski
or watch a brief interview with him,

go to **freibergs.com/boom** *and type
the word* **Kim** *in the BOOM! box.*

Now, some of you are probably thinking, *It's easy to be engaged at work when you ski for a living. Who wouldn't get pumped up if you could figure out a way to make your passion pay?* So, what about those who are caught up in the routine of a dull, ordinary job?

Dance in the Streets

It is Christmas on the corner of Westminster and Dorrance Streets in the heart of downtown Providence, Rhode Island. An exuberant crowd is gathered. Above the applause and honking horns, you can hear one fan yell, "Oh, I love him!" and another shouts, "Whoa baby!" Who's drawing all this attention? He has the swivel of John Travolta, the shimmy of James Brown, the gyrations of Elvis, and the badge of the Providence Police Department. He is retired police officer Tony Lepore, the renowned "Dancing Cop," and he has turned directing traffic into a full-blown performance.

Picture a traffic cop dressed in police blues, white gloves, and an officer's cap in the middle of a busy intersection, dropping to his knees at red lights, whirling his arms like windmills, shaking his body, and

blowing his whistle to a rhythm that has astonished drivers and pedestrians for more than two decades. With a gun dangling in the holster on his right hip, Tony Lepore brings the meaning of "Dancin' in the Streets" to a whole new level. Traffic moves, and Lepore grooves.

People like Tony Lepore epitomize what it means to be alive and engaged at work. When he got bored of his standard, vanilla-flavored traffic duties in 1984, Lepore decided to shake things up with some fancy footwork, and the "Dancing Cop" was born. Four years after retiring in 1988, Mayor Vincent Cianci convinced Tony to come back and do his thing for two weeks during the holidays. He was such a hit then that Lepore has been doing the two-week gig every Christmas season since. Lepore's passion, energy, and creativity have earned him spots on *Dateline NBC*, CNN, *NBC Nightly News*, and even ESPN's *Plays of the Week*. He has also appeared live on *The Today Show*, *Good Morning America*, and *The Rosie O'Donnell Show*. Tony loves his job, and it shows.

Imagine the possibilities if you and everyone in your organization brought the same level of passion and enthusiasm to work as Tony Lepore does to the streets of Providence.

Rave About a Root Canal?

Unbelievable! That's what Kevin said when his dentist informed him that he was headed to the endodontist for a possible root canal. *Unbelievable!* That's what he thought when he walked out of endodontist Jack Pawlak's office after having an incredibly positive experience. How many people do you know who rave about getting a root canal? Here's Kevin's account of his experience with Dr. Pawlak:

Dr. Jack Pawlak, whom I met for the first time during this office visit, is a complete and certifiable nut—but he's a nut who loves his work. It shows in his remarkable approach to the patient, and it shows in his complete devotion to his work. While my tooth was extremely sensitive to cold and gave me some discomfort at night, I did not have a throbbing emergency on my hands. Even so, this busy endodontist was able to get me in for a consult within an hour of my dentist's referral.

After a five-minute wait in the reception area, I was escorted into the dental chair, where Dr. Pawlak was eagerly waiting for me. But before I could even sit down, he started firing questions at breakneck speed.

Dr. Pawlak's demeanor exemplified a cross between the comedic routines of the quick-witted Robin Williams and the sarcastic, in-your-face Don Rickles. When he asked me if the tooth in question had a crown, I said yes. He said, "Is it porcelain or gold?"

"Porcelain."

"Ahhh!" he said, "that's why I came to practice in California. Everyone wants those nice, white porcelain crowns. In the Midwest, where I grew up, it's always gold crowns. Why? Less long-term problems. Sixty-five percent of the porcelain crowns need a root canal within seven to ten years, you know. That's why I came to California—big bucks!"

I thought to myself, *Who is this guy?*

Jack Pawlak is brash, irreverent, unafraid to editorialize about other patients, and very direct—all in a charming way. He is absolutely passionate about his work. Pawlak immediately put me at ease and made me laugh. His stories were captivating and memorable—each designed to make a point that would educate and guide me. Three or four times during the course of our conversation, he pulled out a chart showing me the anatomy of a tooth. Each time he explained possible scenarios causing my pain. I quickly grew comfortable with his knowledge and confidence.

It was obvious that he was interested in thoroughly diagnosing the situation, because the questions kept coming, and each time I answered, he would pick up on little nuances. When I told him the pain was more evident when I was mountain-biking, he said, "That's because you're pumping more blood into the sensitive area, causing more throbbing to occur." When I told him that both the top and bottom molars hurt, he told me it was due to a nerve that wrapped around the back of my mouth. He analogized, "If I stick a knife in the back of your neck, you feel it in your toe. Why? Because the nerve goes from your neck to your toe!"

At the end of the initial consultation, Dr. Pawlak said, "Look, it's up to you, but if it were me, I wouldn't do this root canal right away. I'd take some heavier-than-usual doses of ibuprofen and see if we can get the tooth calmed down.

"You're a bright guy," he said. "In a couple of days you'll know. If it still hurts, call me. I'll see you Saturday; I'll see you Sunday morning; I'll see you whenever you want—I'm here seven days a week. Just don't call me five hours before you get on an airplane; you'll need some time to let the tooth calm down before exposing it to high altitude."

Trying to match Dr. Pawlak's wit and sarcasm, I said, "What kind of nut works seven days a week?"

"Hey, man, what can I say?" he answered. "I love what I do. Besides, I only work with four dentists, and I like yours. If I didn't like him and I didn't like you, it would take you six months to get in and see me, and even then I might refer you to someone else."

Unfortunately, three days later the pain was still there, so I made an appointment to have the root canal. Again, the wait in the reception area was less than five minutes. When I sat down in the chair, Dr. Pawlak explained exactly what he was hoping to find when he got inside the tooth. Then he grabbed my cheek and gave it a little jolt as he inserted the needle for the novocaine shot—I didn't feel a thing.

From that point until the procedure was complete, Dr. Pawlak explained—play-by-play—exactly what he was doing and how long it would take. He said, "I'm in the first canal, and we've got two more minutes to finish it." Sure enough, at the end of two minutes, he was done, and we were on to the next phase of the procedure. The whole process was very educational, reassuring, and—quite frankly—entertaining. When the procedure was complete, Dr. Pawlak demanded, "I want to hear from you by eight o'clock tomorrow morning to see how you're doing."

What Dr. Pawlak knows is what everyone who is truly alive at work knows: it's better to be a player than a bystander. He doesn't just sit back and wait for the mouths to march in and the checks to clear. He's more interested in your teeth than you are, even if he doesn't feel your pain. For him, it's not about watching; it's about running out on the playing field and carrying the ball to make the score. He's made the conscious choice to play the game as hard and as fully engaged as he can. The result is that he's rarely tired or burned-out; instead, he's energized by the relationships with the people he's helping. In the game of life, he's chosen to be a player.

Imagine the possibilities if you and everyone in your organization chose to be a player too, if you chose to live and work at the same level of passion and engagement as Jack Pawlak does. Jack has turned the regular expectations for his profession upside-down, making a lasting difference in the lives of his many patients.

What do these employees and professionals in widely varying jobs—Kim Francom and the ski instructors of the Sundance Ski School; Tony Lepore, the Rhode Island traffic cop; and Dr. Jack Pawlak, endodontist—all have in common? Clients automatically gravitate to them because they are incredibly good at what they do and visibly excited about their work. Colleagues love to work with them because they have an invigorating spirit that is life-giving and hugely contagious. They're fully engaged in playing the game, they're making a difference, and they have built a reputation for being people other people can't live without. They are blowing the doors off business-as-usual.

Your Most Powerful Attribute—
the Freedom to Choose

Do the folks we just met ever have a bad day? Yes. Are there some parts of their jobs that they don't like very much? Probably. Do they periodically need to get away from it all and recharge? You bet. Are they human? Absolutely. But even on a bad day these individuals bring something extraordinary to the game—not always because they *feel* like it, but rather because they *choose* to make a difference regardless of how they feel.

Kim Francom chose to get on with his life and use his disability to make a difference in the lives of children with their own disabilities. Directing traffic and performing root canals can become mundane and routine. Not for Tony Lepore and Dr. Jack Pawlak. They aren't just going through the motions. They choose to be mentally, physically, emotionally, and spiritually engaged in their work. They have decided to turn the tedious into something spontaneous and alive!

THE DIFFERENCE BETWEEN ORDINARY PEOPLE AND EXTRAORDINARY PEOPLE IS *CHOICE*.

What's the difference between the people we've described and others? They have *decided* to make their lives count. They have *chosen* to use their gifts and talents and life experiences to make a mark in the world. The difference between ordinary people and extraordinary people is *choice*.

The freedom to choose may be the most powerful attribute and precious resource you have in your life. It shapes who you become, how you express yourself, the success you achieve, and the influence you have in the world. In his classic work *Man's Search for Meaning*, Holocaust survivor Victor Frankl describes life inside the Nazi concentration camps during World War II. Frankl lived in a number of different death camps during a three-year period, including Auschwitz, Theresienstadt, and Dachau. While he survived the experience, his wife, mother, and father did not. He observed that under the most terrifying conditions, some prisoners acted like "swine" while others behaved like "saints." "Man has both potentialities within himself," Frankl said. "Which one is actualized depends on decisions but not on conditions" (134). This is good news, because it means you are not some sophisticated "Pavlovian dog," relegated to living a life that is solely dictated by the sum total of your past conditioning. You can *choose* how to respond

to every difficult circumstance you ever face with your boss, your job, your coworkers, and your customers. You can choose how much of yourself you will give to your job, or how little. The freedom to choose is yours alone to leverage or not. No one can grant it to you, and no one can take it away from you.

By the time you lay your head on the pillow at the end of this day, you will have made hundreds of choices that will affect the quality of your life. The nature of these choices will determine how much freedom you have and the degree to which you live an empowered life. Many of the choices you make today will enable you to control your destiny, and some of them will put your destiny in the hands of others. Choice is essential to freedom and autonomy, and freedom is at the core of everything we want in life, including feeling strong, secure, and resilient; finding meaning; and experiencing joy and peace. These are the things that make us feel alive and cause us to become more engaged. Freedom, therefore, is critical to your happiness and well-being.

Freedom is yours for the taking—even at work—but the problem is that we all frequently fail to embrace what is immediately available and already ours. That's because many people think that freedom lies "out there" in a better boss, a more enlightened culture, a different job, a bigger office, or a more solid customer base rather than "in here," in them.

But freedom is a choice. Freedom is a state of mind. It is established from the *inside out*.

> THE FREEDOM TO CHOOSE IS YOURS ALONE TO LEVERAGE OR NOT. NO ONE CAN GRANT IT TO YOU, AND NO ONE CAN TAKE IT AWAY FROM YOU.

> IS IT REALLY YOUR BOSS ... YOUR BOARD ... THE CULTURE ... A LEADER WITHOUT VISION ... OR SALES THAT RESTRICTS YOUR ABILITY TO CHOOSE? OR IS IT JUST YOU?

In his book *Let Me Tell You a Story*, Tony Campolo recounts a story about a conversation between Bill Clinton when he was president of the United States and Nelson Mandela when he was president of South Africa. Years earlier, Clinton woke his family up at three o'clock in the morning to watch the press coverage of the historic day Mandela was released from prison. As the television cameras pressed in, Clinton observed the sheer anger and hatred on Mandela's face as he walked from his cell block to the front of the prison. Then, in a heartbeat, Mandela's rage seemed to vanish. When Clinton asked the South African president about it later, Mandela replied, "I'm surprised that you saw that, and I regret that the cameras caught my anger. Yes, you are right . . . that day when I stepped out of prison and looked at the people observing, a flush of anger hit me with the thought that they had robbed me of twenty-seven years. Then the Spirit of Jesus said to me, 'Nelson, while you were in prison you were free, now that you are free don't become a prisoner.'" Nelson Mandela's emotions naturally gravitated toward anger and resentment (whose wouldn't?) until he recognized what was happening. Then he made a different choice.

Obviously, we are not totally free from conditions—tsunamis happen, leadership changes, employees are laid off, people fall ill, and folks die—but we are totally free to take a stand in the face of what life throws our way. Mandela didn't "choose" to live in a world full of racism, but he was able to choose how he would respond to that world. And he chose to be a player, rather than a victim.

BOOM!

When it comes to making choices there is a QUARTER-SECOND that could change your life!

To find out how, go to freibergs.com/boom and type the work Choice in the BOOM! box.

In an age of victimization, entitlement, and excuse making, people have difficulty seeing that they are free. Who among us does not wrestle with circumstances outside our control, with conditions that are limiting and constraining? But the real question is, who ultimately restricts my ability to choose—who gets in the way of the freedom that I crave and deserve? Most of us locate the source of that restriction "out there" and give away our power to choose to other people.

Consider the following grievances:

- "My boss never lets me express my individuality."
- "Senior leadership pays lip service to these innovations, yet we are expected to embrace them."
- "Our board is too conservative; without taking risks we can't be innovative."
- "The culture sucks! People live in fear around here."

- "We need a leader with vision. Things are out of control; we have no focus."
- "Sales always overpromises to close a deal, and then operations is forced to underdeliver."

Is it REALLY your boss . . . your board . . . the culture . . . a leader without vision . . . or sales that restricts your ability to choose? Or is it just YOU?

The truth is, you always have a choice, and you choose how you will respond to the things you cannot control. Between any given situation and our response to that situation lies what Victor Frankl calls "the last of the human freedoms—to choose one's attitude in any given set of circumstances, to choose one's way" (*Man's Search for Meaning*, 66). The problem is that we often disconnect cause and effect. That is, we fail to link the consequences of our actions back to choices we've made. And the choices you freely make do not always lead to freedom.

The truth is:

YOU CHOOSE to compromise who you are by attempting to fit in.

YOU CHOOSE not to stand up to the board because you need a better business case for your intentions.

YOU CHOOSE not to stand up to senior leadership because you fear their response.

YOU CHOOSE to be part of a culture of fear by letting people intimidate you.

YOU CHOOSE to stay in a culture where you feel choked.

YOU CHOOSE not to cast a vision for your own part of the organization.

YOU CHOOSE not to confront sales, so they continue to make life difficult for you.

YOU CHOOSE to be helpless and not make a difference.

The point is, in every case, **YOU CHOOSE**.

Free will is inherently part of what it means to be human. *Not choosing is itself a choice.* When you abdicate or abandon this most basic of freedoms, you imprison yourself. You choose to become helpless, powerless, mindless, less influential, and less happy. You've benched yourself in your own game of life!

If you work in a high-paying job for a toxic boss who makes your life miserable and you say, "I have no choice," what you really mean is, "I am choosing to prioritize making money over my own job fulfillment," or "I'm choosing to embrace safety versus risk, or the known instead of the unknown." In reality there are other jobs that will enable you to pay your mortgage, and other leaders who are more enlightened. For any number of reasons (some legitimate, some not), you are not willing to confront the uncertainty and pay the price for moving on. That, in and of itself, is a choice. By rationalizing that you have no choice, you are *choosing* not to recognize legitimate alternatives that are yours for the taking. You are stuck in a comfort zone of inaction that is functional and safe, but leaves  you dead and disengaged, perhaps even anxious and stressed. Your choice, while seemingly benign, comes with an "unhealthy" price tag, one that could cost you more than the price you would've paid for constructive confrontation or moving on.

We call people like this *dead people working*. You know them, because you work with them. They are in the next cubicle, down the hall, in your department, on the front line, and, yes, even in the executive suite.

They are physically present, but they are psychologically, emotionally, and intellectually checked out! They look like normal people—they talk, they laugh, they complain, they seem to have dreams and plans just like us—but after years of choosing to be helpless, any thought of being a real player who makes an extraordinary contribution goes out the door. When we ask audiences all over the world, "How many of you know dead people working?" the response is overwhelming.

Following the sound of embarrassed chuckles, hands always go up. Research from Gallup, Walker Information, Hudson Institute, Towers Perrin, Hewitt Associates, and others shows that approximately 75 percent of the workforce is either not engaged or actively disengaged in their work and are not loyal to their companies. Unfortunately, the *dead people working* syndrome is alive and well.

But this force of epidemic proportions that threatens to derail your every effort isn't something that just happens in organizations. Boredom, despair, and indifference—symptoms of dead people working—are the result of the choices people make.

The prisons we create by voluntarily imposing constraints upon our lives are often so subtle. We make choices without even recognizing them as choices. We bring our BlackBerrys to the soccer field. We answer the phone in a restaurant or movie instead of letting it roll to voice mail. Or we mentally start the workweek on Sunday afternoon, which begins the process of emotionally and psychologically checking out from our friends and family, and thus we strip ourselves of a full weekend. Technology is always there, and because we allow it to be, we fall under its trance.

Just because a bell rings it doesn't mean you have to *do* anything. Just for the heck of it, leave your BlackBerry at home the next time you have to go to a family function. Or the next time your cell rings, let it roll over, and check the message(s) when you feel like it. Be smarter than your phone or BlackBerry. That's freedom.

Surrendering our freedom to choose may be the worst form of incarceration, because we do it to ourselves. Worse yet, we get so comfortable with the walls we've created that we come to think of them as our safe haven and our excuse for not being a player.

> "MAN MUST CEASE ATTRIBUTING HIS PROBLEMS TO HIS ENVIRONMENT AND LEARN AGAIN TO EXERCISE HIS PERSONAL RESPONSIBILITIES."
>
> —ALBERT SCHWEITZER

How many times have you broken the promises you made to yourself professionally and personally? You said you were going to volunteer for a project with high visibility but chickened out at the last minute because you didn't think you had the skills. You know you need to confront a coworker who constantly fails to meet deadlines that affect your work. Instead you end up whining and moaning about her to colleagues. You said you were going to build a business case for your boss about spending more time in the field, but you never do the work or make the appointment to see her. You rationalize each of these choices (usually based on fear or weakness). But let's be clear: you are *not* a product of your conditions; you are a product of your decisions. As Alsatian theologian and physician Albert Schweitzer once said, "Man must cease attributing his problems to his environment and learn again to exercise his personal responsibilities."

Benefits of Reclaiming Your Freedom to Choose

You can't fix a problem that you don't know exists. So one of the keys to leading where you are planted and blowing the doors off business-as-usual is being more conscious of the choices you make and how they affect your life. And when you do that, you can take ownership of more of the freedom and autonomy that is yours to begin with.

Choice enables you to get what you want and express who you are. Choice allows you to learn from painful or negative situations. As you choose to learn from these circumstances, you create more meaning in your life. Fulfillment and satisfaction will follow. Choice helps you see that you are the cause and not just the effect. It puts you in a powerful position to make a valuable contribution. Choice makes it possible for you to be fully engaged, to create more life at work, and to get better results.

Some of the most capable, responsible, and productive people we know are those who exercise the freedom to choose their attitude, to decide where they will focus their attention, and how they will interpret or explain events, regardless of their circumstances. These people choose wisely!

There is no substitute for a workforce that chooses to be engaged and to fire on all cylinders. People who are engaged infuse passion into everything they do. A fire burns within them that stirs their souls and inspires them to make a difference—enabling them to try things that others are afraid to try, and to be the kind of people others yearn to be. Why is this so important? Because most business leaders now agree that neither building a bigger, better widget nor having some killer business plan will *always* lead to building a great company. But having a workforce that is alive, fully engaged, and firing on all cylinders—a workforce that is booming—is indispensable.

For the last twenty years, our own work has taken us into eighty to one hundred businesses each year, across the nation and around the globe. Before we give a presentation to a group, we talk to people at various levels inside the company to identify major issues and to find out what's really going on in their organizations and in their industries.

We've never heard a client say, "Our people take too many risks, they assume way too much responsibility, and we've got to get them to slow down when it comes to taking initiative." Instead, the people at our events tell us:

- "We want everyone in our organization to be moved by the major threats facing our business and our industry."

- "We want people to respond with a sense of urgency to the significant opportunities the market presents."

- "We want everyone to be obsessed with and fixated on developing themselves and helping others succeed."

- "We want people to be dogged in their pursuit of creating lifetime customer loyalty."

- "We want every person to have the guts to test new ideas and challenge the status quo."

- "When waste and redundancy make people's jobs more difficult, we want everyone in the organization to be agitated—even outraged—as if it were their own money going down the tubes!"

- "When managers become too controlling or departments fall into silos or the practice of tribalism, we want our coworkers to be incensed enough to speak up."

- "When the organization achieves a major breakthrough or wins a new piece of business, we want to celebrate; we want everybody to be genuinely excited and optimistic."

- "When anyone in our organization talks to people at social gatherings or community events, we want them to speak about the business with the sincere affection and genuine enthusiasm of a prideful ambassador."

- "We want people to take more responsibility, assume more ownership, and be more accountable for the success of the organization. We want them to stop waiting for permission to act—and ACT!"

Will You Be Missed?

So, what about you? If you had the opportunity to hire *you* tomorrow, would you do it? If you left your organization tomorrow, would you be missed? Would your customers and colleagues mourn your departure? Would the organization feel a deep sense of loss? Are you indispensable?

In his 1994 inaugural address, Nelson Mandela quoted Marianne Williamson, author of *A Return to Love* (New York: Harper Collins, 1992), saying:

> Our deepest fear is not that we are inadequate. Our deepest fear is that we are powerful beyond measure. It is our light, not our darkness, that most frightens us. We ask ourselves, who am I to be brilliant, gorgeous, talented, and fabulous? Actually, who are you not to be? You are a child of God. Your playing small doesn't serve the world. There is nothing enlightened about shrinking so that other people won't feel insecure around you . . . We [were] born to make manifest the glory of God [that is] within us. It is not just in some of us, it's in everyone. And, as we let our own light shine, we unconsciously give other people permission to do the same. As we are liberated from our own fear, our presence automatically liberates others. (http://jmm.aaa.net.au/articles/4564.htm)

We agree with Mandela: "*We [were] born to make manifest the glory of God within us.*" We participate in this birthright by accepting that we are accountable for creating the world in which we live. You were designed to choose, and you are defined by choice. In front of you are SEVEN

INTRODUCTION

CHOICES waiting to be made. These choices will determine the quality of your life and the significance of your contribution to the world in which you work. They will determine whether you become a person who is truly indispensable or one who is hardly missed.

BOOM! was written to help you embrace your freedom to choose. It's about avoiding the snares of indifference and victimization by embracing the God-given freedom inherent in all of us. It's about acknowledging the power you have to make a difference and to give history a shove. It's your wake up call to be a leader, to create a community of purpose-driven people who—together—will create organizations that can move mountains. If you make these seven choices, you will find the power to lead where you are planted and build a reputation among your team, inside your company, and throughout your community for being the kind of person other people can't live without. And make no mistake, in the end, how you live your life is your choice.

We invite you to join the movement.

BOOM!

Want to create more FREEDOM in your life?

Go to freibergs.com/boom *and type the word* Freedom *in the BOOM! box.*

It's pretty simple . . .
You are a product of your decisions,
not your conditions.
You can choose to lead your life
or let others do it for you.

CHOICE #1

BE A PLAYER, NOT A BYSTANDER

Extraordinary Happens When Ordinary
People Do Whatever It Takes

01

"On the field of life, we are all called to be players and to actively engage in winning the game."

On the field of life, we are all called to be players and to actively engage in winning the game. Players are focused on bringing energy, passion, heart, and soul to the game. Players get joy and meaning through their contributions. Players have a powerful bond and loyalty to their team, and players always strive to win and make a difference. Players choose to "be there," and you can count on them to bring their *all* to the game. We call these people MVPs (most valued players) because of the impact they have on the outcome of the game.

Do *you* choose to bring your all to the game?

To be a player is to have a VOICE, to have influence. It is to speak up and shape policies and practices that support a work environment where people are fully awake, completely alive, and entirely engaged. Players influence the cultures in which they live and work. To be the *cause* of something is to "put it out there," to put a stake in the ground. To be the *effect* is to passively live with it—accept it as it is! What makes a "player" an MVP? How do his or her choices add value and make a difference?

Players Know Who They Are

Players are values-driven people who refuse to check their values at the door in order to fit in. Secure and optimistic, they are not easily affected by negative and dysfunctional organizational politics. They have a strong sense of who they are, what they stand for, and how they want to live. Players rarely get derailed by circumstances that frequently hold "victims" back. They get frustrated just like anyone else. But when things go wrong and people within the organization fail to meet their needs, MVPs have little time for pity parties. Instead, their commitment to who they are, where they want to go, and what they want to accomplish are the important driving forces in their lives.

Stories of MVPs with a fierce focus on what they stand for are as old as business.

In 1878, there was a man who worked as a clerk and assistant to the owner of a dry goods store in Watertown, New York. It was a good job, and he liked it, but he had a level of engagement that compelled him to always look for better ways to do things.

One day he noticed that when clearance items were placed on a table near the front of the store and priced at a nickel or a dime, customers cleaned out the table. There were two innovations here: First, merchandise usually kept behind the counter was now available for customers to handle, which seemed to encourage purchase decisions. Second, discount pricing was being presented in an era when farm families were having a hard time generating cash.

So the young man shared his observations with his boss and suggested increasing the number of tables and having a special sale offering everything for less than ten cents. The store owner said he didn't think it was a particularly bright idea, but since he couldn't see any harm in it either, he gave the go-ahead.

The resulting sales were a huge success, so the young man expanded his thinking and a few months later went back to the boss with an ambitious and audacious plan: open a store where everything was just a nickel or a dime. This ambitious clerk proposed leaving the store to start an all-new store, and he wanted the boss to put up the financing and be his partner.

The boss wasn't impressed and said, "It's not a good idea. It won't work. Sorry to lose you. Your job will be waiting for you when it fails." This would have been an excellent time for the boy to give up; his relationship with his boss and his job were on the line. But he went for it . . .

And failed, BIG TIME! He opened that same year in Utica, New York, and closed before the year was out. Again, that would have been the perfect time to admit defeat, and he would have had lots of support for that decision.

But he tried again the following year, and on June 21, 1879, he opened the *first successful* five-and-dime store, in Lancaster, Pennsylvania. So confident was he that he put his own name on the big sign out front: F.W. WOOLWORTH'S.

It became the first global chain of stores in history. Woolworth was the Sam Walton of his day. Years later somebody interviewed the boss who'd turned his offer of partnership down. He said, "When I kissed Woolworth off, I figure it cost me a million dollars for every word I used to tell him no."

When you know what you stand for, nothing and no one stands in your way.

But it doesn't happen just in business. Ask yourself, "How did Victor Frankl, Rosa Parks, Martin Luther King Jr., Nelson Mandela, and countless others choose to rise above their oppressive circumstances?" Each of these MVPs had a personal constitution that became the fundamental basis for the choices he or she made. In our work lives we obviously don't face the atrocities of Auschwitz or the extreme challenges of fighting for civil rights and abolishing apartheid, but we do face some daunting challenges sometimes. To be a player, to truly engage during times like these, requires a compelling motivator, something more stable and constant to which you are dedicated.

A Personal Constitution

Do you have a personal constitution? Players find enormous strength in knowing who they are and what they stand for.

Senator John McCain was a thirty-one-year-old navy pilot who lived a privileged life until the day his A-4 Skyhawk was shot down over Vietnam. We can talk about our fears, but they pale when compared to those of a man who awakened on the ground to find that he had two broken arms and a broken leg, was surrounded by a mob that had stripped all his clothes off, and looked up to see a soldier with a bayonet. When the soldier started stabbing him, his real horror began.

McCain was transported to the Hoa Loa Prison, also known as the Hanoi Hilton, where he remained for more than five years. No one could blame a man for doing *anything* to avoid that kind of fear and pain. And McCain could have eased his pain a little by at least pretending to cooperate with his captors. But he refused, and every time he said no to his interrogators, he was beaten into unconsciousness.

Then the Vietnamese discovered that McCain's father was the commander in chief of the Pacific Command; they thought they could organize a PR coup by releasing him. But McCain had a strong personal constitution and refused to accept a release. The POWs had agreed that no one would go home unless they all went home, and McCain was true to his word.

In the midst of the most terrible personal horror, McCain knew he had the most important freedom of all: he had the freedom to *choose*.

And his choice—guided by his strong constitution—was to make a difference. But to make a difference you must focus on what you can control.

Players Choose to Focus on What They Can Control

The one thing we all share in common is that our time and energy are limited resources. Energy can be replenished, but time is finite: once it's gone, it's gone. Every day you make choices about how you allocate your time and where you expend your energy. How you spend your time *should* be determined by what you value. Unfortunately, a lot of us spend time in activities that are not of value to us; we find ourselves wasting time doing things to which we should have said no. Perhaps we allow fear to drive our calendars more than we should. Scan your calendar: Are your time choices/allocations controlled more by what you value or what you fear? These choices either move you closer to the individual reputation and personal brand that you are building within your organization, or farther from it.

Focusing on the things you *cannot* control is a waste of your limited resources. It depletes your reservoir and leaves you with less time and energy to focus on the things you *can* control. Players recognize that gaining traction toward a desired outcome is the result of choosing wisely between the two. They ignore the things they cannot do anything about. They simply don't let things outside their control take up too much mental space, or they concentrate on bringing things outside their control into their control.

You can increase your effectiveness by orders of magnitude by simply asking yourself the question, "Right now, at this moment, given this situation, am I focused on something I can control, or obsessing over something I can't control?"

So, what kinds of things *can* you do something about?

You can't control your boss or senior leadership, but . . .

- **YOU CAN CONTROL** your attitude toward your boss and senior leaders.

- **YOU CAN CONTROL** your ability to perform, to become a guru, a thought leader, a go-to person who is seen as adding tremendous value to the organization.

- **YOU CAN CONTROL** your approach when interacting with your boss or other leaders. Are your ideas well thought-out? Do you build an airtight business case for your initiatives? Are you passionate?

- **YOU CAN CONTROL** your conversations with others about your boss and other leaders.

- **YOU CAN CONTROL** your ability to set your boss and others up for success.

Woolworth controlled his destiny by controlling his attitude, his knowledge, and his emotions. He knew what he stood for, and he kept his mind clear of negative influences. He literally chose *not* to fail.

You can't single-handedly change your company's culture, but you can . . .

- **CREATE** a small pocket of success in your own area of influence that inspires others to take notice and behave differently. If enough people are awakened by your approach, the culture will eventually change. But it starts one by one by one, with people like you, who choose to make a difference.

- **LOOK FOR** inexpensive ways to rearrange your work environment so you feel more productive and able to perform at your best.

- **BRING** the right attitude—embrace a spirit of hope and optimism, and share it with a hopeless, pessimistic crew.

- **AVOID** people who are tuned out and actively disengaged— they are toxic and contagious! Make it your professional constitution to try to reengage them. Help people see how their individual contributions help the department, team, or organization achieve future goals.

- **ASK** for tools, supplies, and materials that you absolutely need to improve your performance at work—do not assume that your boss knows you need certain things.

You can't control how much energy, time, and resources your company has to provide you with opportunities for growth and ongoing development, but don't let this become an excuse for doing nothing. Take the initiative; establish a plan. People who have development plans actually perform at higher levels of engagement.

So what can you do? You can . . .

- **ASSUME RESPONSIBILITY** for your own development.
- **GET** yourself into meetings and conferences that enable you to rub shoulders with movers and shakers who can help you expand your competence, your capacity, and your network.
- **LOOK FOR** and volunteer to assist with entrepreneurial projects that tap new skills and build upon your existing talents.
- **LEARN** something new every day—stretch, grow, develop. Whether you're reading a trade publication, a news report, a personal-growth piece, or a book that adds breadth to your spiritual journey, you can learn something from anyone and anything, if you WANT it bad enough.
- **FIND** a mentor who will challenge and inspire you—a "sounding board" to whom you can be accountable. Find a mentor who will tell you the brutal truth about yourself and make you sweat the details. If you're going to go for it, really go for it!

You may not be able to look into a crystal ball and discover the future, but you should do something, because when you understand how your roles and responsibilities contribute to achieving the vision, strategy, and goals for growth, you take a huge step toward being a player! What can you do?

- **TAKE THE LEAD** and suggest a weekly/biweekly or monthly forum, with the goal being open communication between you, your colleagues, and your boss.

- **STOP** rumors, and never trust secondhand information. When it's possible, make data-driven decisions—go directly to the source for accurate information.

- **LOOK** for information that describes the direction, objectives, and vision for the future of the business.

- **THINK** about how your talents and your work projects will help drive business success; then schedule a meeting with your boss for his/her input.

- **KNOW** who you are competing with. Study the competition. Get to know them. Visit their Web sites. Look at their ads, marketing, and PR pieces. Read their press releases . . . and visit them if you can.

- **STUDY** the market realities and trends in your industry, listen to the futurists and industry experts, and then apply their observations to your business.

Assess your own situation, and then decide what you can influence, and what you can't. The more you focus on things you are worried about but can't control, the more you disempower yourself. The more you focus on what you *can* control, the more freedom you have to take a stand!

Players Take a Stand—They Join the Dialogue and Shape the Debate

Martin Luther King Jr. said, "Our lives begin to end the day we become silent about things that matter." Loyalty is not a synonym for blind obedience or mindless conformity, and taking a stand does not equate to being a troublemaker. After twenty years of studying successful businesses, we have learned that irreverence in an organization can be healthy. In fact, great leaders not only tolerate it, they need it, they want it, and they should expect it. Groupthink—even among the most cohesive and well-intentioned members of a team—has been the source of monumental errors and tragic disasters.

Some years ago CRM Films (www.crmlearning.com) released a very popular training video that identified groupthink as one of the factors leading up to the explosion of the 1986 space shuttle *Challenger*, the 1941 attack on Pearl Harbor, and the 1961 Bay of Pigs fiasco. The power of any organization lies in its ability to garner diversity of thought and a multitude of perspectives. That never happens when people are afraid to join the debate. It takes guts to question authority, challenge policy, argue your point, and ask why. But that's what MVPs do.

Every executive team in the history of business has held opinions or implemented strategies that subsequent management teams found wanting or flawed. That's why you must give yourself permission to put

group·think |ˈgroop, θiNGk|

noun

the practice of thinking or making decisions as a group in a way that discourages creativity or individual responsibility

every idea—every process, policy, and plan—on probation constantly. When you aren't willing to join the debate, your ideas are suppressed. When you neglect new ideas, you rob the organization of opportunity and innovation, just as surely as if you walked out of the joint with a boatload of inventory. If you want to make your organization boom, you've got to be a player.

Organizations are political by nature. To ignore this reality is not only naïve, it's foolish. You compete for limited resources to get things done, to build a case for why the business should move in one direction versus another, to embrace the values you deeply believe in, and to convince people to work affirmatively and effectively on things that matter.

This means that leadership is a political process. It's about figuring out what motivates people, what scares them, and what inspires them. It's about knowing who to tap for support and how to leverage their gifts, talents, and contacts. Players jump into this process with both feet; they join the dialogue and shape the culture by shaping the content and character of the debate. Through open and authentic communication, players build trust and respect by letting people know where they stand. Players support, confront, listen, and persuade. They also compromise. In a straightforward way, they play a crucial role in deciding what the organization will become. Contrary to what many people think, the organization is as much the will of the people as it is the will of the CEO.

Players debate and communicate with optimism, hope, and goals for future growth. That's what makes people come alive and become more connected, more accountable, and more involved. The thrill of victory and the agony of defeat that come with risk taking and putting their thumbprints on the organization are better than the lukewarm satisfaction of the sidelines. The opportunity to change some part of the world is more stimulating than just biding time. Players have influence because they give themselves permission to have an optimistic *voice*.

To get in the game, to be fully engaged, requires a point of view, a sense of conviction, the confidence that you have something valuable to offer, and a strong backbone. Whether it's your belief in an opportunity for breakaway innovation, your outrage for the broken status quo, or your passion for lighting a fire under the dead person working in the next cubicle, you must stand for something. God has given you gifts and talents and a perspective that no one else has. Your willingness to engage makes the dialogue richer, more diverse, and more interesting. Even though people in your organization will send you signals that your voice is not valued, withholding your voice denies the organization of something it desperately needs—*you*.

Players Influence the Game

In 1905, the game of football was in a crisis. It had become so violent that players were dying on the field. President Theodore Roosevelt himself called a conference at the White House to say something had to be done. "Change the game," he said, "or else."

The following season fans saw something new: the first forward pass. At the college level the first forward pass was thrown at an Army–Navy game; the first one in the NFL was thrown when George Parratt of the Massillon Tigers completed a pass to his teammate Dan Riley on October 27, 1906.

MVPs don't passively sit around and wait for the powers that be to pass out the rules. They aren't afraid to question authority, because they don't buy into the "senior executive as god" syndrome. People in authority cannot possibly know it all, be it all, or do it all. The business world in which we live is far too specialized and complicated for that.

Warren Bennis, one of the foremost thought leaders of our time, tells a story about his experience as president of the University of Cincinnati. He came into work one day to find his office stormed by students who were outraged about two gorgeous trees that had been cut down to widen a road on campus. After probing for a bit, Bennis learned that the person who chopped down the trees was employed by a local contractor who was hired by the landscape architect to carry out the design. The landscape architect was hired by the university's director of planning, who worked for the vice president of management and finance, who, in turn, answered to the building committee. The building committee reported to the executive vice president. When Bennis got all twenty of them together in a room, everyone was innocent—including himself. His point: bureaucracies are great hiding places and effective instruments for evading responsibility. They breed fragmented decision making and conformity without necessarily being in touch with reality. And the result? Two beautiful landmark trees cut down.

BOOM!

But what if someone along the line—anyone!—had simply raised a hand and said, "Wait a minute. Are we sure we want to cut these trees down?"

The Bennis story shows that people in positions of authority are often just as vulnerable, scared, inconsistent, and flawed as you are. That's why people who live and work at the point of action must step up and take charge. No one knows the issues better than they, and you, do. No one has a better view from which to see the waste, redundancy, and opportunity than you do. The true experts and the most legitimate sources of authority in any organization are those closest to the point of action. It was the pilots at Southwest Airlines who figured out that if you slow the plane down to eighty knots upon landing by using reverse thrust before using the brakes, you can cut your brake maintenance in half. With a fleet of over 450 aircraft flying three thousand flights a day, that is a lot of maintenance saved! And let us assure you, the pilots didn't wait for the director of flight operations or any other executive to figure it out or to ask for their opinion. The pilots played with passion and offered it up without being asked.

If leadership is about serving and empowering people, shouldn't you have an opportunity to evaluate how well your leader has served you? What's stopping you from making your review a two-way process? Take CrimsonCup, an independent coffee-house community that is on a mission to make neighborhoods better, one latte at a time. The team working at the corporate office in Columbus, Ohio, has created a performance and feedback coaching process that is *absolutely* two-way. The goal is authentic conversation and straight talk about what it takes to be an MVP who produces breakthrough results. All of this requires a detailed conversation about the company's breakthrough goals, as well as the employees' and managers' roles in achieving the goals. And the process is guided and documented on a napkin. Why a napkin? Well, at CrimsonCup they believe that the best performance conversations are usually had over lunch (not in the leader's office), with important points jotted down on a napkin. As the napkin unfolds, the conversation unfolds; nothing is left out, and nothing is left uncommunicated!

Wouldn't everyone in your company work smarter, better, faster if more of us took the initiative to start our own performance dialogues and become rule makers? Why not become an extraordinary player and set up a dialogue, a two-way, authentic conversation with your manager? And bring a napkin! Share your performance goals for achieving breakthrough results; define your accountabilities, and discuss the kind of support, coaching, or guidance you might need. And BOOM!—we guarantee that the process will leave you feeling more engaged, more directed, and more in control of your future.

Remember, *you* are the organization. You are its eyes, ears, brains, and brawn. You are its conscience. Your organization doesn't solely belong to someone above you. Sure, there may be a founder who has majority stock ownership, or it might be a privately held, third-generation-run family business, but these people can't make the organization what it needs to be without you. The minute you make this transition psychologically is the moment you will become more comfortable establishing the rules. Edmund Burke, a member of the British Parliament remembered for his support of the American colonies in the struggle against King George III, said, "Nobody makes a greater mistake than he who did nothing because he could only do a little."

So, what will you do with your unique vantage point? Will you exercise your freedom to make a difference by leveraging your insight and assuming ownership at the local level? Or will you take a seat on the sidelines because you believe that it's someone else's responsibility to carry the ball?

BOOM!

Players Choose to Think and Act Like Owners

Entrepreneurs carry the ball; they are a unique breed. They love to play in the arena of high risk / high reward. Not everyone is cut out to be an entrepreneur, but we have yet to meet a business leader who doesn't want more of the entrepreneurial mind-set in his or her organization. Entrepreneurs are self-motivated, self-directed, and self-disciplined. They accept ownership and take responsibility for the outcomes of the projects they pursue, which is why you always find them in the driver's seat. When someone is thinking like an entrepreneur, he or she will ask, "Since this is my business, how will I go to market with my product? How do I convince everyone around me that it will work?" Or, "What resources will I need to get the job done? How do I bring together the right combination of people to make it happen?" Entrepreneurs play whatever roles are necessary and do whatever it takes to achieve the results they envision. If it means stepping out of a job description or crossing a functional boundary, they do it. If it means doing more with less and bootstrapping their way into needed resources, they do it. If it means finding unique market opportunities that others can't see or choose to ignore, they do it.

In our book *GUTS!: Companies That Blow the Doors off Business-as-Usual*, we describe the entrepreneurial mind-set of someone who chooses to do whatever it takes.

> • Owners step out from behind titles and job descriptions to act on behalf of the customer and the company. You never hear them say, "It's not my job." They never throw problems over functional walls ("Let me transfer you to . . .") or make excuses.

- Owners cater to the organization's mission, vision, and values; nonowners cater to the boss.

- Owners focus on the business results of their actions, no matter who is watching.

- Owners have the guts to ask the tough questions. They understand the consequences of complacency, and they aren't afraid to challenge the status quo with the mantra "How can we make it better?"

- Owners disregard functional boundaries to consider what's good for the company as a whole.

- Owners bend, stretch, or even break rules that don't serve the customer.

- Owners pay attention to details. (77–78)

Do you get a sense of the commitment with which owners take on their work? Players have the same mentality.

Recently, we were on Coronado Island in San Diego for our daughter Aubrey's soccer tournament. She had to arrive one hour before the game, so we dropped her off and got on our bikes to go find a bite to eat while we waited. We came upon what appeared to be a cute, quick-serve breakfast joint, so we ordered, and while we waited for the hot items, we had coffee, some fruit, and a couple of muffins. Well, we waited, and waited, and finally it got to the top of the hour, and we needed to race back for the game. So Jackie asked if they could package our food to go. Our order hadn't even been started yet! So we canceled the order.

When Jackie stepped up to the register to ask the order taker for a refund, we fully expected that she'd have to check with the boss and

BOOM!

would then refund just a portion of our bill. Nope! This order taker was an MVP, and she acted like an owner. She asked for our card, refunded the entire charge, and said, "Please come back. We are so sorry for the delay. We are very busy today!" Wow! This MVP's choice to simply take charge and make a difference caused our entire perception of the place to change for the better!

What kind of reputation are you building in your organization right now? If someone were to examine your attitude and behavior over the last eighteen months, would your example suggest that you think like an entrepreneur and act like a business owner—a player—or a bystander? Stop reading for just a moment and ask yourself, "Would those who work with me often and know me well describe my choices as courageous and resourceful? Would they say I am self-directed and accountable?" You may not be ready to mortgage your home to take on a high-risk business venture, but to be a player is to take on a similar mind-set.

BOOM!

Want to get further inside the mind of an MVP?

Go to freibergs.com/boom *and type the word* MVP *mind in the BOOM! box.*

Choose to Play Hard!

So, what about you? How hard are you willing to play? Your future—the quality of your life at work, your reputation, and the significance you glean from making a difference—depends on your answers. Take the following assessment and determine which way you lean. For each of the A and B statements, circle the statement that best describes you. Do *not* go with what you think is the *right* answer. Go with what you *know* to be true about your behavior most of the time at work.

> HOW HARD ARE YOU WILLING TO PLAY?
> YOUR FUTURE—THE QUALITY OF
> YOUR LIFE AT WORK,
> YOUR REPUTATION, AND
> THE SIGNIFICANCE YOU GLEAN
> FROM MAKING A DIFFERENCE—
> DEPENDS ON YOUR ANSWERS.

1. A. I choose my attitude, and it drives my performance, regardless of the circumstances I face.
   B. My attitude and my ability to perform are affected by my work conditions.

2. A. I go for it! I tell my boss what he/she needs to hear.
   B. I tend to play it safe and tell my boss what he/she wants to hear.

3. A. When people in my organization complain, I tend to press for a solution.
   B. When people in my organization complain, I tend to join them.

4. A. I tend to support my ideas with a well-thought-out business case.
   B. I tend to "trial balloon" an idea before putting too much energy into it.

5. A. When I see a problem, even if it is not my job, I own it and do whatever it takes to fix it.
   B. When I see a problem and it's not part of my job, I don't worry about it.

6. A. I admit my mistakes and apologize to those affected by them.
   B. When I make a mistake, my first response is to ask, "Who shares the blame here?"

7. A. I seek out "stretch" assignments; they stimulate and challenge me.
    B. I avoid "stretch" assignments; they intimidate me and wear me out.

8. A. When there is conflict at work, I tend toward finding a way to work it out.
    B. When there is conflict at work, I tend to avoid it.

9. A. People I work with would say I tend to talk positively about others.
    B. People I work with would say I tend to be critical of others.

10. A. If I err, it's usually on the side of seeking forgiveness after acting.
    B. If I err, it's usually on the side of seeking permission before acting.

11. A. I don't let others determine how I will feel or act.
    B. There are people at work who make me crazy.

12. A. My sense of hope and idealism for making a difference at work is alive and well.
    B. My sense of hope and idealism for making a difference at work has diminished.

13. A. The culture in my organization is primarily the will of the people.
    B. The culture in my organization is primarily the will of the CEO.

14. A. My job security and advancement depend on my ability to get results.
    B. My job security and advancement depend on being politically correct.

15. A. I spend my time and energy on things I can control.
    B. I tend to worry about circumstances over which I have little or no control.

16. A. I tend to seek clarity about my responsibilities and the organization's vision.
    B. I tend to wait for our leaders to clarify expectations and share strategy and vision.

17. A. People who work with me would say I play to win—lean toward risk.
    B. People who work with me would say I play not to lose—lean toward safety.

18. A. Once an organizational strategy is set, I am committed to making it work.
    B. Once an organizational strategy is set, I tend to point out its flaws.

19. A. My work matters, and I make a difference.
    B. My work is a job, and my real life is outside of work.

20. A. When things get difficult and resources are scarce, I focus on what I can do.
    B. When things get difficult and resources are scarce, I focus on what I *can't* do.

21. A. When the organization fails to meet my needs, I ask, "What could I have done to be more influential?" Then I learn from it and move on.
    B. When the organization fails to meet my needs, I sulk, pout, and hold a grudge.

22. A. I am motivated by constructive confrontation.
    B. I shy away from constructive confrontation.

23. A. I love my work.
    B. Work is just work.

24. A. I can be myself at work and still get ahead.
    B. Fitting in is the way you get ahead at work.

25. A. I appreciate many things about where I work.
    B. When I look at my organization, I don't see much to be grateful for.

Give yourself one point for every B circled and zero points for each A circled. Then total your points and consult the following table to interpret your score.

EXTREME PLAYER (0–4 POINTS):

If you scored 0–4 points, two possibilities exist. Either you are an extreme player, an MVP whom the organization is most fortunate to have . . . or you are in extreme denial! Ask yourself, "Am I in touch with the way I behave and how others perceive me? Am I willing to face reality? Am I being real?" Everyone periodically chooses to be a bystander, toshift blame and responsibility elsewhere. You and I are no exception. When in doubt, ask a close friend or trusted colleague to do the assessment on your behalf and see how his or her perception differs from your own. Consider your actual score to be somewhere between the two. Then take it again and focus on your most recent behaviors!

As an extreme player, you believe that you have a significant role in shaping what the organization will be. Because you see the organization as a product of your own creation, you "weigh in" more often, engaging in discussions that others tend to avoid. You understand that the organization will change most dramatically when you become an instrument of change in it. Most likely you are a "go to" person, a shaker and mover, who is blowing the doors off business-as-usual. Use this strength to coach, mentor, and inspire others in your organization.

PLAYER (5–8 POINTS):

If you scored 5–8 points, you conduct yourself in a mature manner that garners respect from your coworkers. Most of the time you take responsibility for your own morale as well as for the consequences of the choices you make. Periodically you find yourself slipping into the role of victim, but you catch yourself doing it faster than most. Even though you get discouraged sometimes, you haven't lost your sense of idealism or your passion for making the organization what you want it to be. While you're not perfect, you frequently choose freedom, autonomy, and accountability over dependence and helplessness.

PLAYER/BENCHED (9–12 POINTS):

If you scored 9–12 points, you really are on the fence post. Sometimes you choose to be strong and powerful, taking a stand, taking initiative, and making your point of view known, and sometimes you choose to be helpless. Use the Seven Choices to help you set up permanent residence on the player end of the continuum.

BENCHED (13–16 POINTS):

If you scored 13–16 points, you're benched. You probably have great ideas but fail to share them with people in your organization as often as you should. Work is just a job; it pays the bills. Most likely, you are not out to sabotage the organization, but you are not adding a lot of value beyond just showing up. People don't talk about your contributions to the organization, because there is not a whole lot to talk about. You are in danger of becoming a dead person working. Read the description below and ask yourself, "Is this where I want to end up?"

DISABLED LIST (17–20 POINTS):

WARNING: Dead Person Working! If you scored 17–20 points, chances are you are actively disengaged and draining the organization of the vitality it needs. Given that you spend more time making excuses and pointing the finger than focusing forward and finding solutions, you probably operate out of insecurity and fear. While you may have moments of brilliance, you frequently feel like a victim and are afraid to take initiative. You feel as though the sense of hope and idealism you once had has been beaten out of you. The helpless state of mind in which you choose to reside is also robbing you of life at work.

Your lack of accountability is slowing the organi zation down, making it slug gish, and creating a road-block to creativity and innovation. Personally, you're missing significant opportunities to make a dif-ference. The organization isn't getting what it paid for, and the cycle repeats itself, because you keep making the same choices. Is this how you want to spend your life?

Use this book as a wake-up call.

Commit yourself to greater freedom and autonomy. Then make the necessary changes. The payoffs are—BOOM—more life at work, and a life that matters.

DEAD PEOPLE WORKING

Questions Players Ask

Regardless of where you fall on the player continuum, there is always room for growth in making better choices, and the quality of our choices is determined by the quality of the questions we ask.

For example:

- "Why hasn't our CEO clearly communicated her vision?" becomes "What can I do to help our CEO clarify the future direction of our organization?"

- "When is this company going to start investing in developing its people?" becomes "What knowledge and skills do I need to make a greater contribution, and how do I acquire them?"

- "Why doesn't IT build a system we can use?" becomes "How can I define what 'user-friendly' looks like in our unit, so IT has a better understanding?"

- "Why does XYZ department always have to protect its turf?" becomes "What can I do to reach across functional boundaries and promote more collaboration?"

These questions put the locus of control in your hands. They challenge you to be a player, to be the *cause* versus the *effect*.

Develop the discipline to ask these four simple but very powerful questions in every situation, and BOOM, you will take a huge step away from helplessness and a powerful step toward becoming more in control.

- What do I desire most; what do I want to create?

- What part of the problem do I own?

- To what part of the solution can I contribute?

- What about me must change?

BOOM!

At first these questions may make you uncomfortable, because they won't let you off the hook. You will inevitably feel some pain as they force you out of denial and self-deception and into reality and being a player. But don't give up. Over the long haul these questions will absolutely energize you by giving you the authority to act, the power to effect change, and the freedom to stay the course. You will feel more at liberty to follow your dreams and, ultimately, create more life at work—not to mention a reputation for being a most valuable player! But what is your course, and what have you done with your dreams, your desires?

Players Refuse to Sell Out

Players refuse to sell out their dreams and aspirations, the deepest desires of their hearts. Sound too touchy-feely for you? Think again. Engagement is about pouring your heart *and* your mind into something. It's about feeling something so passionately that you have to dig in with everything you've got. On the other hand, disengagement and its traveling partners—frustration, discouragement, despair, and apathy—set in when you lose heart. "Everybody's got a hungry heart," sings Bruce Springsteen in his 1982 hit single "Hungry Heart". The problem in most organizations is that people have convinced themselves that they are *not* hungry. When you operate solely from your mind, your heart atrophies; it becomes dead and disabled, and you lose a part of yourself. Ask ten dead people working, who are actively disengaged, "How did it happen? How did you get to this place in your career?" Part of the problem is the majority of them will say, "I stopped listening to my heart." Ask ten people who left successful careers for something they've always wanted to do, "Where did you find the courage? What was the major impetus?" If they are honest, the majority of them will say, "I started listening to my heart. I went with my gut."

Not long ago, Kimberly Henshaw, our former Duchess of Details, found her life turned upside down. Kimberly was a mother of two very young children, with a husband who felt as if he was on a road going nowhere. Mike earned a degree in biology, tried it out for a while, and decided perhaps he needed more. So, off to law school! A few years later and a law degree behind him, Mike landed a job with a firm here in San Diego. But it didn't take long for him to doubt his choice. What had life become? The same drive each way; the same reserved parking spot every day; the same lobby in, elevator up, and cubicle for logging in the hours; and the same colleagues' faces. OK, maybe the case numbers were different, but the themes were all the same. What meant security, achievement, and success for some, became a lifeless routine for Mike. The good news is that Mike's heart was still beating, and a dream was stirring his passions back to life. Just when Kimberly wondered what was next, she found herself quitting her job (yes, leaving us), selling her home, and packing to follow a dream in Hawaii. Mike and Kimberly sold out! They sold out a false sense of security (full-time jobs, weekly paychecks, owning a home) and poured their hearts and minds into buying and running their own business. Almost one year later, Mike (thirty pounds lighter, working twelve hours a day and loving it) and Kimberly are ALIVE, living a dream come true—as the owners and operators of a thriving dive shop in Kona on the Big Island of Hawaii. So the question we ask you at this point is, are you listening to your heart?

ARE YOU LISTENING TO YOUR HEART?

Potentially great organizations are crippled by people who kill their desires and live their entire work lives out of duty. They've ignored desire or abandoned it altogether and given up their dreams. They've allowed things like routine, bad habits, fear, and a false sense of security to take control. *Good enough* has become the enemy of *great*. *Routine* has become the enemy of *desire*. *Easy* has become the enemy of *sacrifice* and *hard work*.

What about you? Is there something you long for that you've given up on? Have you sacrificed a dream that could make you come alive for a life that simply "works"? When the journey is over, will you be able to look back and honestly say, "I wasn't afraid to pursue my dream," or will you have sold out? Will you be able to proclaim, "I locked arms with others who weren't afraid to pursue their dreams, and together we played some awesome music—and the music we played, wow, it made a difference in people's lives!"? We want you to *want* to work hard, but that doesn't mean becoming burned-out. Mike Henshaw is working harder than he ever has, but he's full of life because he's turned-on about it. Maybe it's time to dig deep inside, rediscover your dreams, and play like crazy.

Players Know Change Begins from the Inside Out

If anything is going to make your organization the enlightened, impassioned place you want it to become, it will be a conspiracy of people like you, whose dreams, desires, new ideas, and fresh perspectives will trigger critical transformation. But it won't occur until people like you become so committed to making a difference that the rest of the organization can't help but be transformed by your example.

Personal change almost always precedes organizational change. If reform is going to happen in the systems, structures, policies, and culture where you hang out, then change must first make its way into the hearts, minds, and characters of people like you. That's why Mahatma Gandhi said, "Be the change you wish to see in the world." Most of us affirm this famous statement intellectually, but when it comes right down to it, our behavior suggests that we aren't lifting a thumb until someone else leads the charge. Hypocrisy runs rampant in our society. We espouse lofty values

Be the change you wish to see in the world.

but frequently lack the integrity to live them out loud. Karen Shadders, VP of People for Wegmans, a Fortune 100 Best Company, recommits to her values on a daily basis. Karen told us, "I take the same route to work each day, and there is a spot that has become my trigger point where I consciously think about how I am going to demonstrate my values and challenge myself to the highest standards. I recommit and think about how I can take these values and make them real in the work that I do each day."

Karen has become an MVP inside one of the most admired grocery chains in the world. She is like many of the shakers and movers we meet in companies all over the globe. When people do something to become a force for positive change, it gets noticed. Other folks respect their courage and admire their example. They get bigger, more exciting assignments and leverage them into meaningful work that produces tangible results. They become a beacon of success, and everyone—from the CEO to the person in the office next door—wants to know how they do it. This establishes their credibility and creates an opportunity for them to tell their story. As more and more people hear their story, a personal brand, a reputation for being a go-to person, is established. This attracts new opportunities for success, and on it goes. If you want to live your values out loud each day, find your own trigger point, and do as Karen Shadders does—recommit each day.

On June 30, 1859, Charles Blondin, a Frenchman and the greatest tightrope walker in the world, strung a tightrope across Niagara Falls. Over twenty-five thousand cheering people watched as Blondin inched his way across 1,100 feet of rope suspended 167 feet over the raging falls. With forty-two million gallons of water pouring into the raging river below each minute, and no net or safety harness, the slightest error would be fatal. As he approached the Canadian side of the Falls, the crowd went wild and started to chant, "Blondin! Blondin! Blondin!"

The Frenchman silenced the crowd and yelled, "I am Blondin! Do you believe in me?"

The crowd screamed back, "We believe! We believe!"

Again, he quieted the crowd and asked, "Do you believe that I can go back across the Falls carrying a person on my shoulders?"

Another mighty roar erupted as the spectators responded, "We believe! We believe! We believe!"

Then, above the cheering and applause, Blondin asked, "Who will be that person?" You could hear a pin drop. After a long, dead silence, one man came out of the crowd, crawled up the scaffold, got on Blondin's shoulders, and allowed the tightrope walker to carry him back across the Falls.

On that day thousands yelled, "We believe! We believe!" But only one person was willing to act on what he believed. Now, it's easy to write off this example and say, "Who in his right mind would let some idiot exhibitionist put his life in jeopardy by taking him across a tightrope over Niagara Falls?" The answer, of course, is: The person who completely trusted that Blondin would get him safely to the other side—the one who truly believed.

We don't want to know what you *believe* about freedom. We want to know the last time you took on a sacred cow, spoke up when it wasn't politically correct, or did your homework. We want to know when you built a solid business case and voiced your disagreement with someone in a position of authority.

We don't want to know what you *believe* about autonomy. We want to know how often you have stepped out on your own to pursue a new opportunity without waiting for someone above you to suggest it. How often do you need to look up for affirmation and get the "go ahead" before acting?

We don't want to know what you *believe* about authority. If we examined your decisions and behavior over the last eighteen months, would we find that you are an order *taker*—or a self-directed *shaker* and *mover*?

We don't want to know what you *believe* about accountability. We want to know if you admit your mistakes. Do you assume responsibility for your contribution to the problem and offer up solutions? Do you honor your commitments and deliver the results when and how you say you will?

We don't want to know what you *believe* about meritocracy. We want to know: Do your conversations with colleagues in the bathroom, break room, or bar indicate that you feel you are entitled to a promotion or that you must earn it? Do you feel you deserve better assignments regardless of whether you do something extraordinary or just show up?

Change begins from the inside out. It is relatively easy to say, "We believe! We believe!" That's why we call it "lip service." But are you metaphorically willing to climb up on Blondin's shoulders and put your beliefs into action? By its very definition, true belief is action oriented. That's why we say, "Put your money where your mouth is." The more you embrace freedom, autonomy, and accountability, the more you will become an instrument of change in your life and in the lives of others.

Your Playing "Small" Does No One Any Favors

Consider an ordinary man with a small physique walking down the main street of a capital city on a clear day. He is just another nameless, faceless person who blends in with the crowd, until he chooses to seize a moment in history and give us a powerful image of courage and commitment. Armed with only his shopping bags, he steps off the sidewalk and stands in front of a rolling column of more than seventeen Chinese tanks moving in on prodemocracy protestors.

His incredible achievement is not that he permanently stops the tanks—he doesn't. In fact, many think the hero of Tiananmen Square ultimately gave his life because of what he believed in, although his identity and fate were never confirmed. His impact? On June 5, 1989, his act awakened people all over the globe to the transformational power of one committed person. The "Unknown Rebel" was named in *Time* magazine's 1989 list of "the 100 most influential people of the 20th Century."

The world is vast, and it is easy to feel like just another number. We see so many things that need to be changed, so many things that could be better, but we feel powerless. So we shrink from our responsibilities. But we are not nearly as inadequate as we may think. We have unprecedented power; power to change the world, to make it better or to make it worse. Remember the tragic fact that it only took a few people to implode two buildings in New York City and redefine global terrorism. Their ability to create that horror makes it even more important that you and I stand up and make our lives mean something.

To think and act as though you are of no consequence in your organization—or in the grand scheme of life, for that matter—is an insult to our Creator. Many of us become prisoners to fears that are unfounded. As the Eagles' song "Already Gone" says, "So oftentimes it happens that we live our lives in chains and we never even know we have the key."

Disney's box-office sensation *The Lion King* plays out this theme very well. Simba, the only son of the great lion king Mufasa, runs from the kingdom and his own greatness because his evil uncle Scar blames him for his father's death—a murder that Scar engineered himself. Simba leaves his home to live in denial and takes up residence with Timon the meerkat and Pumbaa the warthog. As Simba shrinks from his responsibility and pulls the shade down on his past, the consequences of his pride are devastating. Left with a leadership vacuum, darkness sets in, a famine takes hold, and the lions become demoralized. That is, until the wise old monkey, Rafiki, shows up one night to rattle Simba's cage. Rafiki, the tribal shaman, helps Simba rediscover the true meaning of his heritage as the heir to Mufasa's throne. Simba begins to understand that he has not only run from the kingdom, but he has turned his back on the courage, strength, and wisdom with which he was raised. Then, on the same night, Mufasa confronts Simba in a dream:

Mufasa: *Simba.*

Simba: *Father?*

Mufasa: *Simba, you have forgotten me.*

Simba: *No! How could I?*

Mufasa: *You have forgotten who you are, and so forgotten me. Look inside yourself, Simba . . . you are more than what you have become.*

Simba: *How can I go back? I'm not who I used to be.*

Mufasa: *Remember who you are. You are my son, and the one true king. Remember who you are.*

Faced with the choice to remain a victim or rise to his calling and make a difference, Simba chooses to shed the cloak of shame and self-deprecation and returns from exile to confront his uncle. In the process he is transformed into the image of his father.

It's paradoxical. We frequently run from accountability; yet there is no meaning, no freedom, and no fulfillment in our lives without it. Simba opens the door to these virtues—for himself as well as the pride—but only after assuming responsibility for how he handled circumstances he couldn't control. His choice to play "small" did no one any favors. In fact, it hurt the Pridelands community. But when Simba took charge, other members of the pride were liberated to become more accountable and play a role in the fight against evil as well. Even the two couch potatoes, Pumbaa and Timon, were jolted out of their complacent lifestyle. In choosing to follow Simba, they chose to make a difference, to pursue a life that had meaning.

Every day we are each confronted with choices similar to the ones Simba faced. On a personal level, whether it's facing the brutal facts of reality (after all, life is difficult, demanding, and riddled with unpleasant circumstances), admitting a mistake, speaking up in a meeting, or acting on candid feedback, side-stepping your responsibility and playing "small" may offer temporary comfort, as it did for Simba, but the long-term impact can be devastating.

What happens to your family and friends—what do they lose—when you fail to step up to your own power? What happens when a critical mass of people in an organization chooses to play small and lay the blame on "them"? It creates a recipe for dysfunction that deadens the organization and its people.

Here are just a few examples of what happens when we shrink from our desires to make a difference:

- People with titles are revered regardless of their character or leadership abilities.
- A culture of candor and meritocracy is sacrificed for a culture of politics and entitlement.
- The focus shifts from honor in service and sacrifice to demanding our individual rights.
- People become codependent—on management, on outside gurus, on the person in the next cubicle for answers they already have.
- People lean on rules and policies and legalism instead of gut instinct and common sense.
- The organization moves slowly and sluggishly while people cautiously wait for marching orders or permission to act.
- A culture of narcissism is created that is so inwardly focused that it's out of tune with market realities.
- Fear and paranoia take hold as the mysterious "they" becomes an excuse for not acting.
- People hide anonymously in the bureaucracy to avoid accountability.
- The kind of risk taking and experimentation that precedes creativity and innovation are repressed.

BOOM!

- People who do assume responsibility resent those who don't, and morale goes out the door.

- Expectations become unrealistic as we charge management with being responsible for our success and self-actualization.

- Little mistakes get tucked under the rug and turn into big mistakes.

Our point here is that perhaps we need to expect less from the people around us and require more from ourselves. Maybe we need to stop waiting for someone in charge to give us permission and stop putting so much of our job and life satisfaction in the hands of other people. Perhaps we need to realize that we have more freedom, more power, and more influence than we give ourselves credit for. When we are willing to look in the mirror and acknowledge that *we* have created the cultures we tend to complain about, we will also find that the solutions lie within us.

The challenge we're laying down starts with each of us having the courage to ask, "If it's not THEM, then what am I doing that's meaningful? How am I adding value? What does it mean to be a person who literally creates my own success? And how do I become this person?"

BOOM!

If you want to catch a brief interview with some of the players we've met,

go to **freibergs.com/boom** *and type the word* **Player** *in the BOOM! box.*

In the heat of fast-paced
competition there is no time for
"that's not my job" or "who's to blame."
Great players elevate cooperation
and collaboration to an art form.

CHOICE #2

BE ACCOUNTABLE

There Is No *"THEY"*—
Only You and Me

02

"People who are accountable never walk by a problem intentionally."

Once you've decided to be a player, you have to know who you're playing against—and here comes a big surprise: for most of your life, we're willing to bet, you've been playing against *yourself*! All these years, while you've been blaming *them*— "*they* won't let me grow; *they* hold me back; *they* don't care about my success" —you never knew that there is no "they"; there's only you and me. And no one can stop us but ourselves.

The Real Enemy Is Us, Not Them

Have you ever sat in a meeting where people feel paralyzed and heard someone say, "What do *they* want? *They* need to share their vision more clearly." In other words, how do we please management—at whatever level? How do we figure out what they want and then give it to them? As a manager or a senior executive, have you ever discussed your organization's response to a new initiative and said, "*They* [our employees] need to get on board; *they* need to take more initiative"?

Have you ever been part of a team or a department that isn't performing well and heard some version of: *"They* [merchandizing] don't stock enough inventory. Sales are down because our customers don't have enough choices. If *they* would only do their jobs, we wouldn't be in this mess. We missed the deadline because *they* didn't get us the forecast on time"?

Have you ever heard a front-line person refer to customers as though they are the enemy and say, *"They* don't know what they want. *They* ask the same stupid questions over and over again! *They* have unreasonable expectations!"?

Have you ever heard a senior executive refer to the board of directors and say, *"They* don't understand the specific nuances of the market realities we face. I wish *they* were better informed"? What all of these statements have in common is that they reveal our propensity to shift the burden of responsibility. The whole agenda is about what *they* should or shouldn't do to fulfill me, rescue me, relieve my pain, make me happy, and complete me. It's as if *they* were put on the face of this earth to bring me satisfaction, and *they* aren't doing their jobs. In looking to *them* our codependence is exposed.

Do you know who *they* are? Have you met *them*? The mysterious "they" lurks in every organization. And they are bad hombres! Imagine someone coming up to his boss with a brilliant but gutsy idea and the supervisor saying, "That's a phenomenal idea. Share that with senior management!"

"Well, I was hoping *you* would share it with them; that's why I brought it to you."

"Yes, but it's your idea. You should present it; you should get the credit for this."

"No. I'm OK with you doing it."

"Why?"

"Because I heard about *them*."

"Why, what have you heard?"

BOOM!

"I heard what they do to people with radical ideas. I heard they are brutal!"

"Who?"

"I don't know. I just heard that *they* can be downright mean."

"Well, has anyone been seriously injured; have they ever killed anybody?"

"I think so."

They come in many forms: our board members, bosses, senior management, coworkers, customers, suppliers, spouses, children, parents, friends, in-laws, and outlaws. It's easier to point the finger at *them* than it is to be accountable. Yet if we are intellectually honest with ourselves, when we are done saying,

"*They* won't listen . . ."

"*They* won't cooperate . . ."

"*They* won't give us the resources [time, authority, etc.] . . ."

we still have to look in the mirror and ask, "Is it that *they won't* . . . or *I haven't?*"

"*I haven't* been open-minded."

"*I haven't* earned their trust."

"*I haven't* approached the right people in the right way."

The biggest problem and the real enemy we face is *ourselves*. We act as though we are powerless when we are not. We operate from the belief that change begins from the *outside in*. That is, "If I'm going to be happy, someone or something beyond me must change, because my company, my boss, my circumstances control me." We develop a pattern of thinking that says, *My happiness, my job satisfaction, my sense of accomplishment, and my ultimate success are dependent upon people and forces outside myself.* Far too many of us play the role of victim rather than realizing that we have the power to live intentional lives.

Being a victim is a choice, much of which hinges on our failure to be accountable for our own outcomes in life; instead, we blame others for getting in the way of our progress. We blame bureaucracies that

> **BEING A VICTIM IS A CHOICE, MUCH OF WHICH HINGES ON OUR FAILURE TO BE ACCOUNTABLE FOR OUR OWN OUTCOMES IN LIFE.**

limit our creativity, politics that govern our voices, and uninspiring leaders who have a neurotic need to control us. We hide in the shelter of systems and structures that suppress our action, we falsely flatter bad bosses whom few people respect, and we withhold world-class ideas for fear of rejection—all in an attempt to save face. But our pursuit of safety and self-protection delivers something we didn't bargain for: namely, a dehumanizing sense of inadequacy—dead people working!

Ask anyone who has a membership to the "blame and complain" or the "we're confused; let's procrastinate" club if he likes feeling weak, vulnerable, disabled, incapacitated, and cowardly. Ask him if he thinks these are the key character traits that will earn him a reputation as a go-to person within your organization. The answer is an obvious no. Yet so many people fail to see the connection between blaming, complaining, and helplessness until it's too late. We wake up one day at the end of our lives and recognize that we have become dead people working. With deep regret we wonder, *What happened? Why haven't I been more influential and productive? How come I'm not happy? My life hasn't turned out the way I hoped it would.*

Making excuses weakens our influence, lowers our self-confidence, and renders us helpless.

Yet when people refuse to make excuses, suddenly they are

BOOM!

free to do amazing things. Mike Ullman is the CEO of JC Penney, with a long career in retail at a variety of great companies, including Macy's. He likes to illustrate his stories on engagement by telling the story of how much difference a single person really can make. And, as he makes clear, the difference can be huge.

At Macy's we had a Charter Club specialty store in a strip mall in Princeton, New Jersey, that was one of the worst in the Macy's system at the time. This was not a great place for a store; half the stores were empty, including the other anchor. And where the average Charter Club store was doing about $1.3 million in sales, this store was only doing about $800,000. The manager quit, and we promoted the assistant manager with no big change. Within a year, she had sales up to $2.2 million.

Just like that; nothing else changed. She did a million more than the company average, in just one year. And when we looked at what she did, it was all about engagement—her engagement. She took it on as her store as if she owned it. It was her store, her merchandise, her customers, and her associates. She took on the leadership challenge and got her team engaged, and the results were unbelievable. It all comes down to one person's decision to be engaged.

One person—one woman who refused to be stopped by all the very real problems she faced. One individual who refused to give up and join the dead-people-working club. One soul who checked in and refused to make excuses. She came to work fully engaged and alive, her spirit became contagious, and she awoke the passion in others. One person chose to make a difference!

We've got news for you. There is no *they*—only you and me! Accept the fact that no one is going to ride in on a white horse and rescue you or your organization. No one is going to magically lift the weight of responsibility from your shoulders. Don't wait for others to show you the way. Blaze the trail yourself. Many of us look *out there* rather than *in here* for the answers to difficult problems. The assumption is that someone wiser, better equipped, more experienced, or in the "right" position should solve this problem. If something good is going to happen, it will happen because you looked for the answers inside yourself. and *you* made it happen.

Leadership Is a Choice, Not a Title

One of the reasons we play "small" is our gut-level belief that leadership is a position.

We've grown accustomed to the idea that the only power that matters is positional power—that a title on the door equals the right to hold the floor. Most people would disagree with this intellectually, but if you look at the way the majority of us behave in organizations, a lot of homage is given to people with titles. Theoretically, most of us agree that leadership can and should exist at all levels of an organization, but our manners suggest that we are reticent to assume the responsibility. Most of us deeply believe that critical problems must be solved and major change must be driven from the top.

Authority is comforting; we like to know that someone is leading the pack. It is safer and more comfortable to assume that those in power have more answers and better solutions than we do. Our actions seem to say, "*I don't have a big title, so I'm not in a position to know. Jerry is the senior vice president, and he's supposed to be our leader. It's not MY job to think—he knows what to do.*"

Yet we know that when people act locally, they usually get more of the right things done in a shorter period of time. By the time a problem surfaces to the upper echelons of an organization, it's often too late to take corrective action. Small, manageable problems turn into large, costly problems when they aren't addressed at the individual level. As long as we

BOOM!

are unwilling to step up to the plate of leadership, our reticence will act as a governor on the influence we can have in our organizations.

In our book NUTS! *Southwest Airlines' Crazy Recipe for Business and Personal Success*, we quote Herb Kelleher, chairman and former CEO, as saying, "Leadership is not determined by position or title to any extent, shape, or form. Our people have determined not to regard title or position as especially important because they wouldn't be as free to make things happen" (303). Titles have a smothering effect on leadership; they tend to make people too cautious and too analytical. We spend too much time worrying about how the person behind the title will react to our initiatives instead of doing what's right for the company and its stakeholders. Many people who have made some of the greatest changes in history did it without the power of position, status, money, rank, or intimidating arsenals. Think Gandhi. Mother Teresa. Nelson Mandela. The Dalai Lama. Rosa Parks. Dr. Martin Luther King Jr. If a position doesn't make a leader, what does?

In a word: *INFLUENCE!*

The leaders we just mentioned were people with big ideas, not big positions. If there is any magic to their influence, it's that they were competent communicators. All were able to articulate their ideas with boldness, clarity, and heartfelt passion and BOOM—people joined them and started a movement.

Title, position, and authority may wield power, but influence carries the day. Every parent of a teenager knows this. You can lay an "authority trip" on your kids, but you quickly find out that you are competing for their hearts and minds with a formidable opponent—peer pressure. Your children will *comply* with your authority because you

> TITLE, POSITION, AND AUTHORITY MAY WIELD POWER, BUT INFLUENCE CARRIES THE DAY.

> **POWER AND AUTHORITY FORCE US TO CHANGE, BUT INFLUENCE MOVES AND INSPIRES US TO CHANGE.**

have the power to exert consequences, but they are much more sensitive to and moved by the influence of their peers. This doesn't change just because we grow up and go to work. Aren't you more open to the influence of your friends and coworkers than you are to pronouncements of authority? Power and authority force us to change, but influence moves and inspires us to change. Positional power can control our behaviors, but it will never capture our hearts and unleash our passions.

Influence reaches its pinnacle when someone—who isn't controlled by your power and authority—exemplifies the impact of your influence in his or her life. Isn't this why we are thrilled when an adult child calls home and demonstrates—through a major decision or a significant life change—a commitment to a value system that had something to do with our influence?

If we truly believe that leadership is influence, and anyone within an organization can influence others, then doesn't it make sense to expect more leadership from ourselves and to stop searching for it in others? If leadership is not a position, but rather a choice, *anyone* at any level in an organization can exercise leadership. People who make things happen never use "I don't have authority; I'm not in a position of power" as an excuse. Authority—as long as it's in the best interests of the organization—is better assumed than granted. Expand your influence by changing your view of leadership.

Jackie was invited to do an event for the Jewish Community Centers' Annual Convention in Philly. To prepare for the event, she visited the JCC in La Jolla, met with the president and incoming chairman of the board, toured the facility, and learned about the mission of JCCs around the country. But when she was leaving, Jackie met a guy whose decision—whose choice—to lead is what really put the mission of the JCC into perspective. "EJ," a security guard, stopped her (Jackie obviously wasn't a familiar face to him). He boldly said, "Good morning. Thank you for coming. Was this your first time here?" And yes, it was, so EJ then asked if she had seen the Holocaust Memorial, and if not, did she have a moment to experience the small rock-and-water garden to the right side of the entrance? On that morning (and we're betting on every other day too) EJ eagerly and passionately served, not just as a security guard, but as a leader for this JCC and an ambassador of the memorial. EJ proudly escorted Jackie through the memorial, noting the rocks etched with the names of so many lost to the Holocaust, along with the names of family and friends who wanted to remember them. He pointed to a bronze statue of a woman and commented that her tears run continuously, endlessly, into the bowl that she lifts up toward heaven—a gesture of sorrow, loss, tragedy, and hope. The memorial pulls it all together—the JCCs create a safe haven where all generations come together in memory of the past but in greater hope for the future. This is what you'll read if you visit the Holocaust Memorial at the Lawrence Family Jewish Community Center, Jacob's Family Campus, La Jolla, California, etched into a black marble wall:

"You shall be like a watered garden,
a spring whose waters never fail."

—ISAIAH 58:11

This Memorial garden is composed of the stillness of bronze and of running water, the endurance of stone and nature's fluidity. It represents our desire to carry into the next century and the coming generations the memory of our darkest desolation and the astonishment of our rebirth.

The garden is a place that bears the names of those who were silenced and the names of those committed to remember them. Here in this meditative space we can stroll or sit, reflecting on what can never be repaired and on what continues, despite what we have undergone, to persist and flourish.

Water over rock, green upon stone, a tree whose branches shelter earth while disclosing heaven, the power of memory to transmute grief into eternity.

NESSA RAPOPORT—TOBI KAHN, 1999

Who among us has not felt the tragedy of the Holocaust? This memorial is a symbol of the power of resilience — of choice. To see it is to experience the hope and the desire that has been crafted into all of us just as it was crafted into this memorial — how can we not feel compelled to preserve and prevail?

Given the pervasive feeling of powerlessness in organizations, most people do not understand the full extent to which they can make a positive difference in other people's lives. It's just too easy to underestimate how far our influence can travel, who it will touch, and how

BOOM!

much of an impact it can have. EJ doesn't have that problem, because he made the decision to act like a leader, not just a property guard.

> *"Take your life in your own*
> *hands and what happens?*
> *A terrible thing: no one to blame."*

—ERICA JONG, AWARD-WINNING
NOVELIST AND POET

How Do I Get Rid of "Them"?

Refuse to Play the Blame Game

Blaming is a fundamental part of human nature. It's a coping mechanism we learned when we were young. When we felt threatened or angry or vulnerable, we used it, and it worked. In fact, it worked so well that we perfected it as adults.

Humorist Bern Williams said, "If Adam and Eve were alive today, they would probably sue the snake." Blaming is a defense tactic for those who desire to take the spotlight off of themselves and shift the problem to someone else. Instead of asking, "What have I done to cause the situation I'm in?" the question becomes, "Why are *they* doing this to me?"

If we can't be blamed, we are safe, right? Wrong. The problem is that you will never get to the cause of your misfortune and therefore never get on with living the life you want by pointing the finger at others. Blaming may make you feel good temporarily, but in the end it will only leave you stuck in the situation—a lousy relationship with your boss, a job that sucks the life out of you, a culture that values bureaucracy and politics over making things happen—that is making you unhappy. Blaming only perpetuates the problem.

We guarantee you that moving forward, making progress, and making your life count will never happen if you insist that *they* are the problem. *They* are *not* the problem. You are accountable for your life, and that certainly includes your life at work. If you don't like your boss, you are accountable. If your job sucks, you are accountable. If you work in a culture of fear and bureaucratic red tape, you are accountable. Most of us aren't comfortable with these words. But what is worse, the temporary *pain* of owning your problems—creating a strong probability for long-term healing, freedom, and victory—or the temporary *relief* of dodging your problems—creating a strong probability for broken relationships, unfulfilled dreams, and long-term, self-induced misery?

Breaking the cycle of victimization starts with a commitment to see the world in a different way. Try this exercise; it's a slight variation of the exercise you did in Choice #1.

Identify three to five times in your past when someone or something at work caused you to feel misunderstood, mishandled, or mistreated. These are times when you felt really "ripped-off." Now examine each one of these scenarios and ask yourself:

1. What did I do or fail to do that created this undesirable outcome?

2. In looking at it again, how did I shift the burden of responsibility to someone else?

BOOM!

3. What was I afraid of? What was I protecting? What was I trying to avoid?

4. What were the consequences?

5. If I knew then what I know now about accountability, what would I have done differently?

6. How does this apply to any situations I am currently facing?

By asking these kinds of questions, we learn to think like accountable people. This is the courageous first step to becoming less dependent upon *them.* Being accountable requires big-time maturity, but it is a necessary prerequisite to living a life by design instead of a life by default. When you give up blame and condemnation, you redefine yourself as a leader rather than a victim, and BOOM—you seize an incredible power to change your corner of the world.

Expect No More from Your Boss than You Do from Yourself

A lot of our discontent and disillusionment in life is caused by unmet expectations, and when it comes to our bosses, we expect a lot. But are we in touch with reality? Every organization we've ever been in is a work in progress, an unfinished prototype. The same could be said for the leaders who run these organizations—most are flawed individuals with great vision, attempting to do great things. They are far from perfect. The problem is that the higher we look in an organization, the higher the expectations we have of our bosses. The cure for our disappoint-ment, however, is not to lower our expectations but rather to shift the focus of our attention. We need to expect more from ourselves.

In the blurry world of business, decisions are rarely clear-cut. Leaders caught in predicaments will make judgment calls, trade-offs, and compromises that aren't always right. The decision makers in your organization are not all-knowing. They don't have a crystal ball with which to see the future. They struggle with uncertainty—*just like you*. They worry about what their bosses think—*just like you*. They desire a better culture, less uncertainty, and more stability—*just like you*. They want more time with their families—*just like you*. When it comes to leading major change efforts, their actions may appear to be misguided or self-serving from where you sit, but they are probably doing the best they can with the information they have.

The wiser we become, the more we realize that our bosses are a lot like our parents. As adults we quickly learn that our parents didn't have the leadership thing all figured out either. There was a lot of "parenting" they made up along the way. In their book *The Hidden Power of Social Networks*, Rob Cross and Andrew Parker quote an executive vice presi-dent in the commercial lending industry. With refreshing honesty this individual affirms that even those who reside at the top deal with their share of uncertainty and wrestle with their own insecurities. No one has it all figured out. Here's what this person said:

> It has taken us years, and I think we are still not sure if we are getting things right even after substantial reengineering projects, a move to teams, new HR practices, two acquisitions, and a ton invested in tech-nology. By now we should have reduced costs and created a more nimble company without a focus on hierarchy and fiefdoms. But it's tough to ensure that this is really happening. Most of us in this room have thousands of people that we are accountable for stretched across the globe. It's impossible to manage or even know what's going on in

BOOM!

the depths of the organization. I mean, each of us can fool ourselves into thinking we're smart and running a tight ship. But really the best we can do is create a context and hope that things emerge in a positive way, and this is tough because you can't really see the impact your decisions have on people. So you just kind of hope that what you want to happen is happening and then sound confident when telling others. (3)

If our bosses don't have it all figured out, maybe we should stop acting as if they do. What if *we* took more responsibility for the success of our organizations? Perhaps we should recalibrate our expectations and stop getting angry or frustrated when *they* fail to take care of us the way we think they should. Perhaps we should stop putting our bosses solely in charge of our morale, our education, and our relationships with customers and coworkers. Maybe we shouldn't wait for *them* to be our advocates or send their vision down from on high. Maybe we should take charge of these things ourselves.

Jack Welch told Kevin many years ago, "The organization is infinitely bigger than any one person. As CEOs, we take far too much blame for what goes wrong, and we get far too much credit for what goes right." Expecting perfection from those above us is unrealistic, not only because "perfect" is impossible to attain, but also because everyone in

> "THE ORGANIZATION IS INFINITELY BIGGER THAN ANY ONE PERSON. AS CEOs, WE TAKE FAR TOO MUCH BLAME FOR WHAT GOES WRONG, AND WE GET FAR TOO MUCH CREDIT FOR WHAT GOES RIGHT."
>
> —JACK WELCH

the organization has a different definition of what perfection is. Maybe it's time to take your boss off the pedestal. Remember, bosses can be irrational, emotional, idiosyncratic, hypocritical, vulnerable, and deeply flawed human beings — *just like you*. Assuming your boss will always live the values, walk the talk, fix your problems, and make the right decisions is wishful — flawed — thinking.

If you want to blow the doors off business-as-usual, worry less about your boss's lack of perfection and more about how you can fill the voids in your organization. Give your boss a break by showing some empathy, patience, and support. Start by looking for ways you can compliment his or her shortcomings. Take some initiative; stop waiting for guidance. It just may be that no one has a better understanding of the problem and how to fix it than you do. The organization doesn't expect you to have all of the answers either. But don't make your boss — or anyone else — do your thinking for you.

If the vision and strategic initiatives for the organization are unclear, volunteer to put a team together that can bring clarity to the future of the business. If your boss has been procrastinating on a project she isn't very excited about because it requires a core competence that she doesn't have and you do, step in and take the project over for her. OK, so senior management really doesn't have its fingers on the pulse of your customers because they don't spend enough time in the field. Rather than complain about it, create a reason for them to talk with your customers, schedule a ride along, and make something happen.

Imagine that you are on a personal tour of the incredible museums inside the Vatican. Some of the Vatican's finest paintings are frescoes embedded high on the ceilings. They are difficult to see, but you get to see them up close and personal. Imagine having access to the ancient archives within the Vatican, including photographs and manuscripts. Imagine being able to explore your faith by tapping into the best minds resident within the Vatican and around the globe.

Thanks to Sister Judith Zoebelein, you can.

Shortly after the Internet exploded in the mid-1990s, Sister Judith saw the powerful potential of the Web. She and a small band of Internet pioneers at the Vatican approached Pope John Paul II with the idea of creating a Vatican Web site. John Paul agreed, and www.vatican.va was launched with one page containing the pope's 1995 Christmas message. The site quickly expanded into six languages and a warehouse of information, including an extensive library, 360-degree images of the Vatican's galleries, videos of its restoration projects, and a powerful search engine.

Today, Sister Judith is the editorial director of the Internet Office of the Holy See. She heads a full-blown data center for the Vatican that is set to launch a second Vatican Web site. This one is designed to bring Catholics together in a myspace.com sort of way. The site will include specific opportunities—e-learning and personal news updates—for families, young people, priests, and parishes to connect, collaborate, and learn. The idea is to bring people together online so they can learn from one another and then go back and have a positive impact on their communities.

Sister Judith didn't sit around and say, "The technology is here; someone should talk to the pope about this." She saw an opportunity to reach millions of people and connect them with their faith, she had a plan, and she took the idea to the pope herself. She didn't wait for guidance from above. Instead she provided it to her boss. Have you been guilty of sitting around and waiting for direction? Stop waiting and *lead* where you are planted; choose to play hard and chart your own course to success.

Banish Tribalism and Shatter the Silos

The world is a complex system of interconnected ecological, social, spiritual, political, and economic subsystems. Decisions made in one part of the world have implications for people in other parts of the world. Yet because cause and effect are often separated by time and space, we don't

> **TRIBALISM TAKES PLACE WHEN ANY SUBGROUP OF PEOPLE WITHIN AN ORGANIZATION STARTS TO THINK OF ITSELF AS EXTRA SPECIAL.**

always see the interconnectedness between what we do and its impact on others. When we view the organization as divisible and compartmentalized, tribalism happens and myopia sets in. We begin to see our immediate coworkers and our part of the organization as "special." When this happens, we alienate people from other "tribes" within the same organization, whom we paradoxically rely on to get things done.

Herb Kelleher at Southwest Airlines introduced us to the concept of tribalism. He believes that tribalism takes place when any subgroup of people within an organization starts to think of itself as extra special and believes that its ideas and attitudes are uniquely superior to those of other subgroups. Companies break up, countries fall apart, sports teams are defeated, rock-and-roll bands dissolve, and wars are ignited all because of the destructive nature of tribalism. Tribalism is the enemy of teamwork, diversity, and altruism—the very attributes that make world-class companies unbeatable.

Tribalism is exacerbated by the fact that our needs, desires, and aspirations often conflict with one another because we compete for scarce resources. We allow ourselves to be teased into a *me vs. you* or *us vs. them* mentality where it becomes all too easy to lose sight of the whole. For example, one or more of the following situations may be something you've experienced:

- A salesperson really wants to close a deal and agrees to a delivery date that manufacturing can't meet.

- A manufacturing person doesn't respond quickly to a salesperson who has a time-sensitive issue that the customer must resolve before purchasing the product.

- A scientist marshals the talents of many to pursue a drug for which there is no business case because she didn't involve marketing in the product cycle soon enough.

- A loan officer loses a high-net-worth client because he assumed that the short-staffed people in processing could expedite the paperwork.

- A restaurant server doesn't follow the process and throws off the timing of the cooks.

- A leasing agent asks the tenant to renew her lease without knowing that the accounting people overcharged the tenant twice in the last three months.

- A customer service person can't get her hands on the critical information the customer wants because the information technology people made some unwarranted assumptions about what it really means to be *user-friendly*.

The problem with each of these scenarios is *myopia*. Did the sales or IT people wake up one morning and think, *Let's see how badly we can screw it up today for everyone else*? No. It's not that sales purposely oversold the deal, or accounting deliberately failed to communicate with leasing, or IT intentionally tried to make it difficult for customer service. It's that each group became fixated on its own activities. Each group got caught up in its own tribalistic worldview and failed to look at the whole.

Whether it is departmental, hierarchical, generational, geographical, categorical, or gender specific, tribes are formed in organizations every day. The old-timers resent Gens X and Y for being fickle and disloyal, while the young people impatiently throw their arms up in frustration because they can't dislodge the organization from its "dinosaur" ways. The "home-growns" resent experienced new hires because they create speed bumps on the road to upward mobility. The new hires don't like being considered "green." The old-boys club gets worried about the intrusion of women in their formerly sacrosanct turf. The "creatives" resent the "suits," and the suits can't believe they have to put up with people who think "business casual" means cargo shorts and flip-flops.

What forms of tribalism exist in your business? Where does seamlessness break down internally? Do any of these examples ring true?

- Salaried vs. hourly workers
- White-collar vs. blue-collar
- Home office vs. the field
- Engineering vs. marketing
- Finance vs. sales
- Manufacturing vs. distribution
- Legal vs. everyone

The competitive field on which you are playing the game calls for passion, innovation, speed, and unprecedented levels of teamwork. People who know how to work across departmental boundaries are extremely valuable. Is this what you are bringing to the table? Since the only person you can change is *you*, start by asking yourself:

- Do I suffer from organizational myopia? Am I acting "tribalistic"?
- What issues do I get defensive about?
- How much time do I spend patrolling the fences, guarding the perimeter?

- What do I do to bog people down?

- How is tribalism damaging me? My organization?

- When was the last time I reached across organizational boundaries to bring key players together to make something good happen?

Choose Your Opponent Well

In a complex world where organizations are made up of more and more specialists, MVPs will be those who can bring diverse groups together in a spirit of cooperation to get things done. If we fail to jettison the kind of tribalism, silo building, turf protection, and finger-pointing that goes on in most organizations, our businesses could implode from within. Tribalism wears us out. It chews up physical and emotional energy that distracts people from getting on with their jobs. It wastes resources, costs explode, and productivity wanes. Tribalism disconnects people. It embraces the kind of reductionist thinking that kills knowledge sharing across teams. It stops the flow of information and makes the organization slow to respond. Tribalism severely weakens our ability to compete. While we're busy naval-gazing and blaming each other for things that didn't get done or could've been done better, the competition presses forward and kicks our butts. So all of us have to ask,

WHO IS THE REAL OPPONENT?

Is the *real* opponent *in here* or *out there*? Great teams are fluid. Team members quickly improvise and make adjustments to cover for a player who "drops the ball." In the heat of fast-paced competition, there is no time for "That's not my job" or "Who's to blame?" The collective focus is on doing whatever it takes to win the game. Watch the seamlessness with which a baseball team executes a double play or a basketball team sets up a three-point shot, and you will see what we mean. Watch the urgency with which a soccer team maneuvers the ball between defenders when it's late in the game and they are down by a goal. At that

moment you will see cooperation elevated to an art form.

In a 2006 *Leader to Leader* article entitled "Find a Rallying Cry," Patrick Lencioni made an astute observation. He noticed that you rarely find a silo mentality among firefighters and military squadrons caught in the midst of a crisis. That's because they have absolutely no goal ambiguity. Whether it is containing flames before they devour a neighborhood or extracting a hostage from a hostile situation, the objective is overwhelmingly clear, and the focus is maniacal (no. 41, 41–44).

We asked former San Diego fire chief Jeff Bowman about this, and he agreed. Bowman, who has been a firefighter for thirty-three years, told us about being called to a "child vs. auto" incident as a paramedic. A ten-year-old boy had been hit accidentally and dragged under the driver's car. Bowman and his partner arrived on the scene with other firefighters and immediately sprang into action. He said, "When you have only minutes to save a child's life, there is no conversation about who is in charge or who should do what. It's just not relevant. Everyone moves as one, doing what they were trained to do." The child, who had been badly burned from being scraped against the asphalt, miraculously showed up at Bowman's fire station eight weeks later with his mother to say thank you.

The chief also explained to us that firefighters—as a team—are fiercely loyal to one another. He said that when you live with twelve other people day in and day out, someone is going to get on someone else's nerves. But the minute that alarm sounds, all the finger-pointing and tribalism become insignificant.

Chief Bowman told us that the camaraderie and lack of polarization you see in a team of firefighters called to action has less to do with adrenaline and more to do with their commitment to a cause. He said, "Pulling together as one enables the team to execute on their priorities, which, in turn, allows every firefighter to feel a huge sense of gratification about fulfilling their calling."

Great companies, like a team of focused firefighters, are quick and nimble, because they act like small companies to get the job accomplished. In a small company no one is too big or too important to roll up his sleeves and get his hands dirty. In a small company there is nowhere to hide. A small company keeps its eye on its opponents, because it can't afford not to. It can't afford dead people working; it needs everyone firing on all cylinders. Over the short term, a large bureaucracy can operate under the flawed assumption that a little tribalism won't matter because the cause and effect isn't immediate, but it, too, cannot afford tribalism's dysfunction over the long run. In a small company the cause and effect of tribalism shows up much faster. Regardless of a business's size, the "us vs. them" syndrome will destroy a company from the inside out.

Get Some Perspective

Perspective is the capacity to see things as they are and to accurately evaluate their importance in the overall scheme of things. Have you ever failed to see something accurately and therefore placed its relative importance too high? We are embarrassed to tell you that we've screwed up more good weekends in our marriage due to something petty or because one (or both!) of us took something the other said and blew it out of proportion. When we look back on it, we have to ask, was being right worth it? Was this worth jeopardizing our relationship? Our business? In the larger scheme of things, was it worth any time at all?"

It's easy to take things that are of little or no consequence and turn them into a nuclear conflict. We have a branch of our consulting practice that solely focuses on presentation skills. For almost twenty years we've had a team of trainers working with the U.S. Marine Corps teaching recruiters how to give speeches. Now, the marines are a "buttoned-up" group of people. Their performance expectations of each other are tough and demanding, and what they expect from our training staff is no different. Kevin remembers going in to see the director of Recruiters School, Lieutenant Colonel George Biszak, about a problem we were having with one of our trainers. Kevin was convinced that this problem could potentially damage our working relationship with the military staff at Recruiters School and wanted to set things right. Apparently the marines were not nearly as worried about the situation as Kevin was. On the way out of his office, with a cigar in his mouth, the lieutenant colonel gave Kevin a friendly slap on the back and said, "Now, Dr. Freiberg, let's not be pole-vaulting over mouse turds." It was his way of saying, "We've had a great partnership. One hiccup isn't going to damage it. Get some perspective."

If you want to see people who have lost perspective, become an astute observer of other drivers in traffic. Someone was telling us just the other night that she has a friend who carries a large bag of golf balls in the glove compartment of his car. When another driver cuts him off in traffic, he speeds up to get in front of him, opens his sunroof, and throws the golf balls out the opening so they land on the perpetrator's car. Any loss of perspective there?

Perspective is relative. Sit where others sit and you will change your perspective. Change your perspective and you might find that you empathize more and expect less. We heard an individual from a major hotel chain's lodging division share a story about a time when Marriott had an extraordinary number of workers' compensation claims pouring out of its housekeeping unit. Apparently, most of these claims had to do with some type of back pain. Like any great company, the hotel began to investigate. When the company asked the housekeepers about it, the response was, "When you move as many beds as we do each week, your back starts to give out." The company dug deeper to figure out why the housekeepers were moving so many beds in the first place and found out that when business travelers looked for a convenient place to plug in the power supply of their laptops, they couldn't find one. So they pulled the beds out to get to the power receptacles hidden behind the bed. After they checked out the next day, the housekeepers would come in and move the beds so they were flush with the walls again. Over time this contributed to the back pain they were feeling.

Think about it. This is a world-class company, but even the best need to get some perspective. What would have happened if someone from the executive team had come out and worked with the housekeepers for a day or two? What would've happened if someone in housekeeping, a true expert closest to the problem, had said, "Look, we are moving way too many beds. If we made it easy and accessible for people to plug in their laptops, we could create a win-win-win situation. Customers win because we make it convenient for them to use their computers. The housekeepers win because we eliminate one cause of back pain. And the company wins by deploying precious resources to something more valuable than dealing with workers' compensation claims."

In Harper Lee's novel *To Kill a Mockingbird*, the old lawyer Atticus Finch says, "You'll never understand a man 'til you stand in his shoes and look at the world through his eyes." Tribalism causes us to become dangerously insular. It's almost impossible to think systemically and serve your coworkers unless you truly have an appreciation for the work they do. Many of us grossly oversimplify what others do. We feel that we have the toughest job in the organization—until we get some perspective. When we feel that others have it easier than we do, we automatically tend to think they should bend toward our needs. After all, the person with the easier job has less pressure and more time, right?

One thing is for sure: competition between lines of business does not serve the customer. You can't do service well *externally* until you first learn how to do it well *internally*. The way you treat your coworkers will have a huge impact on the way they treat your customers. The way they treat your customers will have a significant impact on the organization's performance and your job security. And let's be clear: an internal customer is anyone who receives the output of your work or depends on you to get his or her job done.

Get in Touch with the Impact You Have on Others

A few years back, Southwest Airlines set out to burn the barriers of tribalism, help people gain a new perspective, and raise on-time performance with what we call "down-line station visits." For example, the station manager in Los Angeles—who has a lot of originating flights leave LAX every day—put a team together to go visit down-line stations in Albuquerque, Phoenix, San Jose, and Sacramento, who receive those originating flights. The objective was to ask the down-line station team, "What are the top ten things we do in Los Angeles that make your jobs more difficult?" The LAX team would then bring that feedback to the team back at the station, identify the trends, and go to work on making improvements.

Think of the positive impact you could have on your organization if you had the guts to go to those who receive the output of your work and ask, "What are the top ten reasons I'm difficult to do business with? What headaches does our department create for your department?" If you decide to do this, here is a note of caution: Overcome the urge to be defensive by rationalizing or justifying your behavior—no "*yeah, butting*." This will kill the conversation. Instead, we encourage you to listen, probe for a deeper understanding of the issues, take notes, and then decide what you will change. This way people will be more forthcoming with information. Quite frankly, they will probably be blown away by your courage and candor. Once the changes are under way, let the people you've talked to know exactly what you are doing with the feedback they've given you.

As we mentioned earlier, it is the MVPs who can reach across boundaries to make things happen. If you want to banish tribalism, let go of your parochial perspectives and develop a systemic view of the organization. Systemic thinking starts by developing the discipline to ask yourself, *How will the decisions I make and the actions I take, way over here in my part of the organization, affect someone way over there in another part of the organization? How would I receive what I'm proposing?*

Let's assume that right now a group of people somewhere in the organization is having a conversation about people who work fluidly and seamlessly with one another versus those who are always "grinding gears" with others. Your name comes up. What stories will your coworkers tell about you? Do you have a reputation for helping people succeed—or hindering them from succeeding?

Relinquish Resentment—Forgive and Move On

Players are real; they are also resilient. They bounce back from being hurt much faster than most people do. A player who can take a hit, shake it off, and get back in the game is incredibly valuable to the team. What gives players the capacity to stay engaged when they get knocked down in the game of business? Forgiveness. Players not only know how to forgive, but they also see forgiveness as something you choose to do whether you feel like it or not. Players see forgiveness as a strategy for cleansing their minds of the negative thoughts that keep them from looking at the world optimistically and working productively. There is no pay-off for carrying anger and resentment around for even a short period—it's emotionally draining, it distracts you from adding value to the people you serve, and it derails you from doing the things that make you competitive. Players see pardon as a powerful tool for authentic healing and moving on.

Most of us think forgiveness is a great idea . . . until we are faced with the opportunity to forgive someone. Then we find that it is a lot easier said than done. Forgiveness is "major-league" because it requires sacrifice on the part of the person forgiving. When someone forgives you, he takes upon himself the consequences—accompanied by the hurt and pain—of what you have done. And often, the weight of those consequences can seem unbearable.

If you have seen the image, you will immediately know what we are talking about. A nine-year-old Vietnamese girl is running from her devastated village, screaming in agony, naked, with her arms held up and away from her body. Associated Press photographer Nick Ut captured the horrors of war in his picture of Kim Phuc, moments after she and other children fled the village of Trang Bang in 1972. In the midst of an air raid in which enemy planes dropped napalm (ignited jellied gasoline) that covered most of her body, Kim Phuc ripped off her clothes and ran for her life, screaming, *"Non´g Qu´a! Non´g Qu´a!"* ("Too hot! Too hot!"). As fire and smoke engulfed the area, Kim and four other children ran toward Ut, who instinctively snapped the shot. Many credit this Pulitzer Prize–winning photograph with contributing to the end of the Vietnam War. With the help of some South Vietnamese soldiers, Ut

BOOM!

poured water on the girl's horribly burned body and carried her to the Associated Press van. The pain was so severe that she cried all the way to the Cu Chi hospital and finally lost consciousness.

The burns covered 65 percent of Kim Phuc's body and were so severe that most people didn't think she would survive. Nearly thirty-five years later, after seventeen operations involving extensive plastic surgery and skin grafts covering 35 percent of her body, Kim Phuc is alive!

After her physical recovery, Kim dreamed of becoming a doctor and saving other people's lives. It was not to happen. She was accepted to medical school in Saigon, but in 1984 the South Vietnamese government authorities terminated her studies and forced her to be a spokesperson and a symbol for the ravages of war. The emotional stress of being a piece of propaganda and having the Vietnamese Communist government monitor her every move was too much. She successfully defected to Canada in 1992 where she now lives with her husband and children.

Today, Kim Phuc is a United Nations Educational, Scientific, and Cultural Organization (UNESCO) goodwill ambassador. She is a passionate activist, campaigning for peace and committed to the goal expressed in the Preamble to UNESCO's constitution: "Since wars begin in the minds of men, it is in the minds of men that the defenses of peace must be constructed."

In 1996, at a ceremony commemorating the Vietnam Veterans Memorial in Washington, D.C., Kim Phuc was invited to speak to several thousand people. She told the audience that if she could ever meet the pilot of the plane that dropped the napalm on her village, she would tell him that she forgives him and that she would like to join arms with him in the pursuit of peace. She said, "We cannot change history, but at least we can try and do our best to promote peace."

Next to *I love you* the words *I forgive you* may be the most powerful words uttered—in any language. When you forgive someone, you set him or her free, but you are setting yourself free as well.

> "ANGER IS AN ACID THAT CAN DO MORE HARM TO THE VESSEL IN WHICH IT STANDS THAN TO ANYTHING ON WHICH IT IS POURED."
>
> —MAHATMA GANDHI

Forgiveness might sound like another one of those touchy-feely concepts that has no place in business. To you it may seem weak, like you're being a wimp and letting people off the hook. But forgiveness isn't about condoning what others do. We are quite sure that Kim Phuc didn't condone the decimation of her village, nor has she forgotten it. You can radically disapprove of a person's toxic behavior and still forgive that individual. We've all been around people who claim they will "never forgive" and wear it as a badge of honor, when in reality they reveal their weakness and insecurity. Forgiving someone who has hurt you is one of the most courageous things you can do. It requires humility, vulnerability, and strength of character. Gandhi said, "The weak can never forgive. Forgiveness is the attribute of the strong."

Whether *they* are our bosses, coworkers, suppliers, customers, or someone else, we expect an awful lot of *them*. And *they* will let us down. Coworkers shirk, and you wind up doing more work. Incompetent people get promoted. Smart people are handcuffed by stupid systems that truly disable them. A boss says he will go to bat for you, but instead cowers under the pressure of his boss. The organization keeps asking you for more but providing you with less. When *they* don't perform to our liking or give us the things we feel we are entitled to, it's easy to feel hurt and angry. Unfortunately, if you feed and nourish this disappointment long enough, it will grow.

Forgiveness is freeing and helps expose the truth. Anytime you allow someone else's dysfunction to weigh on you, to shape your attitude over the long haul, to send you on an emotional roller coaster, you disempower yourself. You allow the roots of that person's dysfunction to become a stronghold within you and continue to screw up your life. Ask yourself these questions:

1. Would I purposefully drink strychnine or breathe carbon monoxide?

2. Would I fill a backpack full of rocks before hiking ten miles out of the Grand Canyon?

3. Would I leave a gaping wound to heal by itself?

4. Would I invite someone—who has hurt me many times—to coffee for another round of abuse?

These questions are ludicrous, but isn't that what we do when we harbor hostility and carry resentment around for a long time? Trying to forget about the hurt someone has inflicted upon you without actually forgiving that person is like expecting the wound to heal on its own—it won't. Holding on to anger and ruminating over past hurts is no different from inviting someone to hurt you over and over again. When you turn grief and anger and bitterness into a way of living—a lifestyle—you are choosing to prolong your suffering. In his book *You Gotta Keep Dancing*, Tim Hansel says, "Pain is inevitable. Misery is optional."

Since you bring all of who you are to every working relationship you have, what's in you spills out of you. If you are filled with anger and resentment, that's what people get all over themselves when they bump into you. It makes you unpleasant and extremely difficult to work with, and it renders you less valuable to the team. This hardly earns you the reputation of playing hard and being a go-to person.

Had Kim Phuc chosen to carry the hatred, to let her anger disfigure her perceptions of the world, the world would've lost a symbol of hope and an undeniable voice for peace. And worse, she would have lost not just 65 percent of her skin but 100 percent of her joy in life.

Whoever *they* are for you, we challenge you not to let *them* lock you behind the walls of anger and resentment. We dare you to conduct an audit of your gifts and talents and examine the potential you have to make a mark in the world. Is the bitterness you have toward *them* worth compromising all this potential? We challenge you to look at the team-mates whom you enjoy and who add value to your life, and the loved ones who support you. Is your propensity to harbor anger worth the toxic spillover and negative energy that infects their lives? Don't let another day go by; seize the moment. Write the letter, schedule the meeting, make the call, and take a step toward freedom by setting it right with those who have hurt you. The grace you extend to them will reflect your gratitude for the grace that has been extended to you.

Over the years we've heard some powerful messages. We've paraphrased a number of these inspirational themes in the following piece. We commend it to you because it captures what we've been talking about here:

> As we get older, we learn that life just isn't fair. You will risk and fail. People you count on will overpromise and underdeliver, and the one individual you thought you could trust more than anyone in this world will probably let you down. You will invest time, talent, and money in those who will either squander the investment or show no gratitude. Your heart will eventually be broken, and the pain will seem unbearable. You will also hurt others and disappoint those you love—remember how it feels. At some point you will wake up horrified and wonder, *What have I done with my life?* Time waits for no one, so don't take yourself too seriously. Love as if you've never been hurt, learn as if you

will live forever, and live as though you will die tomorrow, because every sixty seconds you spend agitated and upset is a moment of peace, joy, and "aliveness" that you'll never get back. Most of us are afraid to die; perhaps we should be afraid of having never really lived.

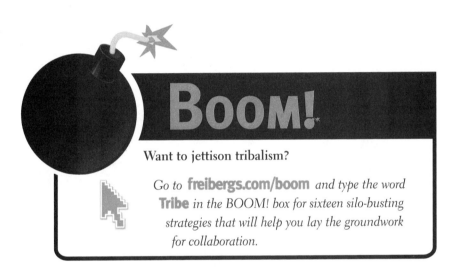

Want to jettison tribalism?

Go to **freibergs.com/boom** *and type the word* **Tribe** *in the BOOM! box for sixteen silo-busting strategies that will help you lay the groundwork for collaboration.*

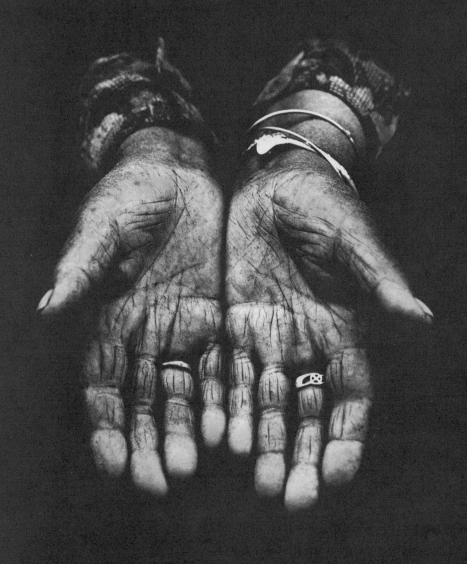

If we dared to live beyond the boundaries
of self-concern and self-indulgence,
the walls of apathy and fear
would be obliterated.

CHOICE #3

CHOOSE SERVICE OVER SELF-INTEREST

Me-First Rarely Delivers the
Desired Outcome

03

*" The secret to happiness and fulfillment:
Never leave a person or a place having taken
more than you have given. "*

When your contribution takes the form of service to others, your work suddenly starts to come alive with meaning. And you don't have to be Gandhi or Mother Teresa. Service doesn't just mean helping the poor, and service also doesn't just mean waiting tables or working behind a counter. It's just like Bob Dylan said: "We all have to serve somebody," and no matter what your job is, there are real human beings—in your company and outside of it—who depend on your service.

But service is more than helping others, because being of service is the greatest gift you can give yourself. As Gandhi said, "The fragrance always remains on the hand that gives the rose." Just as we know that the most joyous holidays are the ones where we give, not receive, the most, so the greatest joy in work is when you make your work a form of service.

In "A Letter to the Rulers of the People," Saint Francis of Assisi wrote:

Keep a clear eye toward life's end. Do not forget your purpose and destiny as God's creature. What you are in his sight is what you are and nothing more. Remember that when you leave this earth, you can take with you nothing that you have received—fading symbols of honor, trappings of power—but only what you have given: a full heart enriched by honest service, love, sacrifice, and courage.

No matter what part of the world you are from, what you do for a living, how much money you make, or what you value and believe in, we all share a common interest—self-interest. We all come into this world narcissistic and self-centered. How do we know this? We have three children! We do not remember any one of the three coming home from the hospital asking, "Mom, is there anything I can do for you?" "Dad, need some money?" "Anyone need to be dropped off somewhere?" It's never happened. Instead it's, "Mom, will you take me to . . . ?" Or, "Dad, will you help me with this?" Or, "Mom, can I have . . . ?"

It's all about *me*—*my* needs, *my* desires, *my* comfort, and *my* will. This natural focus on self-interest is a basic human trait, and it is deeply ingrained in who we are. Our self-centeredness manifests itself in

many different ways. For some of us, it's all about self-promotion, self-aggrandizement, being in the spotlight, or being first. For others it shows up when we become totally focused on self-discovery, self-actualization, and self-improvement, with the primary objective of self-gratification. On your next trip to the grocery store, check out the covers of the mainstream magazines. What will you see? Article titles that entice you with the latest

BOOM!

quick fix to gain more power, stop feeling tired, have better sex, lose more weight, and make more money. Our preoccupation with self is also evident in our self-doubt, self-condemnation, self-pity, and self-destruction. What other reason is there for our spending millions each year on various forms of therapies, treatments, procedures, and self-help literature?

Surely, some of you reading this will have a strong negative reaction to the argument we are making here. Maybe you're thinking, *You're blasting self-improvement? How do people add more value to their organizations, families, and society if they don't get in touch with and improve themselves? And, by the way, don't you both make your living helping people improve their lives? Couldn't this book be categorized as a self-help book?* The answer to all these questions is yes! Still, slice it any way you want, all the forms of self-indulgence we mention make *me*, not others, the point.

Not long ago I (Kevin) had an experience that illustrates this. Many of you who work out on a regular basis know that if you don't get a workout in first thing in the morning, it won't happen. I was at a five-star hotel in Las Vegas for a speaking engagement. It was 5:45 a.m., and I was standing outside the entrance to the spa and workout facility with six to eight other people, one of whom happened to be my client organization's vice president of development, Phil Silberstein. The hours of the fitness facility were 6:00 a.m. to 8:00 p.m.

Phil recognized me and said, "You know, I just walked through the casino to get here, and there were a lot of employees just standing around. You would think they have the people to staff this gym an hour earlier." I said, "I was thinking the same thing." So we commiserated.

The doors opened at 6:00 a.m., and we all got in the elevator to go up to the second floor where the facility is located. On the way up I jokingly said to the group in the elevator, "I'm forming a coalition right now. I want you guys to sign a petition with me to get the gym open an hour earlier, and we'll give it to the general manager." Everyone laughed.

When we got out of the elevator to check in at the reception area, one of the guys (whom we didn't know) said to the receptionist, "We were just talking in the elevator, and we're going to sign a petition to get you guys to open an hour earlier." The receptionist behind the counter, who looked to be all of twenty years old, responded, "Oh no! If we opened an hour earlier, then *we* would all have to get up an hour earlier." That's not what you want to hear when you're paying twenty-five dollars a day to work out. I'm sure it's not what the hotel wants to hear when you've got two hundred dollars in revenue standing there listening.

Phil Silberstein looked over his shoulder at me, as if to say, "Are you paying attention? Are you getting this?" I nodded as if to say, "Yeah, Phil, I'm getting it." So I said, "You know, guys"—everyone was still in the reception area—"if we went over to the hotel across the street to work out, I bet these folks wouldn't have to get up at all." The receptionist replied, "Good idea! That would be fine with me."

> **WHEN WE EQUATE HAPPINESS WITH SELF-INDULGENCE, WE DEVELOP A CHRONIC EGOCENTRICITY.**

Now, what was missing? The spa didn't have a deep-seated knowledge of and connection to the customer—unless we were an aberration (definitely a possibility), there were enough people waiting to open earlier.

Missing was the receptionist's gratitude and passion for the product—it's a beautiful workout facility. It lacks for nothing! She could have demonstrated her passion and pride by saying, "This is our home, we're extremely proud of it, and we want you to enjoy it—of course we'd be happy to open an hour earlier." If she wasn't empowered to do this, she could have at least said, "Your voice is important; here's what I'm going to do. I'm going to take this up with my manager, and if you would permit me to call your room later, I'll let you know what I find out."

Missing was a fanatically engaged employee who was willing to choose service over self-interest. When I left an hour later, I walked through the reception area, where the receptionist was the only one at the counter. Rather than looking up and saying, "How was your workout? Hope you come back and see us again soon!" she was looking down, concentrating on cleaning her nails.

BOOM!

Service or self-interest—where do you reside?

Go to **freibergs.com/boom** and type the word **Service** in the BOOM! box to find out.

When self-indulgence becomes the norm, our egos become the center of the universe, and feeding them becomes priority number one. "I am the world" becomes the refrain in the song that plays in the back of our minds. Of the many addictions that tempt us in the world, none is as powerful as self-addiction.

The problem is that when we equate happiness with self-indulgence, we develop a chronic egocentricity. But a me-first attitude rarely delivers the expected outcome. Focusing on our own happiness to the detriment of others—whether employees, associates, customers, clients, friends, or family—does not necessarily bring us the deep-seated, long-term happiness we desire or think we deserve. After working so hard to feed our egos, we still end up empty and unfulfilled. If all you care about is yourself, you better be extremely happy with *you*, because that's all you're going to have in the end.

If you talk to most parents and ask them what they want for their kids, they will usually say, "I just want them to be happy." If you talk to most kids, especially teenagers, and ask, "What does success look like?" many will talk about what they want to *have* rather than who they want to *be*.

Our strongest hope and prayer for our kids is that they will find their passion and then use that passion to serve others, to create a better world, to make a significant contribution. For passion to be truly fulfilling, it must be dedicated to something other than self.

The old saying "money can't buy you love" also applies to happiness. Consider the words of Berkshire Hathaway chairman and CEO Warren Buffett:

> The hell of it is you're only going to be loved if you're lovable. If you are, you get it back in spades. The truth is you always get back more than you give away. Some people never learn that. They're busy cheating people, cutting corners, lying to them, all kinds of things, and they think they're a success because they have tens of millions of dollars later in life. I don't think they are a success, and I don't think deep down they feel like they are a success. ("Money Can't Buy You Love," Tech Topics, a publication of the Georgia Tech Alumni Association, http://gtalumni.org/news/ttopics/spr05/article1html)

Buffet just put his money where his mouth is by donating the bulk of his $44 billion estate to the Bill and Melinda Gates Foundation. The money ($1.5 billion a year!) will be used to seek cures for the world's worst diseases and improve American education. We suspect Buffet's gift will inspire others to step up and do the same. We also suspect that we know what the answer would be if we asked Warren, "What is the greater source of your happiness, being the second-richest man in the world or being an MVP in finding a cure for a horrible disease?"

BOOM!

We have become a society that is self-absorbed in buying things we don't need, with money we don't have, to affirm ourselves and establish our identities in the minds of people we don't even like. Many of us have used people and the political process to pursue and wield power, because in our organizations, power has become the way we keep score.

Taking the focus off of yourself and putting it on others is not an easy thing to do—you're fighting a lifetime of bad habits and a world full of temptations, after all! As author Rick Warren points out in his best-selling book *The Purpose Driven Life*, "The world defines greatness in terms of power, possessions, prestige, and position. If you can demand service from others, you've arrived. In our self-serving culture with its me-first mentality, acting like a servant is not a popular concept."

Are you here to serve or be served? If you want to make a difference in the world, it's only going to happen through service, and it's only going to happen if *you* make it happen. We're only truly happy when we're serving someone else. Although getting a paycheck every other week, or having health benefits or a nice corner office, are great reasons to show up every day, we'll wager that they are not the main sources of your professional or personal fulfillment, and we doubt that

> **ARE YOU HERE TO SERVE OR BE SERVED?**

someday—when you look back on your life and your legacy—they will merit even a moment's thought. For most people, serving others—clients, customers, coworkers—and making a real difference in their lives is much more fulfilling than any paycheck or perk.

Put even a few people who are preoccupied with feeding their own egos in the same organization, and you have a recipe for disaster. When my needs butt up against your needs, a self-indulgent competition ensues that takes both pairs of eyes off the very things that make the organization productive and competitive.

One way out of self-addiction is to shift your focus and begin to pay attention to the needs of those around you. Retired Southwest Airlines captain Moose Millard told us that he had an unwritten rule that he and many of his fellow pilots followed when getting ready for a flight. After his preflight check was complete, Moose got out of the cockpit and looked for the busiest Southwest employee around to see how he could help. It would certainly be a lot easier for Moose and his colleagues to grab a cup of coffee and schmooze with a flight attendant. This spirit of service among employees not only makes Southwest one of the best companies to work for in the world, but it has also created an altruistic culture that has thus far been impossible for the competition to replicate.

But there's more to this story than just the fact that Southwest's pilots help out their coworkers when time permits. Ask anyone at Southwest about Moose's "likability" factor or the reputation he had for getting things done within the organization and you will find that he had, and still has, tremendous influence. By exercising his freedom to choose service over self-interest, Moose unleashes his potential for influence that runs broad and deep among his peers at Southwest Airlines. The network of relationships he has built is essential to his sense of meaning and significance at work.

As these serving pilots so graciously demonstrate, everyone—no matter how high on an organization's chain of command—needs to serve someone to find happiness and fulfillment.

If you really want to experience the joy of being alive at work, devote yourself to serving others. Never leave a person or a place having taken more than you have given. Albert Schweitzer, the brilliant humanitarian, philosopher, musician, and physician who received the Nobel Peace Prize in 1952, said to his students, "I don't know what your destiny will be, but one thing I do know: the only ones among you who will be really happy are those who have sought and found how to serve."

BOOM!

Happiness, fulfillment, and a sense of significance come from activities that are truly meaningful, activities that we are most certain will make a difference in the world and in the lives of others.

Service Is about Creating a Better World

The aim of purely motivated, unadulterated service is to create better individuals, better organizations, better societies, and ultimately, a better world. That is why people get such a charge out of being a part of world-class service. It is gratifying to know that we are a part of something that encompasses more than ourselves, yet something that would not be complete without our contributions. In this sense we get the best of both worlds—to stand out and be recognized for our heroic efforts and to feel the security of belonging to something bigger than ourselves. Service connects us to a cause, and often what follows is a movement. This is what is happening at Sharp Coronado Hospital, a community of men and women who have dedicated their lives to blowing the doors off health-care-as-usual.

Consider what business-as-usual means in health care. Patients come to a hospital or clinic, expecting to get the highest-quality medical care. But they also want a truly *caring* environment, a setting in which they will be treated with dignity and hospitality.

They come with a sense of urgency, and the system responds by making them wait an hour in the emergency room or radiology department or wherever, seated on ugly, uncomfortable furniture under glaring fluorescent lights, where they are forced to read an outdated issue of *Sports Illustrated* or *People* magazine.

They come vulnerable and scared, and the system responds by isolating them from their loved ones. Patients come seeking to learn, ready to be informed, and willing to take part in their own healing. The system counters with hurried or authoritative caregivers treating them like children, withholding information, and spending more time document-ing procedures than listening deeply and answering questions.

Against this backdrop a new model of service is emerging, a holis-tic, patient-centered model that Sharp Coronado Hospital and others believe will radically change the future of health care.

From CEO Marcia Hall to housekeeper Margaret Reynolds, from chief nurse Susan Stone to volunteer cookie lady Barbara Blei, the people at Sharp Coronado have decided that *how* care is delivered is as critical as the care itself. In 2001 Sharp Coronado adopted the Planetree model of patient-centered care and embarked upon a journey that would literally transform what service and hospitality look like in a hos-pital. Planetree is an alliance of one hundred hospitals and health-care organizations that are committed to the philosophy of Planetree's founder, Angelica Thieriot. She believes that the best health care com-bines "the best of spas with the best of hotels and the best of hospitals to become a truly healing environment, where just being there is healing."

Of course, a critical transformation like this doesn't happen unless a lot of people step up to the plate, become players, and choose to make a difference. Marcia Hall, CEO, humbly admits, "Our house [hospital] is old, but we have learned that creating 'place' out of 'space' has little to do with bricks and mortar and a great deal to do with the spirit and commitment of those who walk the halls within."

Take Mary Margaret Omohundro, for example, a clinical nurse who walks the beach each week and collects seashells that have been bat-tered into smoothness. The shells are offered to patients who are dis-tressed, anxious, and afraid. They serve as "worry stones" or, as Mary Margaret calls them, "angel wings." One nurse's hobby, which started as a simple and small gesture, has become an incredibly important part of this nurturing environment.

Have you ever heard of a nurse promoting bedside spa services? While touring the hospital, Jackie met Karen Moran, RN and manager of the medical surgical department. She was just finishing her daily rounds. Karen personally visits each new patient and presents Sharp Coronado's "Spa at the Bedside" services. She leaves each patient with a blue sheet of paper describing all of the complementary therapies that they can receive (at no charge) at their bedsides!

Susan Stone, chief RN and operations officer, also has a passion for taking service to a whole new level, but she understands that service happens from the inside out. That is, you can't expect your people to take care of their patients in the manner we've described if you are not caring for your team members in the same fashion. Susan took it on as a personal mission to help Sharp Coronado achieve its goal to become the best place to work, the best place to receive care, and the best place to practice medicine.

Susan enlisted the hospital's safety committee, led by safety officer Renee Huslin, to create a wellness, health, and safety program for all employees. It was specifically designed to give the people of Sharp Coronado Hospital what they asked for. Employees overwhelmingly wanted health education, information about weight loss, weekly support groups, and fun activities, like walking and, would you believe, line dancing!

It's amazing: when a small band of people choose to make a difference, that pocket of engagement picks up momentum and takes on a life of its own. Employees from all over the hospital have risen to the occasion and started sharing their gifts, talents, and expertise to promote the health and well-being of their coworkers. Eppie Angeles, clinical lab scientist, has become the resident line-dancing instructor. Rachel Carpenter, manager for the admissions department, leads weight-loss support meetings, and nutrition supervisor Barbara Bauer holds weight-loss classes. There is also a fully active walking group. In 2006, employees demonstrated a 33 percent improvement in injury rates compared to the same time period in 2005 by simply tapping into existing talents and making better use of on-hand resources. The Sharp Coronado team believes you don't have to be the CEO to make a difference.

Is Sharp Coronado's commitment to a patient-centered model working? According to Press Ganey, a world leader in health-care satisfaction measurement, Sharp's patient satisfaction ratings are in the 96th percentile nationwide. And best of all, when you visit the place, you can't help but get a sense that almost everyone who works there feels alive and engaged. They know their work is heroic and meaningful because they believe they are part of a movement that is radically transforming the patient's experience. One patient put it this way: "Although I started out very nervous and scared . . . my stay at your hospital was great, everyone was in a great mood, the water features are very peaceful, and the whole atmosphere was one great ambiance. I was treated as though I was an honored guest at a five-star resort."

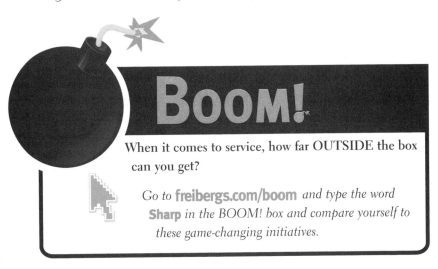

BOOM!

When it comes to service, how far OUTSIDE the box can you get?

Go to **freibergs.com/boom** *and type the word* **Sharp** *in the BOOM! box and compare yourself to these game-changing initiatives.*

Service Is the Most Powerful Form of Influence

People are more willing to follow you, cooperate with you, and support your ideas when you serve their needs. When you serve my needs so profoundly that I become empowered by your actions, I will naturally be predisposed to follow you. Why would I do anything else? What group of coworkers would have difficulty committing themselves to the direction of someone who defines his or her role as their servant?

Why would Southwest's beloved chairman, Herb Kelleher, have hundreds of employees lined up to donate an organ if he needed one? Because for thirty-four years the people of Southwest Airlines have watched Herb live out a leadership that says, through vivid, living, personal example, "I will never ask you to do something I am unwilling to do myself."

How did Elizabeth (Lee Lee) James fast-track her way to the top of Synovus? By serving others. James is the vice chairman and chief people officer of Synovus Financial Corp., a multibillion-dollar, diversified financial services company headquartered in Columbus, Georgia. Synovus, known for its "People First" culture and being a great place to work, doesn't lose very many employees. "But when we do," James told us, "my first response is to ask, 'What didn't I do, or we do, to set you up for success? What could I have done better or different to help you win?'" That's accountability. That's assuming responsibility for making sure the Synovus culture is what people think it is. A servant leader always looks in the mirror first and asks, "What about me needs to change in order to make a difference? Am I / Are we living the values we espouse?"

Service Is Action Oriented

"Right now you are the most powerful person at this bank. You are smart. You are genuine. You are empowered. You are an Umpqua Associate. You are part of something that is making people's lives better. Lives better? From banking? Yep. You have the power to make someone's day. Umpqua is YOU!" These are the words that open Umpqua Bank's *Handbook for Associates*. Apparently, Nicole Bennett, Randy Richardson, and Gary Murphy chose to take them seriously.

When a seventy-four-year-old retiree and Umpqua customer ordered a cord of firewood from a local supplier, he assumed it would already be split when it was delivered to him. Bad assumption. The supplier dumped a cord of unsplit firewood upon this gentleman, stating that he did not have the time to split the massive logs and that the rather frail, elderly man should buy an ax.

Unable to lift and carry the wood to his garage, the customer attempted to stop payment on the $120 check he had written to the supplier. Unfortunately he was too late. The supplier had cashed the check about a half hour earlier. Nicole Bennett, manager of Umpqua's Garden Valley store (Umpqua doesn't call them branches), was sympathetic to her customer's plight, but because the check had already been cashed, she was unable to offer the requested financial help. While many people would've stopped there, Nicole assumed the role of a servant leader, took ownership of the customer's experience, and went the extra mile. She asked her colleagues Gary Murphy and Randy Richardson for their assistance in helping the gentleman. These associates—traveling forty miles—showed up at his home with, as the customer put it, "axes, lots of youthful energy, and three huge, caring hearts." In no time at all the wood was split and stacked, and the garage swept clean. A very grateful man stood in amazement at the kindness of these three people and what they accomplished without compensation.

Obviously these three associates had a huge impact on the customer. They also had a huge impact on the Umpqua culture. Their acts essentially said, *"This is what we are about! This is what extraordinary looks like! This is what makes us different!"* As their story moves throughout the organization, it makes people more cognizant of the opportunities in front of *them* to make a difference. And BOOM, it infects those who hear it with a desire to step up, check in, and be more engaged. And if you think that this customer is ever going to use another bank after an experience like that—or that he's not told all his friends and acquaintances about this remarkable example of caring—think again.

Oregon-based Umpqua Bank is blowing the doors off business-as-usual with extraordinary acts of service like this. Perhaps that is why Umpqua—one of the fastest-growing community banks in the country—has been able to live up to it's billing: "The World's Greatest Bank."

An organization marked by an internal spirit of service is an extraordinary magnet for great talent. This, in turn, is the key to accelerated growth. A business grows not just because of the exceptional skills of its people and its superior strategy, but also because people use their skills and leverage the strategy to serve one another and grow the community.

If indeed we lived a life of service, our ability to make a difference would be far-reaching and profound. If we dared to live beyond the boundaries of self-concern and self-indulgence; if we were a counter-culture to our organizations' lunatic lust for power, control, status, and recognition; if we chose nothing but a compassionate attitude toward our customers, suppliers, and coworkers; if we traded in our propensity to complain, accuse, manipulate, threaten, and condemn for vulnerability; if we decided to hang our egos outside the door and walk into work with an unwavering desire to enrich the lives of others, then the walls of indifference, procrastination, and fear would be obliterated. A spirit of trust and unity would ensue, and the organization would become a force to be reckoned with. One or two of us might be written off as idealistic dreamers who don't really understand the hard rules of business, but a critical mass of such people could change the DNA of our corporate cultures forever.

The greatest change agent to ever walk the face of the earth had a family tree that was less than impressive. He had no army, no nuclear weapons, no political power, no status—and he certainly didn't have unlimited funds. He didn't surround himself with people of impeccable pedigree. Rather, he rallied a bunch of scallywags and misfits and taught them to serve. In two-thousand years the world hasn't gotten over it yet—but the power of Jesus' leadership lay in His passion and His willingness to serve. Whether you're a Christian or not, it's impossible to overlook the incredible power and the huge impact one individual can have when he steps up to the plate of servanthood.

Service Is Contagious

When people feel served, something remarkable happens within them: there is a reciprocal effect that causes them to want to serve others in return. This isn't the ultimate reason we serve, but it is a really cool by-product. A few years ago Kevin was speaking to a large audience about the incredible service USAA offers its members. With an almost 95 percent share of its primary market of military officers and enlisted men and women, this insurance and financial services giant, with more than $81 billion in owned and managed assets, believes it has a sacred bond with its members. There is plenty of evidence to suggest that it does. Many of the mind-blowing stories about how people at USAA demonstrate servant leadership are detailed in our book *GUTS!*

After the presentation, a man came up to Kevin and told him a story that illustrates the reciprocal effect that being served has on people. While on vacation at a resort, the gentleman left a very expensive Rolex watch in the desk drawer of his hotel room before going out to the beach—or so he thought. When he came back, the watch was gone. Assuming that it had been stolen, he filed a claim with USAA for ten thousand dollars and bought another watch. Approximately six months later, he was going through an obscure pocket of his gym bag and found the original watch. He said, "With all USAA has done for me, there was absolutely no question about what I was going to do." He promptly wrote the company a check for ten thousand dollars.

If you've ever had someone at work go the extra mile for you, you know it endeared you to that person and made you more committed to the giver and more aggressive in looking for ways to reciprocate. If you've ever had a boss who expected you to do all the serving, how did *that* make you feel? The opposite is true when you've got a boss who serves his or her employees. We become more motivated to go the extra mile for others when they are in need.

A few years ago, one of the most innovative entrepreneurs we know, Fred Holzberger, came up with a great idea to rerecruit (reengage) his associates, some of whom had lost their passion for work (and life). In the spirit of not wanting to offend anyone, he issued a gift to *all* of his people. He gave four hundred associates one extra paid day off for the coming year. This gift of a day was to be used to find a charity and invest the day there. Fred had just one condition: that the associates bring back their stories and share their experiences with him. You can probably imagine some people saying, "This is one more obligation, one more thing to add to an already overloaded schedule. I don't need this pressure." The results, however, were dramatic. People changed, people's perspectives were altered, they checked back in, their outlooks

> "THIS IS THE TRUE JOY IN LIFE ... BEING USED FOR A PURPOSE RECOGNIZED BY YOURSELF AS A MIGHTY ONE, BEING A FORCE OF NATURE INSTEAD OF A FEVERISH, SELFISH LITTLE CLOD OF AILMENTS AND GRIEVANCES COMPLAINING THAT THE WORLD WILL NOT DEVOTE ITSELF TO MAKING YOU HAPPY."
>
> —GEORGE BERNARD SHAW

improved, and they came to work more energized and more rewarded after having served others.

Will serving others make all your problems disappear? No, it might even increase them. Will it make life and work easier? Probably not, and it might even become more difficult. But it *will* make your life—on and off the job—richer and more meaningful. Meaning, fulfillment, and happiness come when we dedicate ourselves to a life of serving others.

Service Focuses on Responsibilities vs. Rights

Whenever we choose our way into complaint mode or start feeling sorry for ourselves, the words of George Bernard Shaw put it in perspective for us. He said, "This is the true joy in life . . . being used for a purpose recognized by yourself as a mighty one, being a force of nature instead of a feverish, selfish little clod of ailments and grievances complaining that the world will not devote itself to making you happy." We admit it: when we truly examine our lives around the Freiberg house or in our business, Shaw's words are convicting, yet true. The world is not here to make us happy; we are here to serve the world.

In the United States we used to talk about the honor of sacrifice, and there was a lot of dignity in serving others—quietly and without complaint. We've grown into a culture where most people are talking about rights and not responsibilities—what we're owed, what we think we're entitled to. We no longer have a sense of debt or indebtedness to anyone or anything. We have forgotten that we are drinking from wells dug by others.

In a culture that panders to self-expression and individualism, people devote a tremendous amount of time and energy making sure they get what they think they deserve. Look in any direction from where

BOOM!

you are sitting right now, and you'll clearly see that complaint has become a way of life. When we travel, we can pick up the newspaper in almost any city around the globe and find that it is not uncommon to read about employees standing up for their rights. Whether it's demanding their right to fair compensation and benefits, meaningful work, or a decent schedule, the implicit message is: *If we don't stand up for our rights, no one else will stand up for us.*

Management fires back with another set of rights—the shareholders' right to a fair return, the company's right to fair operating costs, and the customer's right to exceptional service. Everyone claims they have a legal, moral, or ethical right to something, most of which is geared toward the acquisition of pleasure or the avoidance of pain. You don't often read about people asking, "What does it mean to live out the virtues of duty and service and sacrifice? What does it mean to confront an issue when others act as if there is no issue? What does it mean to assume responsibility?"

Now the name of the game for many is "look out for number one, because if you don't, nobody else will!" The result? A society in which many forms of self-interest get masqueraded as the virtues of individualism, independence, and competition. Self-interest often leads to tribalism, alienation, and fragmentation—the enemies of great companies. These concepts stand in diametric opposition to true fulfillment and building the kind of unity that is extremely difficult to compete with.

What makes places like Southwest Airlines, USAA, Sharp Coronado, Fredrics Corporation, and others so different is that people talk as much about duty, honor, and service as they do about their rights. They seem to be more willing to sacrifice their privileges for the good of others than people in other companies. When we stop demanding our rights at the expense of one another and start demonstrating the spirit of *service* that we've seen in stellar companies, BOOM, the power of what people can accomplish to change the world is really quite remarkable.

Service Is a Way Out of
Depression, Despair, and Disengagement

When we truly believe in the positive impact we can have on others, serving them becomes more important than our own needs. Knowing this type of happiness and enjoyment leads us to experience something very special: servanthood as a source of meaning, joy, and fulfillment instead of something oppressive, dehumanizing, or taxing. Perhaps the Ken Hamilton Caregiver Support Program at Northern Westchester Hospital best exemplifies the power of how one person's drive to serve can make a huge difference in the lives of so many. After Ken Hamilton lost his battle with lung cancer, his wife, Marian, had a vision of helping others in similar situations. Marian spent two years—day and night—caring for her husband while juggling her role as a mother of two teenage daughters. The journey wasn't easy. She was depressed, she gained weight, and she was exhausted, but she did get through it, and Marian was determined that something positive would come out of her ordeal. And it did. She shared her vision with the hospital—an oasis of sorts, where family caregivers can go to take care of themselves while their loved ones are in the hospital. She wanted the center to be peaceful and tranquil, away from the noise and bright lights of the hospital. It had to be a place of rest, with rooms for private conversations. Marian envisioned phone and computer access, a kitchen, exercise equipment, and most importantly, a place where a caregiver could get counseling from both professional and experienced volunteers. What started as an ordeal in 2002 became a program in 2004, and it will become a center in 2007, offering what Marian dreamed and more. Her determination to serve and make something bigger out of her own ordeal has proved to be a remarkable contribution to Northern Westchester Hospital's patient- and family-centered approach to care.

Consider another story. He had it all—a gorgeous wife, beautiful children, a sensational acting career, and all the trappings of success that go with it. He starred in the smash hit *Superman*, which not only led to the inevitable *Superman II* and *Superman III*, but to other major roles in films such as *The Bostonians* and *Deathtrap*. On Memorial Day 1995 his life radically changed. A horse-riding accident severed his spine and left him paralyzed from the shoulders down. Christopher Reeve had not only been a superstar on the screen but was also an expert skier, cyclist, scuba diver, and outstanding equestrian. Suddenly, as a ventilator-dependent quadriplegic, those days were over. Reeve described his life as unacceptable.

At this point many people would have given up, checked out, and completely disengaged from life—perhaps even contemplated suicide. In fact, Reeve seriously considered it. "Maybe we should just let me go," he said to his wife, Dana. She responded, "It's your decision . . . but I will be with you for the long haul, no matter what." Not knowing what was in store for them, Christopher and Dana Reeve ultimately chose a different road. They committed themselves to finding joy and laughter in their lives and facing this crisis in the best possible way. Dana told CNN's Paula Zahn, "I think, ultimately, part of that feeling is that we would also be able to help people, because his celebrity is wonderful in that way, to be able to use it as a springboard for other people."

It's an incredibly sad story. No one knows until the time arrives, but we seriously doubt we could demonstrate this kind of courage and unselfishness under similar circumstances. It's also a story of hope. Chris Reeve's life had far more impact on the world *after* his accident than it did before. That's because he and Dana found a way to serve even in the midst of conditions others would deem hopeless. Reeve himself acknowledged that choosing to focus on others was a significant factor in his ability to cope with despair. In his autobiography, *Still Me*, he writes:

> When a catastrophe happens it's easy to feel so sorry for yourself that you can't even see anybody around you. But the way out is through your relationships. The way out of that misery or obsession is to focus

more on what your little boy needs or what your teenagers need or what other people around you need. It's very hard to do, and often you have to force yourself. But that is the answer to the dilemma of being frozen—at least it's the answer I found.

Few of us can compare the ups and downs we go through at work to Reeve's circumstances. But isn't that the point? Shouldn't we add to the meaning of the Reeve's lives by learning from them? Shouldn't we look at our own circumstances and say, "Christopher Reeve chose to become a force for positive change in the world. What would he do in my situation?"

When Paula Zahn asked Reeve what his legacy might be, he answered, "I just hope that I won't have spent X number of years on this planet without making some kind of a difference."

If you're disappointed about all the ways your organization fails to meet your expectations; if you're stuck in boredom; if you're wishing for the good old days because your business has changed, your boss is clueless, and your colleagues are checked out; if work is empty, and you're feeling sorry for yourself, look for ways to help others be successful. Find someone to serve. Ask yourself, "Who in my organization is stressed and overloaded? Who just experienced a setback and needs encouragement? Who's engaged in a project that is stalled and needs to be revitalized? Who's new and having trouble getting up to speed? Whose stellar accomplishment needs to be showcased? Who needs someone to pick up the slack because he or she is wrestling with a personal matter?" Don't wait for an associate or your boss to come to you. When you look below the surface, anticipate others' needs, and then act, you blow the doors off business-as-usual!

Eight years after his accident, Reeve published another book, *Nothing Is Impossible*. In it he said, "Given all the inexplicable acts of violence, injustice, and cruelty, mixed with the unexpected small miracles of kindness and happiness that we see in the world every day, I remain convinced that life is chaos, but it is within our power to establish order and meaning."

We agree. "Everything happens for a purpose" and "it was meant to be" are trite, overused phrases that people employ when they don't know what to say to someone for whom something bad has happened. We don't always believe everything happens for a purpose, and it often seems that things aren't meant to be. We live in a world that is filled with evil intent, that is anything but perfect, that is in many ways very messed up. Bad things *do* happen to good people. Life isn't always fair and just. And the places where we work are no exception to these truths. But within each of us is the power to create meaning from the trials we face—if we choose wisely and courageously.

> WITHIN EACH OF US IS THE POWER TO CREATE MEANING FROM THE TRIALS WE FACE—IF WE CHOOSE WISELY AND COURAGEOUSLY.

Service is a way out of the gloom so many of us experience at work and in life. When we take our eyes off ourselves, when we work to do good for others, when we use the difficulties that come our way to make a difference in the world, we create a deeper sense of meaning in our lives. Our jobs become more rewarding, our relationships grow stronger, and our organizations become more unified.

What's ailing you at work right now? If you are giving less than 100 percent of your discretionary effort in your job, what is the reason? What would happen if you turned your focus outward and found an opportunity to serve someone in each of the circumstances that are causing you to disengage? Look beyond *you*! Be determined to find good in your place right now.

Service Is about Bringing Out the Best in Others

Let's face it: some people are just plain difficult to serve. They manifest their unattractiveness in a multitude of ways. Yet, as we mentioned before, a player's willingness to serve is *not* based on people's attractiveness but rather on his or her personal constitution and passion for making a difference. Players have a propensity to look beyond the grumpiness, arrogance, resentment, cynicism, silence, indifference, and ineffectiveness of *dead people working*, to their potential, to something redeemable. There is always more to a person's story than meets the eye. Players recognize that many of us choose to disengage and stop growing because somewhere along the line we concluded that people stopped believing in us. By transferring their belief into others, players help people believe in themselves. It's a profound truth that has been around forever, but a simple "I believe in you" can take a person a long way down the road to engagement.

To invest the best of who you are into someone's brokenness, to transfer glory and praise, to look for the vein of gold in a mountain of dirt, to reach out to the "loser" in the next cubicle, to help people win — these are the attitudes and behaviors that bear the stamp of authentic servanthood. Service is about honoring others, even when they are unkempt, uncouth, unreliable, unresponsive, uninvolved, and uncommitted. Maybe you are saying, "Whoa! This takes humility, vulnerability, and guts. It sounds counterintuitive to everything I've learned about getting ahead. You're talking about a world-class effort here." We agree, and that is why not every organization can be world-class and why so many organizations are filled with dead people working.

Tony Campolo, professor of sociology at Eastern College in St. Davids, Pennsylvania—and one of the most prophetic voices of our time—told us a story many years ago about a teacher who became a hero in the eyes of a little boy—but only after she figured out what it meant to choose service over self-interest. The story also appears in Campolo's book *Let Me Tell You a Story.*

When school started and the students gathered for the first time in September, Jean Thompson began to look over her class. There was one little boy whom she immediately took a disliking to, and his name was Teddy Stollard. The teacher wasn't quite sure why she didn't like Teddy. Maybe it was because he was dirty, not just occasionally, but all the time. Maybe it was because he was always pushing the unkempt hair out of his face. Maybe it was because he had bad body odor. His physical faults were many, and his intellect left a lot to be desired. He sat far away in the back of the room, and whenever the teacher would call on him, he would answer in monosyllables. There just wasn't anything alive about this kid.

When it came time to grade the children's papers, Jean Thompson took a particular joy in putting the red marks near Teddy Stollard's wrong answers. And when she put the F at the top of the page, she did it with a vindictive flair—larger and redder than the other kids. She should have known better, because she had his records from the cumulative file: "First grade: Teddy shows promise by work and attitude, but poor home situation. Second grade: Teddy could do better. Mother is terminally ill. He receives little help at home. Third grade: Teddy is a pleasant boy, helpful but too serious. Slow learner. Mother passed away at end of the year. Fourth grade: Teddy is very slow, but well behaved. Father shows no interest."

As Christmas rolled around, the children brought presents for the teacher, and on the last day before vacation, everyone waited in anticipation for her to open the presents they had given her. When she pulled Teddy Stollard's present out of the pile, she found it was wrapped in a brown

> **SERVICE IS ABOUT HOLDING THE POTENTIALITY FOR GREATNESS BEFORE EVERY PERSON WITH WHOM WE WORK. IT'S ABOUT RAISING PEOPLE TO HIGHER LEVELS OF MOTIVATION AND MORALITY. AND WHEN WE DO, WE OFTEN FIND THAT THERE IS NO HEIGHT TO WHICH THE HUMAN SPIRIT CANNOT RISE.**

paper bag with masking tape holding it together. He had colored Christmas trees and red balls all over it. It read, "For Miss Thompson from Teddy."

As she tore away the masking tape, a rhinestone bracelet with some of the rhinestones missing and an old bottle of cheap perfume that had been half used fell out of the bag. As the kids began to snicker and whisper, Jean Thompson was smart enough to ask Teddy to help her fasten it to her wrist. She held it out for the children to view and said, "Isn't it lovely?" Then she put some of the perfume on her wrist and said, "Doesn't it smell pretty? Don't you like it?" The kids, quickly taking the cue from the teacher, agreed that the present was nice.

When all the presents were opened and the refreshments gone, the children headed for the door with shouts of "Merry Christmas!" and "See you next year!" All except Teddy, who went up to Jean Thompson's desk, quietly clutching his books. "You smell just like my mom," he said shyly. "Her bracelet looks real nice on you too. I'm glad you liked it." And then he left. As soon as he got out the door, Jean Thompson locked the door,

BOOM!

sat down at her desk, and began to cry for deliberately depriving Teddy of what every child needs—a teacher who cares. She realized—perhaps for the first time in her whole teaching career—that being a teacher means more than shoving the information down these kids' throats, testing them, and shipping them off to the next grade.

In the New Year, Jean Thompson came back to the classroom an intensely different person. She began to invest herself in her students. She began to mentor and coach Teddy Stollard until he was caught up with most of the class and even ahead of a few of his classmates. In fact, he ended the year with some of the highest averages in his class. Seven years later, Jean Thompson got the first of three notes that had a significant impact on her life.

NOTE #1: "Dear Miss Thompson, I wanted you to be the first to know. I will be graduating second in my high school class next month. Very truly yours, Teddy Stollard"

NOTE #2: "Dear Miss Thompson, I wanted you to be the first to know. I was just informed that I'll be graduating first in my class. The university has not been easy, but I liked it. Very truly yours, Teddy Stollard"

NOTE #3: "Dear Miss Thompson, I wanted you to be the first to know. As of today, I am Theodore J. Stollard, M.D. How about that?! I'm going to be married—the 27th of July to be exact. I wanted to ask if you could come and sit where Mom would sit if she was here. I'll have no family there as Dad died last year. Very truly yours, Teddy Stollard"

Jean Thompson went and sat where Teddy Stollard's mother would would've sat.

Even in the most apathetic, unimaginative, and disengaged members of a team, there is something waiting to be awakened. Service is about holding the potentiality for greatness before every person with whom we work. It's about raising people to higher levels of motivation and morality. And when we do, we often find that there is no height to which the human spirit cannot rise. Of course, some people won't respond, but that is no reason not to try. Others will respond, their lives will be transformed, and BOOM, you will have made a difference; your life will matter.

In his book *The Only Thing That Matters*, Karl Albrecht says that a spirit of service is "an element of giving—a spirit of generosity that makes people give something of themselves in addition to just doing the job." A corporate community that does not inspire, cultivate, and rein-force a spirit of service is emotionally bankrupt. And this is why people frequently disengage. When you examine the cultures of places like Chili's, Chik-fil-A, Wegmans, Medtronic, Synovus, and Southwest Airlines, you find that they have their share of blemishes, warts, and dys-function. But you will also find that there is something in the way people speak to, look out for, challenge, and laugh with one another that is powerfully appealing. They convey a spirit of service and hospi-tality that makes the person looking in from the outside say, "Break me off a piece of that" or "I want to be a part of it."

BOOM!

Want to experience the joy of being alive at work? We have a story for you to read.

Go to **freibergs.com/boom** *and type the word* **Joy** *in the BOOM! box.*

*Your attitude and motivation in the present
are shaped by your view of the future.*

*The most important thing about you today is not
where you've been, it's where you are going.*

CHOICE #4

FOCUS FORWARD

Your Future Isn't
in the Rearview Mirror

04

"The most important thing about you today is not where you've been; it's where you are going."

A hotel has no room for a frequent guest with a confirmed reservation. A bank rejects the loan request of a high-net-worth customer with a nominal blip on her credit report. An airline loses a passenger's luggage. Each of these scenarios represents a "moment of truth" in which the customer-contact person has a choice— to focus forward and assume ownership or look backward and shift the responsibility to someone else. To focus forward is to ask, "What do I want the outcome of this scenario to look like, and what is the best way for me to move toward that picture now?" To focus in the rearview mirror is to ask, "Why is this happening to me? Who's to blame, and how do I escape?" If the person on the front line—the face of the company— assumes the burden with a sense of service to both the customer and the company and moves toward the outcome she envisions, the customer's faith in the company is renewed and his or her loyalty is possibly even stronger than before the incident ever happened. Also, the front line person's reputation as an MVP, a problem solver, a host of hospitality, grows.

If the company's ambassador looks back by focusing on why he can't fix the problem and shifts the burden, the customer walks—a lifetime of value goes out the door, probably forever—and tells an average of twelve people immediately. In this case the customer-contact person builds a reputation as a victim who throws problems over the firewall, leans on the rules, and lacks the courage to make a difference. One of these people is remarkable; one is average. The difference is in where they focus their energy and attention.

Marcia Hall, CEO of Sharp Coronado Hospital, wouldn't be considered a typical front-line person, but she sure knows how to act like one. Marcia actually reads every patient complaint letter that comes into the hospital and responds to all of them. One afternoon, just before she was getting ready to leave for vacation, she decided to get a few letters off her desk. One complaint was from a patient who was upset after receiving what she perceived to be a standard apology letter from the hospital. Marcia's stomach turned. The patient didn't feel heard and still felt wronged. At this point a victim would've looked in the rearview mirror and said, "I sent her a letter; it wasn't good enough; there's nothing more I can do." Instead, Marcia picked up the phone and got a very frustrated yet very articulate and very concerned patient on the line. Marcia listened and owned it all. Her questions dug deep; she truly wanted to step into this patient's shoes, understand the cause of her frustration, and fix the problem. Once Marcia was confident she had heard all the bitter details, she assured the patient that she would get on it and get back to her with specifics. In the end, a patient who was once very frustrated and very vocal about her negative experience is now part of a formal patient advocacy team charged with helping the hospital become more patient centered. Marcia focused on the outcome she wanted to achieve—making Sharp Coronado Hospital a place where patients receive incredible hospitality and extraordinary care. By assuming ownership and choosing the more difficult road—it would've been a lot easier to ignore the letter—BOOM—she transformed a critic into an ambassador.

If your life is anything like ours, you are hit by hundreds of distractions just waiting to take you off course. In terms of bandwidth, our indi-

vidual capacity is only so big. We can't focus on everything! We do know that where you aim and where you focus your attention either moves you toward building what you want—in your job, your relationships, your organization, and your life—or away from it.

This is a fundamental principle known to all professional athletes. Where you look determines the position of your head, and your body follows where your head goes. Kevin took up mountain biking five years ago. One of the guys he rides with said, "Focus on where you want the bike to go, versus what you want to avoid." That is easier said than done. When you're screaming down a hill on a narrow path, there are a lot of things you want to avoid. But it works! When there is a wall to your left, a large ditch to your right, and a tiny path through jagged rock in front of you, the bike naturally wants to go where you focus. Trust us, Kevin learned this lesson the hard way—on more than one occasion.

We have been inspired by Steven Vannoy's book *The 10 Greatest Gifts I Give My Children*. Vannoy says, "We only have a certain amount of energy, time, and potential to use each day. Of the 100 percent we have, only we can choose where to focus it" (39). Where you focus your energy and attention determines what you see, and what you see has a dramatic effect on your attitude, your demeanor, and your effectiveness. This is illustrated by the figure on page 114. If your focus is *backward* on why it can't be done, what isn't working, what's wrong, what could've

BACKWARD FOCUS

FORWARD FOCUS

Why it CAN'T be done.

What ISN'T working.

What's WRONG.

Ruminating on
the PROBLEM.

Who's to blame.

Making EXCUSES.

Being a VICTIM.

How it CAN be done.

What IS working.

What's RIGHT.

How am I part
of the SOLUTION?

What do I want
to achieve?

Making something
happen.

Being ACCOUNTABLE.

FREEDOM TO CHOOSE

BRAND

Negative	Apathetic
Cynical	Indifferent
Helpless	De-motivated

BRAND

Positive	Energetic
Hopeful	Concerned
Self-reliant	Motivated

A BYSTANDER
who is a victim,
a Dead Person
Working

A PLAYER
who is alive
and engaged,
Making a Difference

been done but wasn't, ruminating on the problem and who's to blame, your chances of being negative, cynical, helpless, indifferent, and unmotivated are pretty high. That is the recipe for becoming a victim, a dead person working.

If your focus is *forward* on how it *can* be done, what's working well, what you want to achieve, what's right, what's happening that gives you momentum, and how you are going to be part of the solution, you will be more positive, hopeful, self-reliant, energetic, concerned, and motivated. This is the recipe for being fully alive and fully engaged. You end up being accountable for your life and making a difference, or, as Steve Jobs would say, "making a dent in the universe." And really, who doesn't want to make a dent and make their life matter?

A Jane Clifford column in the *San Diego Union Tribune* tells the story of a Native American chief who explains his own constant struggle, with an image of two wolves fighting inside his heart:

> An elder Cherokee chief took his grandchildren into the forest and sat them down and said to them, "A fight is going on inside me. This is a terrible fight and it is a fight between two wolves. One wolf is the wolf of fear, anger, arrogance and greed. The other wolf is the wolf of courage, kindness, humility and love." The children were very quiet and listening to their grandfather with both ears. He then said to them, "This same fight between the two wolves that is going on inside of me is going on inside of you, and inside every person." The children thought about it for a minute and then one child asked the chief, "Grandfather, which wolf will win the fight?" He said quietly, "The one you feed." ("Finding Words to Set Daughter on Life's Road," July 1, 2006, www.signonsandiego.com/news/metro/clifford/20060701-444-findingw.html)

What we focus on, the thoughts and feelings we return to from time to time, dominate our outlook on life and affect everything we do. The ones that occupy our minds for only a moment or two tend to fade away and have little impact. Here is the good news: *we* get to choose. The good wolf (focusing forward) and the bad wolf (focusing backward) coexist inside each of us, but *we* decide which one to feed and ultimately which one will win.

We're not asking you to deny or gloss over the reality of your life. Bad things happen. People fail to come through, or they create roadblocks to our progress. Bosses make mistakes and cause others a lot of pain. Dreams get shattered. Windows of opportunity close and can never be regained. We are not suggesting that there isn't value in looking back. History has a lot to teach us if our eyes are open and we are willing to learn. Dissecting a problem or analyzing a mistake has helped many of us face reality, learn valuable lessons, and hopefully avoid repeating it again. The question comes down to motive and intent. If your real motive is to learn versus put someone on trial, periodically looking back works. But even if your motives are good, focusing backward as a matter of habit will force you off the true path of your life, depleting your energy and eventually draining you.

Where you focus can also become a self-fulfilling prophecy. Focus backward long enough and your victimized thinking will drive you toward behaviors that are counterproductive. Ruminate on your problems long enough and your problems will get bigger. Spend enough time blaming others and the bad guys will get worse. And you will develop a spirit of self-righteous indignation that kills the very teamwork you need to get results. What we dwell on gets in us, and what's in us spills out of us.

Develop a habit of focusing forward and—BOOM—you will engage in more activities that support your goals. Spend more time thinking about solutions and your problems will become more manageable. Look for the good, the giftedness that God has built into others, and you will appreciate them more. Do this with enough people, and you will develop an appreciation for coworkers who are different from you. Your associates will become less obstructive and more cooperative. All of this increases the likelihood of getting the results you want, which, in turn, motivates you to stay focused in the right direction.

The reason the concept of vision is so powerful is because of its forward focus. Who we are in the present is shaped by where we want to go, who we want to become, and what we want to do in the future.

Whether it's pumping basketballs through a hoop, drilling soccer balls into a net, memorizing lines for a play, or spotting pirouettes on a stage, what gives a kid the drive, discipline, and tenacity to practice for hours? The answer is that most kids are focused forward. They have a vision of what they want to accomplish—making the varsity team or getting a lead role in a big performance—and they understand that the practice they engage in today makes them better and takes them one step closer to realizing their vision tomorrow. The benefits to focusing forward are many, but here are five that are pretty compelling:

> **WHO WE ARE IN THE PRESENT IS SHAPED BY WHERE WE WANT TO GO, WHO WE WANT TO BECOME, AND WHAT WE WANT TO DO IN THE FUTURE.**

1. Focusing Forward Enables You to Overcome Defeats and Roadblocks

Focusing forward has the potential to elevate hope, and without hope you've got nothing. Victor Frankl said that those who survived the terror of the Nazi death camps were not necessarily the strong, healthy, or able-bodied; they were those who had a sense of hope fueled by something important that they had left to do in life. Their abilities to focus forward, to remind themselves that they had something yet to live for, gave them the hope to hang on.

2. Focusing Forward Enables You to Transcend Petty Preoccupations

Focusing forward is about the bigger "YES" in our lives. It's about what you ultimately want to accomplish. We all get caught up in petty preoccupations from time to time. They are dysfunctional and distracting. They tempt us to waste time and energy on artificial things that really don't matter. They are the fuel for much of the silo building and turf protection that goes on in organizations. They keep us from focusing on the *real* issues. People who focus forward rarely have time for, or interest in, the trivial problems others want to ruminate on. That's because they have a bigger "YES" that mentally catapults them over the superficial toward what is ultimately important.

3. Focusing Forward Enables You to Improve Decisions and Performance

Focusing forward is about emphasizing your strengths versus your weaknesses, what you do right versus what you do wrong, and what you *can* do versus what you *can't* do. This builds momentum and increases your desire to *move* forward. Also, when you have a clear sense of the outcome you're trying to achieve, your decision making becomes more deliberate and happens more quickly. This is because the "rightness" or "wrongness" of your decisions becomes more apparent when you can easily ascertain whether they move you toward your goal or away from it.

4. Focusing Forward Enables You to Raise the Level of Problem Solving

Learning to focus on solutions expands our problem-solving capacities. The more we exercise this muscle the stronger it will become. If enough people choose to focus forward, the organization develops a problem-solving DNA that fosters a culture of creativity and innovation. After all, what are innovations but people's ultra-creative attempts to solve problems?

5. Focusing Forward Enables You to Create Team Unity

When people focus forward, they naturally become less defensive and more accountable. They are more likely to look in the mirror than look for someone to blame. If you are accountable and we are accountable, we can trust each other and we can count on each other. This is the foundation for the kind of collaboration that makes a team a unified force to be reckoned with.

Feed the Good Wolf

If you think we've made a compelling argument for feeding the good wolf, and this has stirred a desire in you to make some changes, here are some strategies to consider.

Strategy #1: Give Complaining a Permanent Rest

Read the newspapers; watch television; listen to the radio. You will discover that the world in which we live has elevated complaining to a major form of discourse, and the battle cry is *I deserve* . . . I deserve better interest rates. I deserve more job security. I deserve better wages. I deserve more concessions. I deserve more respect. I deserve a better contract. It's pervasive.

Why do we complain? Because it gets things off our chest and temporarily makes us feel better. Complaining is a way to establish common ground; it endears us to others who share our discontent. But the root of most complaining is entitlement, a concept we will hit hard in Choice #6. We complain because we aren't getting something we think we deserve. And our narcissistic tendencies take us to a place where we think we deserve a lot. We fall into a trap of exaggerated self-importance that causes us to expect special rights and privileges without reciprocating.

Think about the amount of time spent on complaining in organizations around the globe. If we spent as much time doing our homework

> **IF WE SPENT AS MUCH TIME DOING OUR HOMEWORK AND GETTING PREPARED AS WE DO COMPLAINING ABOUT WHY SOMEONE REJECTED OUR IDEA, MAYBE WE WOULD COME CLOSER TO GETTING WHAT WE WANT.**

and getting prepared as we do complaining about why someone rejected our idea, maybe we would come closer to getting what we want. If we spent as much time trying to understand the changes unfolding in our organizations as we do whining about them, maybe we wouldn't be so intimidated by those changes. If we spent as much time trying to reach out and support another department as we do throwing curses their way, maybe we could develop a better working relationship. If we spent as much time concentrating on the task at hand as we do complaining about taking work home over the weekend, maybe we wouldn't have to. Life *is* hard. Life is also short, and when we stop pretending it isn't, BOOM, we liberate ourselves to stop complaining and take charge of our lives at work.

The problem with habitual complaining is that it's counterproductive; it rarely takes you where you want to go. Complainers often operate under the assumption that pointing out a problem is doing the organization a favor. But complaining is only constructive if it comes with a solution—or a step toward a solution. People chew up their energy by grousing about the horrible boss, the incompetent coworkers, the terrible working conditions, the inadequate product line, and the unreasonable customers, with the underlying hope that someone will ride in and rescue them. The fact might be that you are in a toxic culture or a dead-end job. The market may be mature and your product line may be flawed, but it's not going to get better if you stand on the sidelines, levying your criticism, insulated by the crowd.

When you're done contributing to the "moan and groan" club over drinks with your colleagues, have you changed a thing that will make your organization more successful, your work more meaningful, or your life better in the long run? The answer is no, unless you and your coworkers follow up with ways to fix the problem and act upon them. In fact, complaining is often another form of procrastination that prevents you from getting to a solution.

When levied in the form of gossip, complaining destroys trust and elevates the rumor mill. People instinctively know that if you are complaining or gossiping about others, it probably won't be long before you get around to them. This weakens trust—the very woof and fiber of your organization's culture. Gossip also activates the rumor mill. In the absence of good, solid, accurate, and timely information, people will invent their own. Being "in the know" is intoxicating, because having information that others don't have gives us a distorted sense of significance and temporary power. Like all forms of complaining, gossip distracts us from getting the job done, from focusing on the things that will make our businesses more competitive.

Strategy #2: Nourish New Ideas—The Scarier the Better

Do you want to have a kick-butt, wildly stimulating, adventurous time at work? Maybe not all the time, but most of the time? Do you want work to ROCK? Is the electricity that flows between people who are doing something new and fresh attractive to you? Do you want your organization to be a place that pulsates from the creative surges pouring out of people?

If the answer is yes, be thirsty for great ideas. Be a provocateur of great ideas in others. No matter how new or crazy or threatening their ideas might be, embrace people who don't think like you do. The most innovative and exciting organizations in the world are breeding grounds for new ideas—witness Virgin, Apple, Google, Medtronic, and Toyota. They value off-the-wall thinkers—people who push, prod, and cajole the organization in new, exciting, and often scary directions. They encourage diversity of thought because they know it unleashes creativity. Their restlessness and curiosity drive an obsession for new ideas.

Toyota implements one million ideas a year. That's three thousand ideas a day! Perhaps this is why Toyota plays in a league of its own while most if its competitors are mired in downsizing just to survive. Perhaps this is also why Toyota's market value is worth almost as much as all the other automobile manufacturers combined! Are you obsessed with finding the new, or do you get overwhelmed when someone comes at you with a fresh idea?

New ideas raise the heartbeat, increase the blood pressure, and give the organization an adrenaline rush. They are crucial to the growth of any business, and they are the lifeblood of your career. Right now, the portfolio of assignments and experiences you are amassing to build a successful personal brand depends on new ideas. This is why you must fight with every fiber of your being not to ignore them or shut them down.

If you are like us, you suffer from a severe problem-solving disability, and you might not even know it. You innocently (or maybe not so innocently) squash new ideas before they have a chance to grow, with a nasty little habit referred to as "Yeah, but . . ." We are all afflicted with it. You've heard it hundreds of times as people responded to the ideas *you* put forth:

"Yeah, but that won't work because . . ."
"Yeah, that's nice in theory, but it's not practical because . . ."
"Yeah, but we've tried that before . . ."
"Yeah, but it won't fit into our system because . . ."
"Yeah, but we're not ready for that yet . . ."

"Yeah, but we'll step on too many toes . . ."

"Yeah, but it is too expensive . . . complicated . . . time
consuming . . . off-the-wall . . ."

That list is enough to wear you out. The media also reflects the pervasiveness of our "Yeah, but . . ." mentality. In a 2003 *Wall Street Journal* article entitled "The 'But' Economy" Jack Welch wrote:

> Guess what? There is an economic recovery under way, but you never would have known it last week when earnings reports came out. Even though many companies from battered sectors—including some companies left for dead just two or three years ago—recorded positive results, their successes were almost universally reported with the word "but" prominently featured. The stories in the papers and on TV went something like this:
>
> • Sales were up—but analysts warned that cost cutting explained most of the gains.
>
> • Earnings were up—but the mood of optimism was tempered by concerns about global competitiveness.
>
> • Cash flow was up—but the company still faces harsh tests in coming months.

Welch went on to suggest that the reason for so many *buts* was because analysts and reporters hyped companies with unrealistic business models in the late '90s and were left eating crow when the bubble burst. Now they were covering their bets. With typical Welch passion he concluded the article by saying:

> If we are ever to get competitive again, though, we can't indiscriminately put a negative spin on what is legitimately good news. We live in

a global economy; India and China get stronger and better every single day. To have a fighting chance, companies need to get every employee, with every idea in their heads and every morsel of energy in their bodies, into the game.

The facts are, companies are not bricks and mortar, but people, with blood and sweat and tears. People are the reason for the recent recovery, and people are the reason it will continue—if it does. That's why we need to tell the people who have earned it not "but," but "Bravo."

"Yeah, but . . ." comes in many different forms, but the effect is always the same. When someone approaches you with an innovative idea and you dismiss it, you hijack the creative process and squelch the person's desire to engage. If enough people do this in an organization, it creates a culture of stagnation, boredom, and fear.

To focus forward is to take a strange idea or one you immediately disagree with and ask, "What's good about it? What if it could work? What if it's the right thing to do?" Moving forward is about suspending judgment and building on new ideas with "Yes, and . . ." and "What if . . . ?"

Saying, "No" or "It can't be done" is, in effect raising the white flag before you've engaged in the battle. It is a negative, backward way of looking at the problem, and it gives the problem a strength it didn't have before.

New ideas are fragile. The more creative they are, the more off-the-wall they appear to be. That's why they must be nourished.

> NEW IDEAS ARE FRAGILE. THE MORE CREATIVE THEY ARE, THE MORE OFF-THE-WALL THEY APPEAR TO BE. THAT'S WHY THEY MUST BE NOURISHED.

BOOM!

How could people possibly get their arms around Da Vinci's helicopter in 1490? Of what use was it? Albert Einstein said, "Great spirits have always encountered violent opposition from mediocre minds." Even some of the best thinkers in the world have demonstrated their opposition to new ideas. You can hear the "Yeah, but . . ." in these examples:

The Internet will catastrophically collapse in 1996.
—Robert Metcalfe, 3Com founder, coinvented the Ethernet (1995)

640,000 bytes of memory ought to be enough for anybody.
—Bill Gates (1981)

There is no likelihood that man can ever tap the power of the atom.
—Robert Millikan, Nobel Prize Winner Physics (1920)

The phonograph . . . is not of any commercial value.
—Thomas Edison (1880)

I think there is a world market for about five computers.
—Thomas J. Watson (1943)

Sensible and responsible women do not want to vote.
—Grover Cleveland (1905)

Who the hell wants to hear actors talk?
—Harry Warner, Warner Brothers Pictures (1927)

We don't like their sound. Groups of guitars are on their way out.
—Deca Records, rejecting the Beatles (1962)

The concept is interesting and well-formed, but in order to earn better than a C, the idea must be feasible.
—Yale University business professor on Fred Smith's
senior thesis, which eventually became FedEx (1966)

"Yeah, but . . ." is about choosing between multiple realities that compete with one another. "Yes, I was going to attend the strategic planning retreat, but I scheduled a client meeting that day." In other words, you lose. Some have speculated that the roots of this disease are formed in an education system that teaches us to think in terms of black and white. By the time we are eighteen, we have completed well over fifteen hundred exams requiring a right-or-wrong answer. Think of what this does to our problem-solving approaches. It teaches us to look for one right answer when there may be many right answers. We develop a very narrow-minded approach with which we push to find the one simple solution. When we think we have it, rigidity sets in, and we become less willing to consider other alternatives.

The French essayist and philosopher Émile Chartier said, "Nothing is more dangerous than an idea when it is the only one you have." Players find a way to transcend the tyranny of the *or* by embracing the *and*. Give them a choice between *this* or *that*, and they will figure out a way to have both.

When the dot-com boom descended upon us, many people got sucked into the tyranny of the *or*, suggesting that you could either be an Internet company or a brick-and-mortar company. Of course the implication was that if you didn't become a dot-com company, you'd be dead. The way it has shaken out for most businesses is that you need to be both. With 70 percent of the DVR (digital video recorder) owners in the United States fast-forwarding through commercials, many are saying that television advertising is history. Maybe. But what if this was to become a "Yes, and . . ." for product manufacturers, advertising agencies, and television viewers? What if you could watch your favorite show, click on the actor's handbag, have an advertisement for Prada appear on the screen, order the handbag just as you would a book on Amazon today, and then go back to your show? You would have the option to pause as many times as you were interested in exploring new products, or not at all. Focusing backward is about getting stuck in the tyranny of the *or*, while focusing forward is about transcending the trade-offs with "Yes, and . . ."

Strategy #3: Look for the Best Ideas in Unlikely Places

Another form of the "Yeah, but . . ." paradigm is: "If it wasn't invented here, it's no good." Or its derivative: "If it wasn't my idea, I can't get behind it." As we said, players will take ideas from anyone, anywhere, at any time. Manufacturing giant Procter & Gamble (P&G) has been around for 165 years and created one of the greatest research and development operations in corporate history. For years P&G held research and development close to the chest. That is, until CEO A. G. Lafley transformed the invent-it-ourselves model in which P&G was steeped and broadened the horizon with a new program called Connect and Develop.

P&G estimates that for every one of its seventy-five hundred researchers, there are two hundred scientists and engineers somewhere in the world with equivalent gifts and talents. We are talking about 1.5 million people with new ideas that P&G could potentially tap into! The idea was *not* to replace P&G's researchers (a tyranny of the "or" approach) but to use them more wisely. All of P&G's researchers would continue to innovate from within and work on products initiated from or supported by scientists and engineers outside the company (a "Yes, and . . ." approach).

Two major transformations were required to make this new model a success. First, people needed to move from "not invented here" to "proudly found elsewhere." And second, they needed to transform their perceptions of the R&D organization from seventy-five hundred in-house researchers and support staff to seventy-five hundred insiders *plus* a network of 1.5 million people outside the organization—all of whom are connected.

Connect and Develop appears to be working. Innovation consultant Doblin Inc. estimates that nearly 96 percent of all innovation attempts fail to beat targets for return on investment. Today, P&G's cost of innovation has decreased, while its innovation success rate has more than doubled—think of products such as Crest Whitestrips and Swiffer cleaning products; both launched whole new categories. Almost 50 percent of the new ideas in the company's product-development portfolio have key features that came from outside the formal organization. P&G has introduced more than one hundred new products, many coming from its growing external network. Since its stock crash in 2000, P&G has doubled its share price and boasts a portfolio of billion-dollar brands—twenty-two and counting—business is booming!

Other companies are embracing the concept of Connect and Develop or "open innovation." At Cisco, what started as chat rooms for customer engineers has turned into a full-blown channel for collaborative design—forty-five thousand customer problems per week are solved on the World Wide Web via customer collaboration. Cisco estimates it gets $1 billion worth of free consulting and new ideas from its customers.

These companies have discovered the power of "Yes, and . . ." by throwing "not invented here" overboard. They are open to good ideas, regardless of their source, and are willing to share them, knowing the energy and excitement this pours into the organization. Great ideas are like compound interest: the more you have—BOOM!—the faster they grow. The faster they grow, the stronger you are.

Adventurous people get to "Yes, and . . ." and "What if . . . ?" quickly because they are rarely ever satisfied with the way things are. Their mantra, "Is this all there is?" makes them mentally flexible, comfortably spontaneous, and more willing to explore new ideas. Their passion for a deeper understanding, for pushing the boundaries of an idea, can be heard in the way they probe:

- "Keep talking, I want to understand this better."
- "Where did this idea take root? What got you to this point?"
- "Why is it useful?"
- "What assumptions are you making?"
- "Why are you so passionate about it?"
- "If it worked the way you envision, what would it look like?"
- "What are the possibilities?"
- "How does it line up with what we are doing now?"
- "If we were to pursue this idea further, how would you approach it?"
- "What needs to change if this is going to work?"
- "What impact will it have on . . . ?"

Skepticism is often presumed to be based on logical thinking and anchored in an objective evaluation of factual data. The problem is that most radical innovations are only rational in hindsight. Loads of analytical data showed that BMW was crazy to bring the Mini Cooper to the United States: the research suggested that Americans were hot on SUVs and that an ultrasmall car would fail. The "crazies" at BMW launched the Mini anyway and created a profitable new market. Most breakthrough ideas defy convention and shatter the traditional mold. Consider how you might have addressed these "What if . . . ?" questions five or ten years ago:

What if, instead of punishing people for breaking traffic laws, we recognized and rewarded them for keeping the law? It's happening in parts of Canada as well as the United States. In Southern California, Moreno Valley police have received national awards for their good driver program. No department under three hundred officers in America is more successful when it comes to enforcing speeding, drunk driving, and unlicensed-driver laws and teaching the importance of wearing seat belts and using child restraint seats.

What if all medical prescriptions were digital instead of hand-written? Pharmacists who wouldn't have to decipher the physician's handwriting might just create fewer prescription and dosing errors. Physicians could be warned about prescribing medicine that might have dangerous drug-to-drug or drug-to-food interaction effects. According to the *Wall Street Journal* and the Institute of Medicine, there are one million serious medication errors per year due to illegible handwriting, misplaced decimal points, and missed drug interactions and allergies. How many lives could be saved?

What if eyeglasses could be programmed with photographs? Val Halamandaris, president of the National Association for Home Care & Hospice, says these will be available soon. People with memory loss will be able to download pictures of friends, loved ones, and acquaintances into their glasses. When a person sporting the glasses runs into a friend and can't remember her name, the glasses flash the friend's name on the inside of the lens. Imagine what this can do for people in the early stages of Alzheimer's disease? With millions of baby boomers who are absolutely passionate about aging gracefully, the potential market for such a product could be massive.

What if everyone in your organization traded feedback on the quality and creativity of their ideas? What if potential borrowers could side-step banks by listing their requests online, showing their credit scores, and describing the purpose of the loans and interest rates they are willing to pay? Individual investors willing to take the risk could then bid on financing all or part of the need. That's exactly how the fastest revenue growth company in history operates. At eBay, buyers and sellers are connected in an open market. The process is held in check by a feedback system that puts the reputation of participants out in the open for everyone to see.

What if, for $150 more per ticket, a major airline provided a hassle-free door-to-door trip? The airline greets you at your door, checks you in, and escorts you to the gate through a private security area. When you reach your destination, the airline checks you into your room on your way to the hotel. You don't touch your luggage once until you are safely tucked into your room. The total cycle time reduction at both airports is two hours. Virgin Atlantic currently offers some version of this now for its premier flyers.

What if toothpaste didn't come in a tube? What if all meetings were voluntary? What if you could check into a hotel by swiping your credit card on any door lock with a green light? What if you could track your teenager's location and driving behaviors via satellite from the comfort of your home computer? What if your refrigerator could talk to your cell phone and say, "Hey, pick up some milk"? What if your tires could talk to your dashboard and say, "We are low on air"? What if you could determine the demographics of people driving by an electronic billboard by capturing their radio signals? What if your "smart toilet" could warn you of an impending heart condition? These innovations might have sounded off-the-wall years ago, but they're all either being used now or are in development.

We live in a world where consumer expectations are rising, customers are more demanding, technology continues to grow explosively, and new competitors enter the game daily. The demand for creativity and innovation has never been more profound. If we can leverage the power of "What if . . . ?" and make it a permanent part of our dialogue and a way of doing business, the potential for creative problem solving is enormous. And this is critical, because ideas are the lifeblood of your organization and your career. To a large degree, your success will be determined by the quality of ideas you bring to the table. Your ideas will often be stimulated by being open to the ideas others bring to the table—by "What if . . . ?"

"Yeah, but . . ." is exclusive. It deadens the tone of our conversations, because when our ideas are shot down, we feel shot down. Alienation sets in, and the organization's creative capacity is diminished. "Yes, and . . ." and "What if . . . ?" are inclusive. These words keep the conversation alive and moving. Rather than feeling dismissed, people are invited to share their voices and make a contribution. Rather than getting stuck in the same spot, the realm of choices opens up, and the possibility for radical innovation becomes more real. Rather than being threatened by change, we entertain it, we embrace it, we inspire it, and we grow!

"Yeah, but . . ." is a crutch, a defense mechanism, a crafty way of procrastinating. It's a lot easier to say, "Yeah, but . . ." than it is to put ourselves on the line and commit to some form of action. When we drop "Yeah, but . . ." from our vocabularies and move toward "Yes, and . . ." and "What if . . . ?" we become accountable; we become players. Our requests for outside opinions and authentic feedback are sincere, and our focus is forward. We no longer become a stumbling block to others by slowing things down or putting them on hold. We break away from the familiar, becoming adventurers in pursuit of the next big breakthrough. It's an untamed road filled with mystery and uncertainty, to be sure, but the excitement of exploring new frontiers will add a new dimension of life to work if you let it.

> THE NEXT TIME YOU FIND YOURSELF COMPLAINING, ASK YOURSELF, "WHAT IS THE ROI HERE? WHAT'S THE RETURN ON INVESTING IN THIS DISCUSSION?"

Perhaps we all need to look in the mirror and ask,

IS MY "BUT" TOO BIG?

Complaining is just another way of saying *yeah, but,* and it also feeds the bad wolf. MVPs don't want to hear about how unfair you think things are or how life is stacked against you. They don't run to their bosses or human resources or whoever will listen every time they encounter a problem. They gravitate toward people who, like themselves, are truly interested in and hopeful about fixing things, about making their little corner of the workplace better. The next time you are invited to participate in a dialogue where others are complaining or *yeah, but*-ting, be courageous and ask them, "What is the ROI here? The next time you find *yourself* complaining, ask yourself, *What's the return on investing in this discussion?* Starve the bad wolf by focusing on and running toward the bigger yeses in your life and your work.

Strategy #4: Remember, You Are Drinking from Wells Dug by Others

Want to know the fastest way out of being a complainer and feeling sorry for yourself? Gratitude. Gratitude stems from a sense of indebtedness, from the acknowledgment that we have not arrived at where we are solely on our own. To whom or to what do you give credit for your freedom and where you were born? For your health and your ability to think? For your parents and friends? For the opportunities that came to you by no means of your own? Do *you* take credit for all of this? Who among us is not "drinking from wells dug by others"? What do you have that you have not received? Yet we live in a world that screams, "You owe nothing; you have a right to everything!" And so we forget; we take what we have for granted and live as if the world owes us everything.

An ungrateful heart always sees what is wrong with the world and cynically makes *nothing* out of *something*. Gratitude, on the other hand, sees what is right with the world and usually finds something meaningful in nothing.

How Grateful Are You at Work?

For each of the A and B statements below, circle the statement that is most like you. Respond thoughtfully—do *not* go with what you think is the right answer. Go with what you *know* to be true about your perspective most of the time at work.

1. A. I have so much in my career to be thankful for.
   B. There really isn't much in my career to be thankful for.

2. A. If I had to list everything about my work that I feel grateful for, it would be a very long list.
   B. If I had to list everything about my work that I feel grateful for, it would be a very short list.

3. A. At least once a week, I express my gratitude for someone at work.
   B. At least once a week, I complain about someone at work.

4. A. I have nothing that I did not directly or indirectly receive from others.
   B. I have nothing that I did not work for and earn on my own.

5. A. I am grateful for the diversity of talents my coworkers bring to our organization.
   B. I complain about the lack of competence my coworkers bring to our organization.

6. A. I am grateful for the relationship I have with my boss.
   B. I complain about the relationship I have with my boss.

7. A. I frequently stop and count my blessings; I am *mindful* of the things I am grateful for.
   B. I rarely stop and count my blessings; I could be more *mindful* of the things I am grateful for.

Give yourself one point for every B circled and zero points for each A circled. Then total your points and consult the following table to interpret your score.

HIGHLY GRATEFUL (0–2 POINTS):

If you scored 0–2 points, you are conscious of the good things going on at work. You see the blessings of people, circumstances, and opportunities in your life and rarely take them for granted. You understand that behind every gift is a giver. You ponder the deeper questions: How has grace manifested itself in my life? My workplace? To whom am I indebted? How do I give back? You frequently take time to express your appreciation. The volume on your sense of wonder and appreciation simply for being alive is turned up higher than it is for most people. When bad things happen, this attitude enables you to focus forward and deal with them more constructively. Most likely, people at work respect your maturity, admire your humility, and are attracted to your positive outlook on life.

SOMEWHAT GRATEFUL (3–4 POINTS):

If you scored 3–4 points, sometimes you are aware of the good things going on at work, and sometimes you overlook them. Periodically you take positive things for granted because you feel entitled to them. Your questions ebb and flow between "Who owes me?" and "To whom am I indebted?" You are thankful for the blessings of people, circumstances, and opportunities in your life, but frequently miss opportunities to express your appreciation. We believe you can raise your level of job satisfaction and effectiveness and increase you overall happiness at work by using the strategies at the end of this section.

UNGRATEFUL (5–7 POINTS):

If you scored 5–7 points, there is a strong possibility that one of two things have taken place at work. Some recent event—an argument with your boss, budget cuts, layoffs, or some other significant problem—has precipitated your lack of gratitude. On the other hand, a string of more subtle disappointments and limitations—assignments that lack meaning, coworkers who routinely fail to come through, leaders who don't live the values they espouse—over the long haul might have led you to a lack of gratitude. In either case, you are unaware of the good things going on at work. Instead, you are focused on the things you think you deserve, but aren't receiving. You often complain that life isn't fair, but your expectations of your boss, your coworkers, and the organization might be unrealistic. Most likely, people at work disrespect your immaturity, disapprove of your arrogance, and are turned off by your negative outlook on life. Your chronic complaining is probably driving people in the organization away from you. We guarantee it is distracting you from doing what it takes to be competitive and derailing your ability to make a difference. It's time to change your attitude.

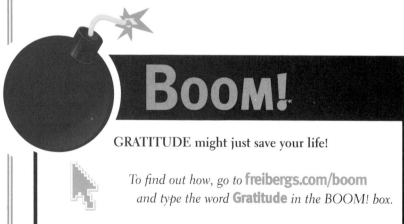

BOOM!

GRATITUDE might just save your life!

To find out how, go to **freibergs.com/boom** *and type the word* **Gratitude** *in the BOOM! box.*

If you agree with this assessment, commit to engaging in the exercises at the end of this section—*today*. They are well researched and they work. The extreme benefits for doing this will become more evident as you read on.

Gratitude transforms our perspective and changes our whole orientation. When you are in awe of what you have, the immediate response is a deep sense of appreciation: "Whom do I repay?" "What does it mean to give back in life?" "How do I discharge my deepest debts for what life has given me?" These questions leave little room for envy, false expectations, or complaint. It's hard to complain when we are truly thankful, but it's hard to be thankful when we take so much for granted.

About a year ago Jackie found herself in one of those ungrateful places. With three children, ages fifteen, eleven, and five, coming and going from dance to soccer, T-ball, and football, the weeks were busy. At the end of a crazy day of chauffeuring, Jackie found herself complaining, "These kids have no clue what a sacrifice we make for them. Running them back and forth, chewing up the day, this sucks." Complaining, like the bad wolf, grows when you feed it. Jackie continued, "Does it matter? Does all of this time on the road really make a difference? Have I accomplished anything significant?" Then, unexpectedly, our son, Dylan, had to go to Children's Hospital for some blood tests. In the midst of such uncertainty, your mind begins to explore all of the possible scenarios: *Is this serious? If it is, how will we handle it? He's so young.* Fortunately, everything turned out fine, but that one trip put life's blessings into perspective. After contemplating trips to and from Children's Hospital to treat Dylan, Jackie thought, *Never again will I complain about taking our kids, who are in good health, to and from activities in which they are fortunate to participate.*

American philosopher Eric Hoffer said, "The hardest arithmetic to master is that which enables us to count our blessings." So you didn't rock the world today; maybe you just changed it slightly. Or if you didn't change it even slightly, at least it didn't get worse. You didn't wreck your car, run over your dog, or cut your finger off. And if you *did* cut your

> C. S. LEWIS SAID, "IT SEEMS TO ME THAT WE OFTEN, ALMOST SULKILY, REJECT THE GOOD THAT GOD OFFERS US BECAUSE, AT THE MOMENT, WE EXPECTED SOME OTHER GOOD."

finger off, at least you're not dead, and you get a whole other chance to try again tomorrow.

C. S. Lewis said, "It seems to me that we often, almost sulkily, reject the good that God offers us because, at the moment, we expected some other good." We have been able to work with people in some of the most admired companies in the world. Yet we are constantly amazed at how many people working in great companies complain about what they *don't* have. On more than one occasion we have felt compelled to say, "What you have in terms of culture is incredibly special. You better protect it and promote it with your life." Sometimes we wished we could offer them a sabbatical and set them up in another work environment. After a year we would send them back. In reality, the grass is rarely greener. Perhaps this would give them a deeper appreciation for what they actually have.

Look, we are not big on funky exercises that promise a lot and deliver a little. But if you want to focus forward and give complaining a permanent rest, try making a daily list of ten things for which you are grateful, or try keeping a gratitude journal. The discipline of being grateful will have a powerful effect on your life. This daily discipline has the potential to radically transform your perspective about life and work. Whether you decide to work with a journal or a list, the idea is that you are forcing yourself to reflect upon and become more conscious of the grace you have experienced in your life. When you make your entries,

BOOM!

don't forget to consider the pain and frustration you have avoided, as well as the blessings you have received. Commit to making your entries every day for the next thirty days, then go back to the gratitude assessment earlier in the chapter and see how your score may have improved.

Is there a compelling case to be made for doing this? In their book *Character Strengths and Virtues*, Christopher Peterson and Martin Seligman document a growing body of research highlighting the benefits of gratitude. People who keep gratitude journals on a weekly basis are more alert and enthusiastic, energetic and attentive, and determined than those who focus on the hassles or neutral events in their lives. Those who replace bitterness and resentment with gratitude report higher levels of fulfillment, vitality, and optimism, and lower levels of stress, frustration, and depression. They exercise more regularly, report fewer physical symptoms, and are more likely to live longer than the ungrateful. Does this sound like a key strategy for becoming more alive and engaged at work? We think so!

Scientific inquiry has only served to substantiate what the world's major religions—Christianity, Judaism, Islam, Buddhism, and Hinduism—have taught us for centuries: that gratitude is central to spiritual growth, physical health, moral maturity, relational competence, and fulfillment. If the research about gratitude hasn't convinced you to make a daily gratitude list, perhaps this story will.

Dain Dunston is a great friend and colleague of ours. Dain is a leadership consultant who's the best in the business at helping CEOs and other leaders zero in on why their strategies aren't getting traction with their people. He's also one of the great speechwriters and speech coaches in America. With a successful career that keeps him constantly in demand and takes him into the inner sanctums of executive suites around the world, Dain has clearly found his sweet spot.

But it wasn't always that way. When Dain turned thirty, he'd lost his job as a realtor in a real estate crash and was trying to support his wife and three children by working in a phone sales boiler room in Los

Angeles. He was discouraged, angry, blaming, and irritable. The table from which he made his sales calls all day long looked out on the parking lot of a psychotherapist-to-the-stars, and each morning he'd watch famous actors and musicians arrive in their flashy cars and go in to talk about their problems. It enraged him. He told us, "I envied their problems, which were nothing compared to mine. I envied their success and bitterly despised my own failure." He was, he admits now, the biggest jerk to work with that anyone could possibly imagine.

One day Dain had a screaming match with his boss, who accused him not only of being a failure as a telephone solicitor but even of not having an "attitude of gratitude" for having a job at all. Furious at the manipulative way this sweatshop owner had suggested he feel gratitude for the demeaning way in which he was treated, he stormed out of the office. When he reached the street, he started to turn left to walk the steam off when something caught his eye. It was a billboard on top of the fire station across the street, advertising some kind of high-dollar whiskey with the slogan "Living Well Is the Best Revenge."

It stopped him in his tracks. He could continue to complain about his boss, the movie stars, and everyone who had called him a failure and dig himself into a deeper rut, or he could take responsibility for his life and learn how to "live well." Dain didn't even go back to work that day. He turned on his heel, went straight home, sat down at his desk, and began to work on a way to live well. He said, "At that time in my life, I knew I couldn't buy my way into living well, which was a blessing in disguise. I knew I'd have to think my way into it." But Dain also knew he couldn't think until he got over his anger at his boss. "The nerve of the guy, to suggest that I wasn't grateful!" He said, "I was grateful, all right! I was *filled* with gratitude, damn it!"

Or was he?

BOOM!

Dain decided to write out a list of the things he was grateful for. At first, nothing much came. He drew a second column and started writing the things he was bitter about. That list was far easier, but as it grew, it seemed less genuine to him. Was he really that bitter about his boss, an economic downturn, or the fact that if he'd tried a little harder out of college, he might not be in the position in which he found himself? Come on.

So he started in on the gratitude list again. His wife and his children. The weather in Los Angeles. The way his mother had taught him to appreciate art. His father's sense of humor. His health. Häagen-Dazs ice cream. He told us, "Man, it was slow in coming, at first. For everything I grudgingly admitted I was grateful for, there were ten items that made my blood boil. But as the afternoon wore on, my list began to grow."

He was grateful for his own sense of humor, for the fact that he could almost always make a roomful of people crack up. He was grateful that, for some reason, people seemed to like him and trust him. He was grateful for his talent for writing and his ability to clarify confusing messages so people got them. And most of all, he was grateful to be alive, living in a wonderful country filled with opportunity, and to be young enough to take advantage of it.

That afternoon's dive into the pool of gratitude changed his life. He began focusing on pursuing a writing career, got a job as a volunteer editor for a sports magazine, and picked up some freelance work with small high-tech companies, helping them to explain their products. With each success—and with the occasional failures—he tallied up the things he was grateful for. Each time, as the list grew longer, weights were lifted from his heart.

As Dain pointed out, "Living well didn't happen overnight, but my capacity to be a contributor in life did." He still struggled. It took nearly six years for a breakthrough into a real career and financial success. But one day he came home to find a message on his answering machine. He had sent an article to a prestigious car magazine, outlining what had caused Chevrolet to lose its market dominance, and what they had to do to fix it. He was hoping they would publish it, but instead, they sent it to the Chevrolet brass. On his answering machine, he heard the voice of the head of General Motors' Chevrolet-Pontiac–Canada division. The man wanted to know who Dain was, how he knew all of the things he had written in the article, and if they could work together. That was the day the door to living well swung wide open. And as far as it being the best revenge? He had long since forgotten what he'd been so mad about.

For Dain, a simple list of the things he was grateful for was essential to changing his perspective, and BOOM,that change was the key to living well.

For many of us, gratitude does not come naturally; it must be cultivated. Forcing yourself to make a daily list of your blessings is essential to making this practice a habit. Will conducting a gratitude audit be easy? Hardly. Especially when you're having an extremely difficult week, but it is exactly what you need. When you feel as though you're in a dead-end job, your boss is dysfunctional, your colleagues are just biding time, work is killing you, you're frustrated and fed up, the last thing you'll want to do is write down the things you are thankful for. But that's the point of developing this daily discipline. It teaches you to look for what *is* working in your life and trains you to focus forward. It's paradoxical. The very thing you need to do most to get out of a funk and stop complaining is the very thing you *feel* least like doing. This is why focusing forward must be based on a gutsy, visceral decision of the will, and not on a feeling.

If you really want to take this exercise to a higher level, consider the specific changes or challenges going on at work right now. Given these situations, what are you thankful for? Perhaps the following scenarios will stimulate your thinking. Choose one or two scenarios from the list below and find *ten positive things for which you could be grateful* if it were to happen to you:

- You are part of a sales team that has been radically restructured
- The funding for a major project you are extremely excited about gets cut
- A boss who had a vision you deeply believed in leaves the organization
- Your computer at work crashes, killing a week's worth of work
- A major client walks because a competitor underbid you
- An unexpected maintenance problem in your plant delays your customer's product launch
- You have three business partners, none of whom think alike
- You are passed over for another person to lead a high-visibility project
- A significant financial investment you made goes bust
- You lose your job

Use this exercise as a way of teaching yourself how to think beyond the major things going on in your organization. As your sense of gratitude increases, you will find that the meaning in work and your satisfaction and happiness in life will increase as well.

In his book *Authentic Happiness*, Martin Seligman describes another exercise that has life-changing potential. Seligman asked students in his Positive Psychology class at the University of Pennsylvania to select one important person from their past who had made a positive difference in their lives and whom they have never properly thanked. Each student was to bring this person to class and present a testimonial—just long enough to cover one laminated page—to the unsuspecting guest. Seligman called it "Gratitude Night." Invitees were restricted to one-third of the students, to stay within the class's three-hour time frame. You know what happened. People got choked up, and the fear of embarrassment gave way to tears of joy and appreciation as the students found a vehicle for expressing how thankful they were for those who meant the most to them. At the end of each discussion, the laminated version of the testimonial was given to the guest.

Written evaluations at the end of Seligman's class indicated that "Gratitude Night" was not only the high point of the class but, for many of the students and guests, one of the greatest nights of their lives. What's to keep you from identifying several people at work and doing the same thing? What's to keep you from initiating a monthly, quarterly, or biannual gratitude night? If you move on this idea, Seligman suggests several criteria:

1. Choose the person because of your deep-felt gratitude, not because of romance or an opportunity for future gain.

2. Take your time (several weeks is not uncommon), and be thoughtful in the words you write.

3. Do it face-to-face. Writing a letter or making a call will not have as much impact.

4. In making the appointment, do not tell the person what it is about, only that you want to meet.

5. Give a laminated version of your testimonial as a gift.

6. Let the recipient react without being rushed; then spend some time reminiscing about the significant events that brought you to this point.

We agree with Helen Keller: "Self-pity is our worst enemy and if we yield to it, we can never do anything wise in this world." Gratitude is a sign of wisdom and maturity, a hallmark of confident humility. Show us a corporate culture infused with gratitude, and we will show you a culture of civility, compassion, and courtesy—a culture where people are not weighed down by the toxicity of complaining, a culture where people find the freedom to soar. We live in the greatest time in human history, when more opportunities are available to more people than ever before. Perhaps it is time to get a new perspective. Charles Dickens wrote, "Reflect upon your present blessings, of which every man has many; not on your past misfortunes, of which all men have some." Gratitude is about focusing forward, choosing optimism, and feeding the good wolf. A spirit of gratitude will raise your passion and energy for work, positively influence your reputation, and ultimately improve the quality of your life.

BOOM!

If you want some more practical ways to focus forward and feed the good wolf,

go to freibergs.com/boom *and type the word* Forward *in the BOOM! box.*

Don't
just do what
the world needs,
play to your genius,
play to what makes you
come alive and the world
will beat a path to your door.

CHOICE #5

PLAY TO YOUR GENIUS

Your Work Is a
Statement About You

05

> *"Life is what happens to you when you're busy making other plans."*
>
> —JOHN LENNON

Your work matters. And the sooner you realize that, the sooner you can begin to change your life. As John Lennon said, "Life is what happens to you when you're busy making other plans." If you don't *plan* for your life to matter, guess what? It won't, at least not to the extent you wish it did. The work you do—in fact, everything you do—is a statement about who you are. Why not choose to make it a masterpiece?

So, how do you get there? Where do you start?

You begin by changing your perceptions about your work. Whatever it is you do, look for the meaning and value beyond the task itself. And here's a hint: work is not meaningless. *All* work has meaning. All work can make a difference. Tom Morris, author of *If Harry Potter Ran General Electric*, says, "Every job can be given either a trivial description or a noble description. Ultimate motivation requires that we have in our minds a noble description of what we do!"

What's Work Like for You?

How many things are you working on right now that will be remembered and cared about long after they are done? Have you done anything spectacular in the last five years that you will tell stories about for the rest of your life? Is your work worth asking about, and is it worth talking about? Does it stimulate curiosity and intrigue on the part of others? Are people standing in line to be the next to take your job?

> HOW MANY THINGS ARE YOU WORKING ON RIGHT NOW THAT WILL BE REMEMBERED AND CARED ABOUT LONG AFTER THEY ARE DONE?

Imagine that you are back in third or fourth grade, and it's craft time. The teacher walks into the classroom, sets a lump of clay in front of you, and says, "You can make anything you want!"

Your mind starts to race with excitement as the creative juices begin to flow. You think, *Letter opener? Nope, too sharp. Paper weight? Nope, too easy. Coffee mug? That's it!* And you begin to shape it and mold it until it's just perfect (in your eyes). The teacher puts your mug in the kiln and fires it. Several days go by, and then you get an opportunity to paint your mug. The design and color scheme are uniquely you. The mug goes back into the kiln. Finally, after sitting on the shelf to cure for another three or four days, the teacher announces, "Class, you may take your art projects home today."

At the end of the day, you blast into the kitchen with a spring in your step and proudly announce to your parents, "Look, Mom! Look,

BOOM!

Dad! It's for you, and I made it!" At this point your parents know enough *not* to ask, "What is it?" They know that would disappoint you. Instead they look at your "mug" in awe and say, "Wow! Did you make this? It's beautiful!"

They treat it with the reverence you know it deserves; they put it up on the family altar—the refrigerator. You probably know that the "fridge" isn't for keeping food cold. Its primary function is to display great works of art behind little plastic magnets for all to see. So they proudly display your very creative coffee mug on top of the family altar for weeks.

One day you come home from school, and your beautiful mug has been placed in the basement for "safekeeping."

While you are not quite old enough to articulate it, you think to yourself, *You didn't just put some* thing *down in the basement; you put that which is a statement about* me *in the basement! It expresses who I am, what I think, and how I feel.* That mug was meaningful because the work of making it was a meaningful expression of who you were.

> WE LONG FOR MEANING, TO BE CAUGHT UP IN SOMETHING BEYOND OURSELVES, A DRAMA OF HEROIC MAGNITUDE.

What if you felt that way about your work? Isn't that what each of us wants? The truth is, we long for meaning, to be caught up in something beyond ourselves, a drama of heroic magnitude. It is how we are made; that desire is part of our very nature. The ability to create something valuable, making the world a better place, acting courageously to serve others, is what it means to be human. Deny this and you run the dangerous risk of becoming dehumanized, empty, unfulfilled, a dead person working.

Here's the key: either our work can define us . . . or we can define our work. Either our work can cast us as meaningless . . . or we can give our work meaning. Which will you choose?

Doing Work That Matters

When we first went looking for men and women who are alive at work, we went to visit SAS Institute, the most successful privately held software firm in the world. In addition to some of the most sophisticated business intelligence software in the world, SAS is known for its country club–like campus and how well it takes care of its employees. We talked to two software engineers, and we asked about the perks at SAS — on-site day care, 36,000-square-foot fitness facility, eight full-time trainers, gourmet dining rooms, thirty-five-hour work week, and a fifty-five-staff member medical clinic — they said the benefits were great, but the really cool thing was getting to create exotic software. What mattered most to them was the work. It was *that* meaningful to them. Given that SAS invests 25 percent of its *top* line in research and development, this should come as no surprise. Every day these guys go to work, they are like kids in a candy store, with a very generous budget. And they are absolutely convinced that the software they build enables companies all over the globe to do things they simply were not capable of doing before SAS came along.

> TO KNOW THAT OUR WORK COUNTS IS TO KNOW THAT WE COUNT.

To know that our work counts is to know that *we* count. The projects you are working on today are statements about who you are, what you think, and how you feel. This begs the obvious question: What do your projects say about you? Further, what do they say about your attitude? About the brand you are building within your organization? How you answer these questions determines how alive and engaged you are and how meaningful your work is. It has an impact on the levels of passion and commitment you bring to your work and ultimately how fulfilling your life will be.

Tony Campolo described the work of his father, and how it provided meaning to his life. He said, "My dad was a craftsman. He worked for RCA making stereo cabinets, back in the days when the wood cabinets were handcrafted. Inevitably we would visit someone's home who had the model my dad made. I would run to my dad and whisper in his ear, 'Dad, it's one of yours, it's one of yours!' and my dad would smile with satisfaction, because on the back of the cabinet was hand-etched the signature of the cabinetmaker." Tony may have come from a poor Italian family, but his father had a sense of pride and dignity about his work — he was engaged in his work because his work mattered.

Meaningful work doesn't just belong to old-world craftsmen, though. Meaningful work happens even in big corporations. And when it does, it makes them even bigger.

In the early 1980s, at a time when the name IBM was synonymous with the words *personal computer*, Steve Jobs brought a group of people together at Apple who deeply believed in their ability to reimagine the future by creating a computer that could be understood intuitively and that could make personal computing user-friendly and fun. Jobs and his team became catalysts to an event of historical proportion — the creation of the Macintosh. Lift the casing off the first Macs and you will find etched inside the signatures of the project team — so passionate about their product that they changed the world! Think we are exaggerating? In the last twenty years, Jobs and company have brought the world three "game changers" — the Apple IIe, which created personal computing; the Macintosh, which brought personal computing to everyday users; and the iPod, along with its cohort iTunes, which transformed the way we access and listen to music. Each of these products set an industry standard. Each rewrote the rules by which others would have to play the game. As we write, Jobs and company just introduced the iPhone, a revolutionary new mobile phone, a widescreen iPod, and a breakthrough Internet communications device all in one product. The fanatics at Apple are working on really cool stuff, stuff that makes a difference in people's lives, stuff that *matters*.

Walk into any Apple store and you can feel the buzz. You quickly get the sense that these Mac fanatics love what they do. Their contagious enthusiasm spills out onto the customers and turns them into fanatics as well. During our work on this book, the power supply on Kevin's Macintosh burned up, destroying the processor along with it. At 4:00 on a Friday afternoon, Kevin took it into the Genius Bar at our local Apple store and explained how mission critical his computer was to our project. The technician indicated that it could take three to four days to fix the problem. That same day, at approximately 9:30 p.m., Kevin got a call from Mac Genius John Nunes, indicating that his Mac was fixed and could be picked up first thing in the morning. When Kevin questioned what John was still doing at the store late on a Friday night, the reply was, "We knew you needed it right away; besides, we love this stuff; we're always here late."

Why are Apple customers so loyal? Steve Jobs would tell you it's the passion behind the product. He said:

> It's because when you buy our products, and three months later you get stuck on something, you quickly figure out [how to get past it]. And you think, "Wow, someone over there at Apple actually thought of this!" And then three months later you try to do something you hadn't tried before, and it works, and you think, "Hey, they thought of that, too." And then six months later it happens again. There's almost no product in the world that you have that experience with, but you have it with a Mac. And you have it with an iPod. ("The Seed of Apple's Innovation," *Business Week*, October 12, 2004, http://www.business-week.com/bwdaily/dnflash/oct2004/nf20041012_4018_db083.htm)

Apparently, now you can have it with the iPhone too. Apple just dropped the word *Computer* from its name. Now, it is known more simply as Apple, Inc., to better reflect its steady but relentless passion to change the world of consumer electronics. BOOM, with a portfolio now spanning software, retail, the online distribution of electronic media, home entertainment, digital audio players, cell phones, *and* computers, Apple is serious about expanding its repertoire of work that matters.

Work has always been one of the most important places where we seek a sense of meaning and identity. Finding meaning in the work we do is essential, because work is a central activity in our lives. When our work becomes meaningful, it's usually because it has become a channel through which we can express the gifts and talents God originally built into us. Discipline and opportunity enable us to develop our gifts and talents. The question is, does the work in which we are engaged allow us to do what we've been designed to do? Further, does it contribute to something larger than ourselves? Does it fully engage us? When the answer to these questions is yes, significance will follow.

Does YOUR Work Matter?

Take a moment to complete the following self-assessment to determine how you feel about your work by checking either YES or NO.

MY WORK MATTERS: SELF-ASSESSMENT

1. **My work inspires me.**
    YES ❏   NO ❏

2. **My work creates meaning in my life.**
    YES ❏   NO ❏

3. My work enables me to fully express my natural gifts and talents.
   YES ❑   NO ❑

4. I make a difference at work.
   YES ❑   NO ❑

5. I am grateful for the opportunities I have at work.
   YES ❑   NO ❑

6. My job gives me an opportunity to work on really cool things—things that matter.
   YES ❑   NO ❑

7. Our products and services make the world a better place.
   YES ❑   NO ❑

8. I am proud of what I do.
   YES ❑   NO ❑

9. People at my work care for one another, look out for one another, serve one another.
   YES ❑   NO ❑

10. My family and friends think my work is important.
    YES ❑   NO ❑

11. I can be myself at work.
    YES ❑   NO ❑

12. I have fun at work.
    YES ❑   NO ❑

BOOM!

13. I love the people I work with.
    YES ☐   NO ☐

14. My work is connected to a higher calling, a noble or heroic cause.
    YES ☐   NO ☐

15. I look forward to coming to work every day.
    YES ☐   NO ☐

Give yourself one point for every YES response and zero points for each NO response. Then total your points and consult the following table to interpret your score.

0–5 POINTS:

You don't feel that your work is meaningful or valuable, and that means your own feelings of value and meaning are at risk. You are probably actively searching for another job or searching for something outside of work that will give your life significance. In either case, there is a good chance that you are disengaged at work. You may frequently feel frustrated, bored, resentful, anxious, or depressed. This could be affecting other important dimensions of your life. If you don't change the direction of your life at work, your spiritual, emotional, psychological, and physical well-being could suffer more than it already has. Pay close attention to this issue, and make a new choice to either redefine your current work or find new work that matters.

6–10 POINTS:

You periodically feel that your work is meaningful, but most of the time it's still just a job. The times you experience a deep sense of meaning at work are overshadowed by the times you get discouraged. The potential for creating work that matters is there, but you must capitalize on it. Don't wait around for someone else to do it for you. Make a choice to either redefine your current work or find new work that matters.

11–15 POINTS:

Congratulations—you love what you do, and you are convinced that what you do makes a difference! You are passionate and excited about your work, because it maximizes your natural gifts and talents.

Most likely, you are fully engaged, because you experience a lot of meaning and joy in your work. Your passion is contagious. People around you are either very irritated or inspired by your example. Assume the best, and use your credibility to help others fall more in love with their work.

Also, remember that meaning is something you create and re-create every day. Don't take what you have for granted.

BOOM!

If you love what you do, consider yourself most fortunate, because you have found a way to link your gifts, passions, and contributions to making a living. But keep in mind that you are an exception to the rule. Most people are in survival mode—just getting by at best and clinically depressed at worst—living for the weekend. Dilbert has become the iconic spokesperson for dead people working. The cartoon character Scott Adams created wouldn't enjoy such huge success if we didn't identify with his cynicism and futility at some level.

We all yearn to be engaged in work that matters, to come home at the end of the day physically tired but emotionally charged because we know we've done something worthwhile. The problem is that too many of us are looking around, hoping that someone will bring us an assignment that will make a difference. When "they" don't come through with that dream assignment, we sulk, complain, or just check out. But we can't expect others to make work meaningful for us—*we* have to make and find meaning in our work. If the work you are doing or want to do truly has the potential to give history a shove, you will become a magnet for other adventurous types who want to make a difference. You will also become an enemy to those who like things just the way they are, those who want the organization to move in a different direction, those who are intimidated by change, and those who envy you for finding something you love to do while they remain stuck and resentful in their own mundane jobs.

A few years ago we worked with a large global hotel chain to help them transform their culture. We started with a group of forty associates who were known as "internal change agents." One young woman (we'll call her Barbie) was selected to represent the help-desk area. After participating in a two-day, off-site meeting, the executive team was so impressed with Barbie's passion that they invited her to cohost an all-employee meeting to share the future direction of the company. When word got back to the help-desk team that Barbie was cohosting this big meeting, it created a buzz. One colleague even did the unthinkable:

when Barbie walked into the help-desk area, he grabbed her jaw and said, "I just wanted to feel the muscles of someone who has bitten off way too much to chew!" Barbie saw the value of change; she stood her ground to fight for the future of the company, even when some colleagues were way outta line!

Pick your change agent du jour: Joan of Arc, Gandhi, Winston Churchill, Rosa Parks, Martin Luther King Jr., Lech Walesa, Lee Iacocca, Jack Welch, Anita Roddick, Carly Fiorina, Steve Jobs, Bono, or the Dalai Lama. An eclectic group, no doubt, but what they share is the courage to choose, to step up to the plate and engage in work that matters, work that altered history! Not one of them has succeeded without facing formidable opposition. Why should we expect to be any different?

Engaging in work that matters comes at a cost: the bigger the breakthrough in your work, the stronger the opposition and the higher the price. Nothing worth having is free. But the courage and perseverance it takes to pay this price comes from the passion and conviction generated by the work itself—work we love doing. If engaging in work that matters has its costs, then not engaging in it has an even higher price: your life. So, when it comes to creating work that fires you up, any price is better than giving up your life's meaning.

Redefine, Reshape, and Recast Your Role

Remember the Sharp Coronado Hospital story from Choice #3? Let us add to the story. The housekeeping team at Sharp Coronado prides themselves on cleanliness and sanitation, but they also pride themselves on being the "hosts of hospitality." They have literally recast their role and turned janitorial services into something really cool. In addition to patient satisfaction, Press Ganey also measures housekeeping courtesy and cleanliness, and Sharp Coronado scores in the 97th percentile for courtesy and the 96th percentile for cleanliness. Why? It's because of

BOOM!

artists like Margaret Reynolds, who realized that she could make a difference by recasting her role. She loves origami and thought it would be fun to surprise the patients with towel origami, now known as towel art, in all the rooms. Margaret then shared her skill with other members of the team, and now housekeepers Rocio Castro and Adela Larios are also infamous Sharp Coronado Hospital towel artists.

To add to the hospital's spalike feel, the housekeeping team recast their role and made housekeeping even "cooler." Instead of just serving as housekeepers, now they also serve as *hosts*. These hosts visit each patient's room four times a day. They bring patients warm, wet towels to refresh them and then ask if there is anything else they can do to make the room and stay more comfortable. They want it to feel more like a five-star resort than a hospital. Each interaction offers another opportunity to individualize service beyond the daily routine of cleaning and sanitizing the patient's room. Think about the power of this kind of personalization. Patients come into the hospital with different wants and needs. One might be an early riser, used to having breakfast at 6:00 a.m. Another patient might like to read late into the night and sleep in until 11:00 a.m. Tuning in to these needs says to the patient, "One size doesn't fit all. You are unique, and we are going to treat you this way." Patients often say, "This feels like a first-class hotel." Others have said, "It feels like home; it's so comfortable and clean." And there is no doubt the hosts are finding significance in their work by participating.

Either you define your work, or your work will define you. So if you want to turn your boring, mundane, plain-vanilla job into something noble and heroic, you'll have to redefine it. Because no matter what your job is, you have the opportunity to mold it and shape it into something you want it to be. Let's be clear: not all work can be exciting, fulfilling, and heroic all the time. Few jobs are completely devoid of some drudgery. But drudgery done for others can give significant meaning to our work and inspire us to be exceptional even in the ordinary things.

How much fun can it be to clean a hospital or stand in a cold intersection and direct traffic? So what makes Margaret Reynolds, the towel artist, or Tony Lepore, the dancing cop we told you about in the introduction, so unique? Simple: they did what not many dare to do. Margaret and Tony took routine jobs and redefined them. Margaret used art, and Tony used fancy footwork. They didn't join the moan and groan club. They didn't have a pity party. They didn't psychologically check out. They didn't sit around and wait for the chief of staff or the chief of police to give them a job with a bigger adrenaline rush; they created their own. Instead, Reynolds and Lepore recast their work into something really cool by entertaining others.

Peek in on our neighborhood Vons grocery store. All customers are asked at checkout, "Did you find everything you were looking for?" One day our neighbor, Kathy Roberts, was greeted at checkout by the store manager, who asked the standard question. Kathy responded honestly but nonemotionally, "No, actually, I did not. I've been in a couple of times to get your famous meat loaf, and it seems I'm always too late. By the time I get here, it's all gone." In response, the manager did not just apologize and suggest a better time to come back for the meat loaf; he asked her how many she wanted, got her home address, and personally delivered one meat loaf to Kathy's door later that day! This Vons manager literally recast his role as an ambassador in that very moment. Now, in the larger scheme of things, is delivering meat loaf huge? For you, maybe not, but for Vons and the loyalty and good "press" that this manager created in our little neighborhood, it's big enough to matter!

> # COOL PROJECTS STIMULATE THE PASSION IN EVERYONE. THEY ARE THE THINGS FROM WHICH LEGENDS AND LEGACIES ARE MADE.

It's not the work that is boring, mundane, and meaningless; it is our *perceptions* about the work that make it meaningless. All of us have the freedom to choose how we view our work, and these choices either give meaning to the work we do or strip it of significance. When we bring meaning to our work by redefining our jobs—our jobs in turn become more meaningful.

Make Every Project a REALLY COOL Project

Transform *your* projects into *really cool* projects by giving them a context and a meaning that's bigger than just the task at hand. World-class people want to be involved in cool stuff, that is, projects that matter, that have meaning, missions that are memorable, ventures that will change the world! Cool projects stimulate the passion in everyone. They are the things from which legends and legacies are made.

CHOICE #5: PLAY TO YOUR GENIUS

When we were looking for a home back in the mid-'90s, we fell in love with a Spanish house that was originally built in 1929 but had recently received a facelift.

We didn't have much of a backyard, but we did have a canyon that seemed to go on forever. What we discovered with a bit of exploration was an overgrown canyon, with about five different levels of terracing. Deep down, somewhat hidden by the growth, was a pool that must have been built by hand in the early 1940s. A cool find indeed, but it sure wasn't very inviting. You had to walk through winding pathways inhabited by all sorts of critters to get there. There wasn't any deck for sunbathing, and the long north side literally dropped about twenty feet deeper into the canyon. So it wasn't a pool we expected to use very much.

On the first level—our actual backyard—there was no fence, just another huge drop to level two. Not the kind of yard suitable for our young children. But we made do and placed our trampoline in the far corner of the backyard.

A few years later, Jackie came up with an interesting project idea. She said, "Let's drain the pool [which we never use anyway] to create a pit for the trampoline, add a small deck around it, and make a safer place for the kids." Cool concept. But not cool enough for Kevin. It didn't take long for him to redefine Jackie's project into a BHAG (big, hairy, audacious goal). What could have been a very functional but not so exciting trampoline pit became a full-blown re-landscaping project, including an upgraded pool with an expansive deck, new stairs, retaining walls, a grassed-in area around a true trampoline pit, and a sandbox.

We took an initial idea—small in scope and low on the game-changer scale—and transformed it into a dream—something memorable. Since its completion, the project has become a haven for our family, a recreation area for our children, and a magnet for friends and neighbors.

REALLY COOL PROJECTS
HAVE SEVERAL THINGS IN COMMON:

- They venture into uncharted waters. They involve doing something new and different that hasn't been done before.

- They transform the mundane into the exciting. The people working on them have the wisdom, creativity, and guts to take a routine task and turn it into something that has high impact.

- They move with speed; they're charged with momentum—even if it means breaking some rules to get things done. Part of the excitement and passion behind a really cool project is how fast it moves. When things get weighed down, people lose interest and enthusiasm.

- They leave a legacy that lives on in the organization long after the project team is on to something new. A cool project is memorable; it's lasting; it's worth talking about.

- They attract the attention of bright, intelligent, idiosyncratic, creative, strong-willed, hardworking people with a revolutionary spirit, who want to make a difference.

What about your projects? Where do they reside on the game-changer scale? If the project you're working on now isn't adding value, isn't cool, isn't exciting or energizing, if it's not making a contribution, then transform it, reframe it, and redefine it until you fall in love with it. What if you were to share your ideas with someone else whom you know has bigger vision, better ideas, and can see things that perhaps you'd never see? It may be more risky, take more time, more energy, and even more money, but it could also turn a mundane assignment into something you get turned on about, something that unleashes your passion, raises your performance, increases your impact, and causes your business to boom! Define every project in terms of the five criteria just listed. Be relentless; don't settle for *done* when it could be *done better*. Your life is now! Your projects are a statement about you. Just do it!

Play to Your Genius

In our business we meet a lot of people who make six-figure incomes. But many of them admit they are unhappy and unfulfilled. Sure, they love the power, prestige, and perks that go with the high-level positions they have devoted so much of their lives to, but when they reach the top, something's missing. They live lives of outward abundance and inner poverty. Deep inside, something big is missing. The sad part is they spend fifteen to twenty-five years chasing their dreams of wealth and power only to realize it didn't deliver the meaning they thought it would. Their standard of living is at an all-time high while their quality of life is at an all-time low.

> CONGRUENCE IS THAT PLACE WHERE YOUR GIFTS AND TALENTS AND YOUR PASSIONS ARE ALIGNED WITH WHAT NEEDS TO BE DONE.

So, why do they go on suffering? At this point, they've invested so much time and energy chasing their empty dreams that they can't bear the thought of giving them up. And learning to do something new is too scary. So they live in their misery and die a little bit each day. They work ten to sixteen hours a day and get the life sucked out of them. They go home at the end of the day emotionally drained and have noth-

BOOM!

ing left to give their families. The best they hope for is to plop down on the couch in front of the television and garner some sense of gratification by vicariously living other people's "meaningful" lives.

We often ask these people, "If you're not happy, why don't you change?" The answer we most commonly hear: "I don't have a choice. It's too risky. I've invested twenty years of my life in this career!" We then respond, "You always have a choice. If you've lost the last twenty years of your life, don't lose the next twenty!" But do they change? Sometimes—but not always!

> "MOST OF US
> GO TO OUR GRAVE
> WITH OUR MUSIC
> STILL INSIDE
> OF US."
>
> —OLIVER WENDELL HOLMES

Sadly, these people have rationalized their resistance to change because they are convinced that the lives they really want aren't attainable. Somewhere along the line they bought into the notion that they can temporarily defer their deepest desires and aspirations in order to get ahead. The problem is that "temporary" becomes permanent. Just one more raise, one more move up to a bigger house, one more college payment always leads to *one more*. And so they end up selling themselves out. They become posers: they work at a job that doesn't inspire them, with people they don't care about, in an industry they aren't excited about—all for the sake of a buck. As they become more and more disconnected from their work, disillusionment takes hold and becomes a major roadblock to change. After all, who is willing to take an emotional, physical, or financial risk to pursue something they think is impossible? What's their problem? *Lack of congruence!*

Our premise is this: you will experience more life at work and have a greater opportunity to make a difference when you are congruent.

Congruence is that place where your *gifts and talents* and your *passions* are aligned with *what needs to be done.*

The people we've described aren't accounting for what happens if they *don't* change. The dehumanizing effect that living an incongruent life has on us can be seriously harmful. The reason wellness is such a hot issue today is because so many people are *not* well. Oliver Wendell Holmes said, "Most of us go to our grave with our music still inside of us." What a shame. Being engaged comes from unleashing the music within and sharing it with others.

Most of us don't become dead people working overnight. It gradually sneaks up on us. We slowly get seduced and sucked into someone else's definition of success, only to reach a crisis point years later and say, "What happened?" If we are wise, we will accept responsibility for the quality of our lives and wake up. We will admit that joining the dead-people-working club is a consequence of the *choices* we made.

Create Congruence—Work in Your Sweet Spot

Do a mental survey of the businesspeople you personally know who get great pleasure out of their work. What do they have in common? In our experience with businesspeople in different positions and different industries around the world, we have found that it is a sense of fulfillment. Most people who are happy in life spend time doing things they are gifted at, tasks they are genetically, psychologically, emotionally, and spiritually engineered to excel at. These gifts and talents express who we really are and make a valuable contribution to others.

John Coltrane, the world-renowned saxophonist and titan of improvisation, provides a wonderful example of how a gift, powerfully expressed, can unleash the passion within us. In the early 1950s Coltrane almost died of a drug overdose. Retreating from the drug and alcohol addictions that almost killed him, Coltrane put his faith in God. Many music aficionados agree that his most mature period as an artist came after this experience. One of his most revered pieces, *A Love Supreme*, is a deeply spiritual thirty-two-minute cauldron of emotions expressing his thankfulness to God for His grace.

After one electrifying and overwhelming rendition of *A Love Supreme*, this legend of jazz was so completely moved that he stepped off the stage, put down his saxophone, and uttered the Latin words *"Nunc dimittis."* Coltrane was referring to the words sung in an ancient prayer from the Canticle of Simeon: "Lord, now lettest thou thy servant depart in peace, for mine eyes have seen thy salvation." Coltrane was in that moment where his gift was never more vibrant and alive. He knew he would never play another rendition of the piece that would equal or better this one. At that moment, he experienced a  state of "joy in being" so profound that he knew he had become completely fulfilled and fully expressed as a human being.

Imagine how you would feel if you were *completely* fulfilled, *fully* expressed in your work! John Coltrane found congruence. The fact is, engagement increases when you lean into your strengths, not your weaknesses.

Players assume ownership for finding congruence and taking responsibility for figuring out how to work there as often as possible. They understand the power of what can happen when their work requires what they are good at and passionate about. They work at finding assignments where they can excel, where the "turn on" value is extremely high, and where they can make a difference.

Congruence starts to happen when we challenge ourselves to address three critical questions:

What are my natural, God-given gifts and talents—what am I good at? Congruence requires talent. You must be great at what you do. You must have the knowledge and skills needed to perform at an extremely high level. Simply being satisfied isn't nearly good enough!

What am I passionate about—what turns me on? Congruence requires more than talent: it needs a corresponding, deep-seated desire to apply that talent in a particular way. Congruence assumes a love for the game, a love for the project, a love for the role—despite the parts we dislike. The challenge with this part of the sweet spot is that we often get caught in the tension/trade-off between what matters and what works. We rationalize our behavior by claiming, "It would be great to someday be able to find work that I'm passionate about, but right now I have to be practical; I have bills to pay; I have to do what works."

Where can I make the greatest contribution—what needs to be done? Congruence/harmony is not a hedonistic call to self-indulgence; it's about using our gifts and talents to serve some part of the world and make it better. You can be both good at what you do and love your job, but if you aren't doing the work that the organization needs you to do, then you will not be in your sweet spot. On a practical level, it will be difficult over the long haul to get paid for something that doesn't need to be done and is not considered a valuable contribution.

Congruence challenges the traditional way we keep score in business—that those who make the most money win—and offers us a different criterion for success—that those who are fully expressed add the most value, make the biggest difference, and win. In this model success is waking up in the morning and leaping out of bed because you can't wait to get to work!

Ultimately, the degree of congruence you have in your work will determine the size of your sweet spot. The larger the sweet spot, the more passionate and engaged you are. In some cases there might not even be a sweet spot at all.

How Do You Know If You Are Not in the Sweet Spot?

That's like asking how you know you're in love. You'll KNOW! Are you in love with your job, excited by your life, free to fully express your gifts and passions in your work? No? Then you haven't found your sweet spot.

If you're working outside your sweet spot, at best it's just a job that pays the bills. At worst, you feel as though you are grinding gears. Few things about your job come easy. You feel overwhelmed and stressed or bored and restless most of the time. You don't look forward to going to work in the morning, so you hit the snooze button and roll over until you absolutely must get out of bed. You feel guilty about the work time you spend for personal use on the Internet. You fantasize about your dream job and envy others who appear to have found it. You drink too much, eat too much, or exercise too much as an escape. You live for time off. These danger signs are a good indication that something must change.

When we asked a good friend and successful attorney here in San Diego, "So, how's work?" he replied, "Ah, it's just work!" Fortunately he recognizes it and is taking significant steps to move toward his sweet spot. If it's *just* work for you, too, then maybe you need to do the same.

How Do You Know If You Are in the Sweet Spot?

There are some sure signs that you have arrived at your own personal sweet spot at work. It's as if the mold was made especially for you, as if there is a void in the world that has long awaited you. The work in which you are engaged takes full advantage of your gifts and talents, and you are fully engaged in applying them. You, in turn, make your job look effortless. Things just flow together. You lose track of time because you are energized by what you do. You are excited about getting up in the morning, and you can't wait to get back to work tomorrow. Think of the famous people we all know who appear to be working in their sweet spots. Bono of U2 says he wakes up every morning with a melody in his head. He was made to write and sing.

The Power of Congruence

But there may be things on the job—barriers that get in the way of your getting into your sweet spot. By identifying your sweet spot, and then building a solid business case for why the barriers should be removed, you do something incredibly positive and energizing—both for yourself and the organization, and the benefits are many:

Congruence fosters authenticity. We are more human, more alive when we are doing what we've been made to do. When you find the sweet spot, you aren't trying to do something or be someone you are not. You get to play to your genius. You spend your time honing and developing your gifts and less time on your inadequacies or weaknesses. You become more confident and action oriented. One of the fastest ways to extinguish the flames of engagement and expression is to force a fit, to squeeze yourself into a mold for which you were not made, like trying desperately to "develop" your weaknesses.

Congruence promotes autonomy and self-direction. When you hit the sweet spot, you require very little supervision. If you've ever been in a job with a high degree of congruence, you know how compelling and enthralling it can be. Your focus is maniacal, your energy is explosive, and your commitment is over the top. No one has to tell you what to do. Your inner drive puts the wheels of initiative in motion. The best anyone can do is to remove the obstacles that get in the way of what we're already turned on about. Think of what can happen when a critical mass of people reach this level on a team.

PEOPLE WHO DEVOTE THEIR TIME TO THINGS THEY LOVE BECOME MORE OPEN-MINDED, MORE ENERGETIC, SEXIER, MORE PLAYFUL, MORE ALIVE . . . AND MORE INTERESTING.

Congruence cultivates commitment. We invest more of ourselves in work we love. We also work harder and more passionately to protect this investment. The fact is, we give more of our discretionary time and effort to the things that bring us the most meaning and joy in our lives. Commitment comes most naturally when we are thoroughly excited about what we do.

Congruence is what makes work fun. Aristotle said, "Where talents and the needs of the world cross, therein lies your vocation." We would say, ". . . therein lies your avocation." Ultimate congruence takes us to a place where work stops feeling like work, and BOOM— "I have to" becomes "I want to." Creativity and productivity rise. We move closer to maximizing our potential, and we have more fun. People who devote their time to things they love become more open-minded, more energetic, sexier, more playful, more alive . . . and more interesting—all of which makes them more fun to be around! Confucius said, "Choose a job you love, and you will never have to work a day in your life."

Congruence is a key to standing strong. When you are doing what you love, you develop an inner security that makes you more resilient to criticism and mistakes. You don't feel that you have to please everyone. Your significance comes from being in a job that fits you perfectly instead of from the approval of others.

Congruence makes it easier to say NO for a bigger YES. When you absolutely know what you're good at, what you're passionate about, and what needs to be done, it is easier to say no to assignments and opportunities that fall outside of your sweet spot. With three very busy children and careers that take us both on the road, we sometimes find ourselves having strayed too far from home for too long. Last year Jackie created some personal and professional boundaries that helped her know when to say no, because being around and available for our children was our bigger and more clearly defined *yes*. When we know what we've been made to do and what needs to be done, we are also better able to define what we are *not* made to do. This can even create opportunities for others who are more capable—who have different sweet spots—to fill in the gap.

Congruence stimulates personal growth. When you are doing what you love, you want to do it more and better. Consequently, you work harder at your job, you give more to it, and—ultimately—you grow more. The famous Nobel laureate George Bernard Shaw clearly had a gift and a passion as a playwright. But it was years before he got his first published work. Shaw continued honing his writing skills and growing as a writer because he believed in what he was.

Congruence cultivates team unity. Congruence raises the level of trust and respect among team members. When players operate from their sweet spots, the focus turns to the strengths that each person brings to the table. If you are doing a job that doesn't put you into your sweet spot, you're doing a job that someone else really ought to be doing. You lose because of the frustration you experience as you try to get by each day— knowing that you're not doing what you're meant to do. Your coworkers lose because they are denied an opportunity to work in their own sweet spots. And, of course, the organization loses because people aren't firing

BOOM!

on all cylinders. Dissect a high-performing team: we think you will find an extraordinary number of individuals working in their sweet spots.

Working in a job where there is no congruence is damaging to us and to our organizations. We simply end up going through the motions—living from one paycheck to the next. Eventually we become hardened and embittered or indifferent. Finally, we disengage from our work and from those with whom we work. The tragedy is we become dead people working!

How large is your sweet spot? Use the diagram below to determine how much congruence you have in your job. Place a number between 0 (totally unsatisfied: dead) and 10 (totally turned on: alive) in each of the three circles to express the degree to which you are satisfied with each circle in your current job. For example, if you feel that you fully get to use your gifts and talents in your current work, and that makes you feel more alive, you might put a 9 or 10 in that circle. If you are only moderately passionate about your current work, and it makes you die a little bit inside, you could put a 5 in that circle. You get the point. Total the three numbers.

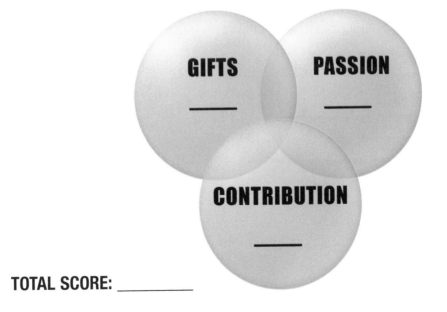

TOTAL SCORE: _____

If your total score equals 30, all three circles have complete overlap and you have perfect convergence. If you didn't score a 30 (most people don't), identify the circle or circles that are most out of alignment and ask, "What's missing?" Use the following questions to guide you:

- What are my natural gifts? Why aren't they being fully expressed at work?

- When am I most happy and fulfilled in my life, what am I doing?

- How can I transfer what I love doing into my job?

- What would make my contribution at work more meaningful to me? To my organization?

- What important projects could I sign up for that could be well served by my natural gifts and talents?

- What projects, initiatives, hobbies, or extracurricular activities should I engage in to further develop my gifts and talents?

- What is holding me back? How am I rationalizing my resistance? What am I going to do next?

You have two choices. You can find your sweet spot and unleash the most wonderful gifts God has given you; to employ those gifts where you find the greatest need, and set them free in the service of others. Or you can write off the search for your sweet spot as an idealistic pipe dream and let your profoundest talents atrophy, making your life a blip on the radar screen, when it could've been so much more.

And if you did score 30? Take another look. One trait of highly engaged people is a lingering hunger or discontent with the status quo; yes, they're engaged and excited in what they do, but they're not complacent. They're actively criticizing themselves and their work, actively looking for ways to improve, and often dissatisfied with even their best

BOOM!

work. Why? Because they're so engaged that they can see over the top and imagine even greater things to do.

So, If You're Not in the Sweet Spot, What Can You Do?

Declare it. Make a declaration to yourself and at least one other person that you are out of alignment. Either you don't have the skills for the job, you don't have the passion, or you're unable to make a contribution. Declare it; don't try to hide it. Wave the biggest flag you can find, and get attention to the problem, because if you don't, you'll die the quiet death of meaninglessness every day.

What causes us to be dead people working is fear—we're afraid to admit it's *not* working. We sort of know what congruence would look like; we might even know how we could get there. But the distances look too great, and the obstacles seem too high. Some people are that way about clothes. They'll buy a pair of pants, hoping they'll fit, only to discover that they don't. But they wear them anyway, because they're either too stubborn to go up a size or too embarrassed to admit it.

So *if your job doesn't fit, don't wear it.* Don't force the fit.

If you know that you're not in your sweet spot, take a moment and write this down:

I, [YOUR NAME], AM IN SEARCH OF MY SWEET SPOT. I AM IN A JOB WHERE I DON'T HAVE EITHER THE TALENTS, OR THE PASSION, OR THE ABILITY TO MAKE THE MEANINGFUL CONTRIBUTION I WANT TO MAKE.

Now sign it and put it in your pocket. And as soon as you can, find someone appropriate to share it with, someone who will hold you accountable, *declare* it to them. Think about what would happen if you marched into the office of your boss, your partner, or a colleague and declared it out loud. Real change means asking for help in figuring out how to (a) get the skills and talents you need to make a passionate contribution, or (b) get out of your current job and into one that works for you, one that can grow to be your sweet spot.

If you really want to change, if you really want to find your sweet spot, you better be prepared to put it all on the line, because if you're not willing to take big risks, don't expect big returns.

But don't quit your job just yet. In fact, don't declare it to your boss until you've done a little bit of self-evaluation and asked yourself a few questions.

What Are Your Talents?

Do you know yet? Many younger workers don't have a clue, often not until they're well into their thirties. If you're in your twenties, you may not have had the time to find out. Other than music or math prodigies, many of us have to try a series of different activities until we begin to home in on our talents. But here are some questions that may help you find yours:

What Have You Done That Felt Effortless, That Came Easily to You?
Have you ever been thrown into a project where others are struggling, but, to you, it's all obvious and clear? Talents tend to help us organize a view of the universe that others just can't grasp.

Are there any tasks around your workplace that others hand over to you because they know that, for you, they're no-brainers? That's where you can start to look for your talents.

When Have You Felt Like You Were Grinding Your Gears in Hopeless Work?
One way to identify your talents is to single out the areas where you are sure you have *no* talent (other than, for many of us, singing). Have you

BOOM!

ever been given a task where you felt like a fish out of water—where you felt completely ill suited to the job, even while others seemed to have no problems? By identifying ways you're not talented, you may begin to clear the underbrush from around your true talents.

Our young son is very active and athletic, and while he's too young to know where his true abilities will lie, we've noticed something interesting. In some sports, he seems a natural. In others, he seems to struggle. Put him on skis, and he's like lightning. Put him into a peewee football game, and watch out! He throws a mean spiral pass and loves to mix it up on the line. But put him on a basketball court, and he's all thumbs and elbows, absolutely out of his element. He has gifts in one area that abandon him in another.

What are your gifts, and when have you fully expressed them?

If You Asked Ten People Who Know You Well What You're Good at, What Would They Say?

You may be surprised at the answers you get from people who will give it to you straight. They may already have very clear ideas about where your talents lie. We're not talking about your mother, who wants you to be a doctor, or your uncle Charley, who wants you to follow him into the dry-cleaning business. We're talking about objective observers who watch you do something that's effortless for you and think, *Darn, I wish I could do that like she does!*

What Do You Get Affirmed For?

If you think about it, there are probably common compliments that you get, possibly compliments that you tend to dismiss as not important. But they might be important affirmations of where your talents lie. Do people comment that you write well or that you're good with numbers? Do people say you're a good driver or that you have an eye for design? When a project is in trouble, do people say you're good at getting your teammates focused? Listen to what they say: these affirmations are based on genuine and generous observations of you in action, of you at your best. Take note of such observations, write them down, and review them frequently.

What Are Your Passions?

Once you begin to have a strong idea of what talents you possess, you can start to look at what makes you passionate at work.

What Projects Have You Done That Turned You On?

If you've identified some talents, we'll bet that projects where those talents were used were tasks that really lit you up, assignments that you couldn't wait to get back to work on every morning. So imagine what it would be like to feel that way every day of your work life.

Make a list of the projects that have turned you on over the past few years. Make a second list of the projects that have been a living hell for you. What makes the great projects stand out? Identify that, and you'll start to understand what makes you passionate.

When You Look at Projects You've Done, What Makes You Most Proud?

Chances are, the work you're proud of is the work you're passionate about. If you were part of a task force planning new office space for the company and look back at that as something you're proud you were part of, that's an indication that you have a passion for creativity and planning. If you were part of a team that did extraordinary work during Hurricane Katrina, pulling long hours to make sure everyone affected was taken care of, you may discover you have a passion for managing mission-critical logistics. Whatever it is, what's available in your workplace that can give you more of that experience, more often?

What Needs to Be Done?

Finally, if you're sure your talents are being fully expressed in work that makes you passionate, but you're still not feeling fully congruent, you need to ask yourself this question: *Am I doing the right stuff?* Or are you just so absorbed in playing with your talents and passions that you don't care about the results? If so, that's as bad as being a dead person working. In fact, it may be worse, because you're a person who's in the right place with the right skills and passions—the kind of position in which most readers of this book truly long to be—and you're wasting your time, actively ignoring goals and deadlines.

Or it may be that you're in a place where your talents are being used, but not in pursuit of worthwhile goals. Maybe you're a talented and passionate designer or engineer being asked to work on substandard products or with people who don't care about quality. That's understandable.

The question is, what are you going to do about it? What have you *tried* to do about it? We encourage you to go back to the ideas of recasting your role and turning mundane projects into really cool projects.

Before you blame the organization for failing, you have to at least have worked to your best ability to change it. Talents and passions will open the doors to opportunity. But sometimes you have to reach out and try turning the knob. Sometimes you have to pound on the door and make some noise.

Have you *really* done all you can to make a positive change in your workplace, or are you just going to take your ball and leave the playground? Before you do, we suggest you take a long, hard look at yourself and at the way you're taking responsibility for your own engagement, your own talents, your own passion, and your own contribution.

Total freedom is when you can stand on your desk to declare yourself—declare yourself *for* meaningful work with engaged people—and be willing to take the consequences.

Once you're able to freely and truly express your talents and your passions to accomplish what needs to be done, BOOM—you'll be amazed at how your influence will grow! Maybe it's time to risk more.

When recasting isn't even an option, and you can't find your sweet spot—move on!

Not all jobs can be recast. Sometimes the most meaningful stand you can take is just walking out the door.

Take Anita Sharpe and Kevin Salwen, for instance, who made their marks in journalism, both as writers for the *Wall Street Journal*. Before working there, Sharpe was editor-in-chief of the *Atlanta Business Chronicle*, where she helped increase the circulation nearly tenfold. Under her leadership, the publication twice won the national Gerald Loeb Award. As a writer for the *Wall Street Journal*, she won a Pulitzer Prize for her investigative journalism.

Salwen spent eighteen years with the *Wall Street Journal*, most recently as national small-business editor. While there, he launched two publications, covered two presidential administrations, wrote two different columns, and appeared on CNBC's *Power Lunch* each week for his view on small business.

All meaningful work, right? But while both Sharpe and Salwen had envious careers, they grew tired of opening the closets and pointing their fingers at the dark sides of business and government. The work began to lose meaning for them. And so they made the decision to turn their backs on their jobs and walk out the door. They put everything on the line so they could restore the meaning to their work lives.

Instead of just going to another newspaper, they opted for a radically different approach: they founded *Worthwhile*, recently renamed *Motto*, an inspiring business magazine that asks one simple question: "Do you enjoy what you do?" Sharpe said, "People are seeking a way out of the darkness and looking for those who can help light the path." *Motto* is for

BOOM!

the next generation of business leaders who are reaching for greater meaning in their work lives.

In the March 2005 edition of *Worthwhile*, Salwen describes coming to a point where the impressed "oohs" and "ahs" rendered at cocktail parties in response to what he did for a living were not enough anymore. Essentially a self-admitted dead person working, he said:

> In truth I had begun "career sleepwalking" . . . Now, having created the magazine and heard from readers, I can't be blunt enough: "If you are unhappy with your work life, change something. At least start on the path to bringing yourself more fulfillment (and by the way, that can be at your current company)." Are you waiting for someone to say "Go for It?" Let me fill the role: "Permission Is Granted." (From the editors, 8)

Don't settle for work that doesn't matter.
It ALL matters.

It's your life, and it's the only one you've got. The work you do is a statement of who you are. If you want your life to matter, then *you* have to transform your work into something you are turned on about.

BOOM!

Want more PERSONAL POWER to play to your genius?

Go to **freibergs.com/boom** *and type the word* **Power** *in the BOOM! box.*

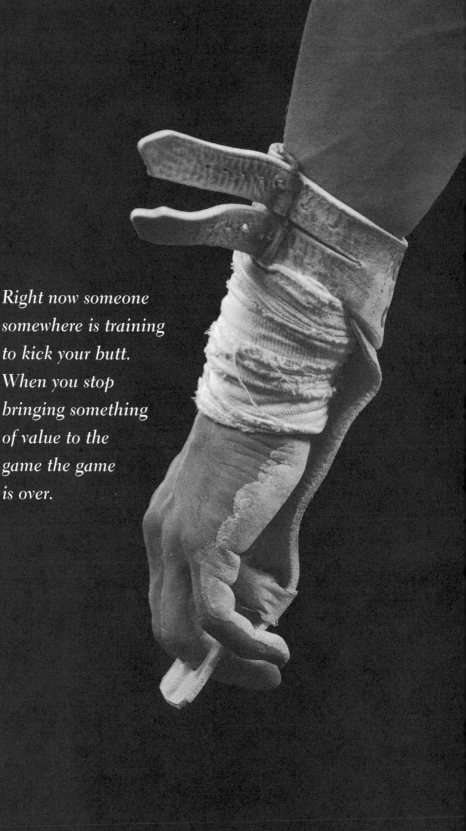

Right now someone somewhere is training to kick your butt. When you stop bringing something of value to the game the game is over.

CHOICE #6

GET IT DONE

Success Is the Reward
for Those Who Make a Difference

06

"Great companies elevate and protect people who champion a culture of results over a culture of rhetoric and red tape."

an your organization get along without you? Are you a person that great companies will fight to keep? Do people like to be around you? In our experience, far too many people talk about what they shoulda, woulda, or coulda done. MVPs *get* it done. They don't make their bosses do their thinking for them, they don't make their coworkers carry more than their share of the weight, and they are constantly looking for something new to bring to the table. Great companies elevate and protect people who champion a culture of results over a culture of rhetoric and red tape. There are a lot of ways to expand your influence, but you must first believe that it starts with *you* — that you are personally and professionally accountable for leading where you are planted and causing your influence to grow. Here are a few ideas.

Create Vitality, Energy, and Buzz

Walk the colorful hallways at Southwest Airline's General Offices long enough, and you will eventually run into a character who is "holding court" with a small group of people or standing nose-to-nose with one other person—completely (and comfortably) oblivious to what's going on outside the dialogue. He is always deeply engaged and contagiously engaging. Energy and enthusiasm flow from the epicenter of the conversation. If you watch for a while, you will see that each of the participants walks away from this conversation more alive and more engaged. Is the person with whom they have been talking the Energizer Bunny? No, it's Herb Kelleher, the cofounder, chairman, and former CEO of Southwest Airlines. We are not exaggerating when we say that Herb has become one of the most beloved CEOs in the world. Even competitors who fear him will tell you they like him.

What is it about Herb that is so magnetic, so engaging, so contagious? He is one of the smartest people we know, and he is a fierce competitor, but beyond that he seeks and exudes vitality, energy, and a buzz for life, for growth, for people, and for learning. When Herb is in a conversation, he is 100 percent *there*; you will never see him looking around or diverting to an issue he finds more fascinating. His self-effacing humor, intense curiosity, and the fact that he always finds something interesting about what you have to say immediately makes you feel comfortable with him. People feed off his energy, and he in turn feeds off theirs—the conversation and interaction are always positively intoxicating! Organizations and teams would do well to get buzzed with the same kind of energy, engagement, and enthusiasm that Herb brings to learning, stretching, and growing from others.

One of the qualities engaging people have is their ability to cultivate energy and create a buzz. In their book *The Hidden Power of Social Networks*, Rob Cross and Andrew Parker refer to these people as *energizers*. This quality is very hard to replicate and, therefore, becomes an incredible competitive advantage. It's like fuel: if you build a reputation as someone who can infuse the organization with passion and enthusiasm, you stand out; you differentiate yourself from everyone else who just shows up, waiting to be inspired.

Most of us have worked with someone in our career who had a "wet blanket" effect on the organization. You know the type of person we are talking about: they have a knack for sucking the life out of people. Your interactions with them are dampening, disheartening, and discouraging.

Kevin served on a board of directors with one such person. A very bright and well-meaning individual we'll call "Ed" would use each board meeting to pontificate. Ed would take up all the space with his preconceived ideas. While he verbally acknowledged that he valued other people's perspectives and insights, he rarely got out of their way. He was blinded by his self-importance and had no clue about what a drain he was on the board. To be fair, Ed had some very good ideas, but he lacked the ability to create buzz, to get people excited about them.

Now, shame on Kevin for being a spectator—for letting Ed dominate board conversations, for complaining instead of confronting, and for acting like a victim. Had Kevin chosen to be a player by helping Ed uncover his blind spots, several positive things could have happened: board members might have taken more initiative to leverage Ed's expertise instead of avoiding it, the board meetings would have been more productive, the leadership team would have felt more passion and energy coming from individual board members, and the organization would have received better strategic direction from the board.

We know the same kind of people socially as well. They have this tendency, a knack, a bad habit of controlling the conversation. They take the stage, they interrupt, and they share their own experiences and don't reciprocate with an interest in yours. The conversation is one-sided and all about them. Sadly, too many of us let it happen, yet we go home at the end of an evening and complain to our spouses, our partners, or ourselves about how obnoxious the monologue was. When you find yourself in this situation personally or professionally, you have a choice. You can let it happen, or you can chime in, become a "buzz agent," and redirect the conversation toward a more engaging dialogue, where you and others can contribute and experience the buzz of learning, debating, sharing, and growing.

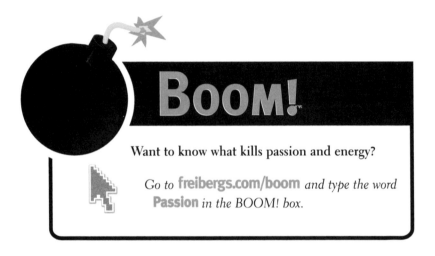

Want to know what kills passion and energy?

Go to **freibergs.com/boom** *and type the word* **Passion** *in the BOOM! box.*

What happens when you create vitality, energy, and buzz in an organization? Well, you are certainly more visible, and you have more of a voice than others. Your ideas will carry more weight and have more influence on the business. That means you have a better shot at getting other people to rally around your ideas. Whether it's calling to check in from a different time zone in the middle of the night, going the extra mile to research an issue, filling in when you are short staffed, or connecting you to significant others in their network, people will give you more of their discretionary time and energy. The best-of-the-best will want to work with you, because thoroughbreds like to run with other thoroughbreds. People seek out people who energize them. That means you have a better shot at putting together project teams that win. Do this enough and BOOM—you will build a reputation as someone the organization can trust with bigger or more important assignments. Do you bring the same level of energy and passion to the game as those you admire—or envy?

Here are some things to consider if you want to become a "buzz agent" and bring more life to others and infuse more energy into the organization.

> DO YOU BRING THE SAME LEVEL OF ENERGY AND PASSION TO THE GAME AS THOSE YOU ADMIRE—OR ENVY?

Give People a Voice

When you create room for people to "weigh in" with their ideas, you value them—even if you disagree with them. When we are valued, we feel more vital to the organization. One of the greatest ways we can energize people is by asking for their insight, listening without distraction, and acting upon what we learn.

We have found that a dramatic shift in the way we teach and learn takes place between undergraduate and graduate education. As you progress from one to the other, you are increasingly expected to bring a point of view and share it with the rest of the class. Your classmates are then expected to listen and react. You move from understanding to contributing and adding on. The quality of the learning is determined by the quality of the insight generated. We learned early on in our doctoral experiences that the very best classes were those in which a lively debate developed over a critical issue. You had to be on your toes. You had to strike a balance between defending your position and being open to other points of view. You couldn't just know the facts; you had to be able to draw conclusions, create an argument, and convey it with passion.

There were often heated disagreements, but everyone felt valued and energized, because everyone was invited/expected to be a player. What would happen if *you* built a reputation for being a catalyst who stimulates the same kind of dialogue in the culture of your organization?

When you *don't* have a voice, you don't feel valued. Bruce Bochy, former manager of the San Diego Padres and current manager of the San Francisco Giants, recently told us about a situation in which the Padres club released veteran third baseman Vinny Castilla. Bochy was against the move and asked that management sit down with the coaching staff to discuss it before making the change. At the time of Castilla's release, the Padres were leading the National League West division and had a lot of momentum. Castilla was released, no discussion, end of story. Now, if you follow baseball, you know that Bochy has a reputation for making the best of less-than-optimal circumstances, but the dampening effect this had on the coaching staff, not to mention the players, was significant. Bochy said, "If you respect the opinions of your coaching staff, those who know what these players bring to the game beyond the statistics, wouldn't it make sense to have a roundtable discussion about major moves like this?"

Even though Castilla's future might not have changed, the former San Diego skipper would have welcomed the opportunity to have a frank discussion about it. Unfortunately that didn't happen. Perhaps this is one of the reasons why San Diego also lost a coach—who is arguably one of the most talented and seasoned managers in baseball—to one of its rivals.

Things are not always going to go your way, but simply to have a voice and be heard is energizing; to be a part of the debate is engaging. Bruce Bochy couldn't control the Padres' front office, but he certainly did sit down with his players and staff to have a candid discussion about keeping the team's momentum alive. He asked them to focus on what the club had going for it versus what and whom they were losing. Apparently it worked: under Bochy's leadership the Padres went on to win their fourth division title.

Build Momentum

Have you ever arrived at the end of an extremely busy day and felt as though you accomplished nothing? We all want to know that we are making a difference.

People get energized when they are going somewhere. You can help this along by being action oriented—by creating a sense of urgency. If you've ever driven a car at one hundred miles per hour or more, you know that you are definitely more alert and engaged than when you are cruising down the freeway at the speed of traffic. Speed is exhilarating! Jump in! Push for daily progress toward meaningful objectives. Get known as a person who dramatically shrinks the cycle time for getting things done.

You can create buzz by reminding people to lift their heads off the grindstone and celebrate the victories they've achieved. Publicize even the smallest results. One small win creates momentum and leads to another. And with each success another naysayer is either silenced or transformed into a player. Let's face it: people tend to check in and engage when things are "clicking." That's because everyone wants to be on a winning team.

You can create energy simply by never concluding a meeting without celebrating an accomplishment and defining next steps and who is accountable for what. You can help people feel a sense of vitality simply by helping them see how their individual contributions link to a larger cause. The importance of doing this cannot be underestimated, because momentum energizes and encourages us to go for more. When you build a reputation as a momentum builder, you become indispensable, because people see you as someone who can step in and change the outcome of the game.

Break the Back of Entitlement—Banish It from Your Thinking

Recently, during a morning-drive show in San Diego, the hosts did a spot highlighting an editorial that had been written to a paper in the Midwest. Apparently this guy found an uncashed paycheck for one thousand dollars on the ground. He did not know the person to whom it belonged, so he looked up the name in the phone book, got the address, and drove the check to its rightful owner. A woman answered the door, took the check, and offered no reward other than a big, huge, appreciative "Wow, thank you!" The guy felt ripped off. He thought, *Shoot, I've driven out of my way to do you this good deed. Don't I deserve a reward?* So he wrote to the local paper and asked for public opinion: Was he entitled to a reward or not? Eighty-nine percent of those who responded said, "No. A reward is not necessary."

Clearly this guy was operating out of an entitlement mentality. Apparently several questions never got on his radar screen: What does it mean to be a citizen, a servant, a contributing member of the community? What are the responsibilities that go with these roles? What happens to a society in which rights and responsibilities are out of balance, a culture where people focus more on what they are owed than on what they owe? Entitlement is grounded in the belief that if I make a sacrifice for you or for the organization—guess what?—you owe me, baby! Who would dispute the fact that this guy clearly did a nice thing? Going out of his way to deliver the check was certainly a sacrifice. But let's not forget that for whatever sacrifice he made, it was his choice—a choice for which he must assume responsibility even though the intended consequences didn't pan out. Clearly this guy was driven to *get*; we think life is so much more fulfilling when we are called to *give*!

At some point each of has to wake up to the fact that society is better served and we are better served when we stop claiming rights that we haven't earned and step up to the plate of meritocracy. You stand a much better chance of making a difference when you recognize that you *earn* your way into more responsibility, more autonomy, higher visibility, bigger jobs, more important roles, and better pay.

There are three myths, three points of confusion that entangle many of us. Each contributes to an entitlement mentality, and each diminishes our effectiveness as energizers, and "buzz agents":

Myth #1: Fairness = Equality

People who operate from an entitlement mentality frequently complain that they are not being treated fairly, when what they really mean is they want equality. But equality in a meritocracy is unrealistic, and a meritocracy is key to an organization that becomes world-class. It's easy to confuse these two concepts, but they are *not* the same. "Fairness" by definition is to be just and honest. "Equality" is to have the same privileges, status, or rights as others do.

Like most teenagers, our fifteen-year-old, Taylor-Grace, is anticipating the freedom and excitement of driving next year. A couple of years ago, based on the example set by our financial advisors, Bob and Peg Eddy, we made our expectations for buying a car very clear to Taylor-Grace. We agreed to match (up to a certain amount) whatever she saved for a car. We indicated that no matter how many of her friends received a car as a graduation gift from parents or grandparents, she would have to earn the money to buy her own car. And we let her know that upon graduation, there would be no crying, "That's not fair!" or "XYZ's parents did it for her!"

We are betting (praying) on the fact that she will gain more confidence in her ability to make money, develop more discipline to save what she makes, and have a better appreciation for delayed gratification if she has some "skin" in the game. We also believe she will take better care of a car she has earned. Now, are we being fair? We think so. Is she going to be treated equal to some of her friends? No way. Will it work? Check back with us in a few years and we'll let you know.

When we are treated differently from others in the organization, it's easy to scream, "Unfair!" But maybe the expectations we have of our organizations aren't realistic. Is it realistic to assume that the organization will continue to give you a Christmas bonus and an annual raise even though you haven't done anything extraordinary to grow the business, add value, or contribute? Is it realistic to think that you will be given more autonomy and responsibility when you've been resisting change rather than embracing it? Is it realistic to get the nod for a promotion just because you've been with the company longer than the person you are competing with? Many people have come to expect it—equality!

Differentiation based on performance is a way of life. Businesses that perform better than others make more money and grow faster. Artists who fill concert halls and stadiums sell more records. Baseball players with a consistently high batting average stay in the game longer. It's not equal, but assuming performance expectations and the rules of the game are clearly articulated, it is fair.

> **PLAYERS ARE MANIACS ABOUT MAKING THE PLAY.**

Imagine a business where everyone was treated equally in the name of "fairness." Everyone got paid the same and had the same opportunities regardless of how they performed. All were given a job based on some formula that made things equal regardless of whether or not the job was a fit. Whether the business performed well or not, everyone had job security. Come on, that's ludicrous. It would shut down individual expression. Innovation would go through the floor. Underperformers would be protected, and those who make the most significant contributions would leave, or worse yet, check out but stay. It would literally kill the human spirit. Organizational vitality would be gone in a heartbeat.

People are treated differently in organizations because they *are* different. The sooner we come to grips with this, the sooner we will be able to jettison entitlement from our expectations. MVPs don't want to be treated equally; they want to be treated fairly. They don't want to milk the system or take advantage of others; they want to experience the rush of making a difference, and they want to be able to look in the mirror with

BOOM!

dignity, knowing they've made a significant contribution. Maybe it's time to give the whole equality thing a break and ask the following questions:

- Am I worthy of what I want?
- Have I earned what I expect to get?
- Do I deserve what I desire?

MYTH #2: BUSYNESS = RESULTS

Sure, you've been busy; maybe you're even exhausted, but what have you done personally to actually find new revenue streams, cut product development cycle time, manage costs out of the business, deepen relationships with customers, improve interdepartmental collaboration, or turbocharge creativity and innovation? Think about what the organization pays you—$30,000, $50,000, or over $100,000 a year. What is its return on investment? Just because you put in a lot of time and expend a lot of effort doesn't mean you are adding value. Players are maniacs about making the play. Yes, they are absolutely concerned with improving process and finding the right methodology, but they believe that process and methodology should be subservient to outcomes.

What kind of reputation are you building in your organization? Are you a person people can count on, or who makes them nervous? Do you make things happen, or make excuses? Do others in the organization see you as a go-to person, or someone who slows the go-to person down? Go-to players get results. They don't confuse activity with accomplishment. Consider these questions:

- How much time do I spend in meetings, in hallways, on e-mail, and over the phone that has very little to do with the results I'm seeking?

- Are the performance expectations I have of myself as rigorous as the expectations my organization has of me?

- When was the last time I sat down with my boss and initiated a specific, candid feedback session regarding my performance?
- Are the results I've achieved consistent with the resources, rewards, and recognition I expect from my organization?

MYTH #3: LONGEVITY = LOYALTY

If you work under the assumption that your tenure or seniority entitles you to job security and special privileges from the organization, you are sadly mistaken. No one is paying you today for what you did yesterday. The shelf life of your contributions keeps getting shorter and shorter. Seniority is no substitute for results. Technology waits for no one. The marketplace doesn't reward your company for the number of years you've been cashing paychecks; it rewards your company for the *results* you create and the contributions you make. You must earn the right to play a role on the team over and over and over again. Customers are asking your company, "What have you done for me lately?" You're asking it of the company, and your company has the right to ask the same question of you.

> NO ONE IS PAYING YOU TODAY FOR WHAT YOU DID YESTERDAY.

If loyalty means an unyielding devotion to "the way we've always done things around here," then it is likely to cripple the business. If loyalty means being a tried-and-true "company person," then you may be committed to an organization that should no longer exist. Loyalty defined the old way perpetuates mediocrity—it will make you expendable.

We believe in protecting the core of what makes any company great. But agile and adaptive organizations must be willing to let go of the past

BOOM!

in order to grow and protect the future. Loyalty must be defined in terms of making a valuable contribution. It's about constantly finding new ways to increase your worth to the organization. It's about anticipating what capabilities and competencies the organization will need next, and then going there first. Let's be candid. When you stop bringing something of value to the game, the game is over. Here are a few more questions you should ask yourself:

> **WHEN YOU STOP BRINGING SOMETHING OF VALUE TO THE GAME, THE GAME IS OVER.**

- Do I define loyalty as tenure, or performance and contribution?

- Is my organization adapting to shifts in the market faster than I am?

- Am I as quick on my feet as the "movers and shakers" in my organization?

Don't let these myths entangle you and deflate your potential. Instead, understand and embrace fairness, results, and loyalty as rights that you are not simply entitled to; they are rights you earn. In addition, we've come up with a few helpful strategies for earning a reputation for blowing the doors off business-as-usual.

Declare War on Complacency

Complacency is the deadly enemy of progress. It arises out of a false sense of security that makes our commitment to change lukewarm. Complacency takes root when we are blinded by either ignorance or arrogance. It is a subtle killer that slowly and often subconsciously creeps into our lives. It destroys marriages, businesses, friendships, teams, careers, dreams, and even entire societies. Unfortunately, it usually takes something dramatic to jolt us out of a state of complacency. The great Danish philosopher Søren Kierkegaard said, "All change is preceded by crisis." You know this to be true. Someone you know at work religiously buckles up after being in a serious automobile accident. A friend goes on a rigorous exercise program and low-cholesterol diet after experiencing a minor heart attack. A workaholic father decides to check in, reengage, and "be there" for his children after his teenager enrolls in drug rehab. In each case the change was preceded by the crisis. The key question is, do we have the wisdom and courage to read the warning signs, to wake up and change before it's too late? Let's look at some examples:

The United States is still the only superpower in the world. Yet no nation has the corner on ingenuity. Success is never final—it requires a continuous effort to renew, reinvigorate, and reinvent. Our greatness today could disappear tomorrow. Hard to fathom? Sure, but who in Rome at the height of its dominance would have predicted the fall of the Roman Empire?

IBM executives believed they were working for one of the most admired companies in the world. With such an illustrious history of success, who at IBM would have guessed that they could be blinded by their own success? Who would have predicted that "Big Blue" could miss the dramatic shift from mainframes to microprocessor-based technology?

In the early 1980s the Japanese humiliated American automobile manufacturers with superior quality. Part of the problem was insulation. A General Motors executive driving a new GM car, maintained by a GM mechanic, parked in the garage at GM headquarters, didn't think there was anything wrong with the cars. GM believed that everything was okay. They were out of touch with reality because they lived behind closed doors.

How many partners at Arthur Andersen would have believed that

BOOM!

their premier accounting giant would be dissolved so quickly in the wake of the Enron scandal? There are *no* guarantees. That's why each one of us must declare war on complacency—starting with ourselves. Here are five places to start:

1. ***Take responsibility for your own education.*** Who is most affected by the quality of education you receive? The portfolio of skills and experiences you establish? The personal brand you build? You are. Who is in the best position to determine what you want and need to make a valuable contribution? You! Doesn't it make sense then, that *you* should be responsible for your own learning? Why put something so critical in someone else's hands? It's foolish to wait around, expecting the organization to provide the training, skills, and knowledge you need, so go after it yourself and start by creating the University of YOU.

First, find a mentor. Don't sit back and wait for the company to set up a mentoring program for you. Recruit your own support team; if you want a mentor, go out and get one. A mentor doesn't have to be someone you know. We have several mentors who have had a significant influence on our lives and on our work. We've never met them, but we follow their work, we read their books, and we listen to what they say in speeches as well as in print, on the radio, and in television interviews.

If your organization wants to be competitive, if it wants to attract and retain top talent, of course it should invest in you, but don't depend on this. Today, job security lies in *your* ability to continue to produce what the marketplace wants—and those wants are constantly changing. If you want to better serve another department, arrange for an opportunity to learn how they operate; if you want to be more business literate, take responsibility for learning to read financial statements and the competition's annual reports. Next time you attend a training program, don't just

> **"IN TIMES OF DRASTIC CHANGE, IT IS THE LEARNERS WHO INHERIT THE FUTURE. THE LEARNED USUALLY FIND THEMSELVES EQUIPPED TO LIVE IN A WORLD THAT NO LONGER EXISTS."**
>
> **—ERIC HOFFER**

evaluate the presenter; evaluate *yourself*: Did you assume responsibility for the learning experience, or sit back skeptically and wait to be entertained? People who make things happen take personal responsibility for their own professional progress and growth.

2. *Learn as though you will live forever.* American social writer Eric Hoffer said, "In times of drastic change, it is the learners who inherit the future. The learned usually find themselves equipped to live in a world that no longer exists." Are you equipped to live in the world your customers are in? Your vendors, suppliers, and channel partners? Your competitors? How about your children? Think about it: a little boy or girl who saw the Wright brothers fly for a few seconds at Kitty Hawk in 1903 could have watched *Apollo II* land on the moon in 1969. That same person could possibly see Richard Branson's Virgin Galactic commercialize outer space travel in the next few years.

The message is clear: We can make one of two choices. We can reeducate and retool ourselves, or we can eventually become impotent and obsolete. We can become agile and adaptive learners, or we can find ourselves living in a world that no longer exists.

Gary Pierce, senior vice president of Human Resources at Wegmans, told us a story about deli manager Dan Jackson, who saw an opportunity to improve his deli and took the initiative to do some research. Jackson, who is not Jewish, wanted to learn more about kosher practices, given that his store is in New York and serves a large Jewish population. So he took it upon himself to go visit several synagogues to talk with rabbis about the meaning of *kosher*, Jewish law and tradition, and the importance of being kosher to the Jewish faith. He brought what he learned back to the store and suggested new product offerings and changes in the way the deli was laid out. The adopted alterations not only increased deli sales, but they were implemented in every store serving an extensive Jewish population. Did Dan Jackson have to do this? No. Did it raise his visibility on the radar of store leaders? Yes, he's since been promoted. Did it make him more valuable and a more engaged member of the store? You bet it did!

3. Get comfortable being uncomfortable. We live in a world that quickly forgets—a world that takes no pity on the person who gets lazy about learning, about finding ways to get smarter, better, faster. Nobel Peace Prize recipient Henry Kissinger said, "Each success only buys you an admission ticket to a more difficult problem." Each success merely buys you an opportunity to continue to play the game, and the game is constantly changing.

If you have achieved a great deal of success in your life, congratulations! But of all the people reading this book, those who have achieved tremendous success are the ones we are most concerned about. We've seen it in our clients, and unfortunately we have learned it the hard way ourselves. We are never more vulnerable to complacency, arrogance, indifference, and inflexibility than when we are riding the wave of success. The more successful you are, the more you have to lose; the less willing you are to change, the more likely you are to fail. Former U.S. Army chief of staff General Eric Shinseki said it well: "If you don't like change, you're going to like irrelevance even less."

When Tiger Woods joined the PGA, everyone anticipated his arrival. He was a gifted amateur, but the question remained, how would he do under the rigorous scrutiny of the gallery and the fierce competition among those who made their living in the PGA? Sponsors such as Nike and Titleist were quick to get behind him—to the tune of a combined $60 million—even though he had yet to prove himself. Well, it didn't take long.

In his first Masters—the ultimate proving ground—Woods not only won, but he won by twelve strokes! He blew the field away. Experts who watched the careers of Jack Nicklaus and Arnold Palmer said that Tiger was in another world, a league of his own.

When the tournament was over, Tiger reflected upon his game. According to his own assessment, he had played pretty well but not good enough to be the greatest athlete to ever play the game, not good enough to achieve unprecedented success over the long haul. So he called up his coach and said, "I want to reinvent my swing." Now, can you imagine being the coach on the other end of that conversation? In the first Masters he ever competed in as a pro, your guy sets a record for the widest margin of victory. His name is plastered on every major newspaper around the world. Wouldn't you be asking, "You want to reinvent what? You want to reconstruct what? Are you kidding?" Unwilling to let *good* become the enemy of *great*, Tiger persisted. As is often the case when you make a change in any sport, things get worse before they get better.

For the next two years the world of professional golf began to question whether or not the Master's victory was just a fluke. People were asking if Tiger was really the "phenom" that everyone originally thought he was. Then, in 2000, he came back and won four majors in a row. His competitors started to say things like, "When Tiger is in the tournament, the rest of us are competing for second place." Most would agree that Tiger Woods is still the dominant golfer to beat on the circuit today.

When the final page of history is written about Tiger Woods, the writers are surely going to say, "He was an extremely gifted athlete. His talent was like no other. His father, Earl, did a magnificent job of mentoring him." There is something else the writers will say: "He had an incredible level of character and maturity for someone his age."

Nobody decides where the performance bar will be set for Tiger except Tiger. That's because no one understands what Tiger is capable of better than Tiger—including his competitors, his sponsors, and his longtime friend and caddy, Steve Williams. Not everyone can be extraordinary, because not everyone has the guts to step out of the comfort zone, face the harsh realities, and make the necessary changes. Tiger's passion for becoming the best in the history of the game is apparently bigger than his fear of what the press will say when he is making adjustments to his swing.

Neither of us is a golfer, but what impresses us about Tiger Woods is that he refuses to rest on yesterday's headlines. How many athletes his age have become complacent after initially earning their way into fame and fortune? What about you? When the customer satisfaction ratings on you or your department come back 99 *percent satisfied*, when the performance review comes back *stellar*, and when the organization awards you *employee* or *executive of the year*, do you have the guts to experiment with and reinvent those parts of your game that you know could be better?

4. Be a guru—a junction box for knowledge. Imagine this scenario. You are the third generation of a family farming operation. You grew up in the heartland, watching your grandfather make the seismic shift from a horse-drawn plow to a John Deere tractor. You knew John Deere as that stodgy old manufacturer of farm machinery and heavy equipment, right? Wrong. Deere has rapidly established itself as a leader in data warehousing and information-based farming. On a new Deere tractor you can find a computer that captures three simple measurements: *latitude* and *longitude* to the nearest square yard, and *yield*, which tells the farmer how much wheat or alfalfa or barley he or she can cut in that square yard.

These three bits of information are sent from the tractor's computer up to a satellite that scans the light waves of plants—determining plant quality and soil conditions—and back down to a computer in the farmer's office, that has a bitmap of the farm. The system is so precise that the computer in the kitchen can talk to the computer in the tractor and tell it to add more fertilizer just north of the tree line, where the shadows fall, to increase the farmer's yield. This smart system enables the producer to garner information that creates new knowledge with which he or she can add new value to the business of crop production. It ain't your grandpa's farm anymore.

How well connected are you? How well do you share, use, and apply information? Are you seen as a person who can take data and ideas and transform them into knowledge? Are you connected to information in such a way that you can offer truly meaningful insight to your organization and its customers—insight that substantially adds value and positions you as an industry expert, a thought leader, and a guru? How *distinctive* is your knowledge?

In the opening paragraph of his book *Business @ the Speed of Thought* (New York: Warner Business Books, 2000), Microsoft chairman Bill Gates said, "The most meaningful way to differentiate your company from your competition, the best way to put distance between yourself and the crowd, is to do an outstanding job with information. How you gather, manage, and use information will determine whether you win or lose" (3). A junction box is an enclosure in which electrical circuits are connected. Electricity flows into the box and is then rerouted to energize other locations. When people tap into you—whether it's on the telephone, in the office, or over the Internet—do they feel as though they've tapped into a junction box for knowledge or a circuit breaker that kills the electricity?

5. Play to win vs. playing not to lose. The life strategy of those who play not to lose is, *I survived. I was never hurt, rejected, lost, or wrong.* A person who plays not to lose will have an epitaph that reads something like this:

BOOM!

He didn't take too many risks, he didn't trust too many people, he didn't do too many adventurous things in his life, and he didn't accomplish as much as he could have, but he did arrive at death unscathed.

What is so fun about that?

Not too long ago, Jackie got one of those chain e-mails that is all about playing to win:

> Life should NOT be a journey to the grave with the intention of arriving safely in an attractive and well-preserved body, but rather to skid in sideways, chocolate in one hand, wine in the other, body thoroughly used up, totally worn out, and screaming, "WOO HOO, what a ride!"

Playing to win is about taking chances—to risk more and try new things. It's about taking an honest look at yourself, facing reality, and having the courage to jettison excuses so you can change for the better. Playing to win is about making decisions and creating an environment that enables you to thrive and live life to the fullest. It's impossible to be complacent and play to win at the same time.

In his book *Wooden on Leadership*, UCLA coach John Wooden admits that he let himself get sucked into a "playing not to lose" men-

tality and that his attitude probably infected the rest of the coaching staff. After thirteen years coaching at UCLA, he'd grown complacent about the woefully inadequate, out-of-date facilities that limited his ability to train and recruit. He said, "While I didn't like the great disadvantages imposed on us by our practice facility, I accepted it as the way things were going to be. We might do fairly well on occasion, but we would never get all the way to the top" (193).

As the 1961–62 season unfolded, John Wooden came to see the self-imposed barrier he had constructed. For the first time in Bruins' history, the UCLA basketball team—shocker of all shockers—made it to the Final Four. No one expected this to happen—especially Coach Wooden. Despite all the disadvantages, Wooden knew he could no longer use the men's gym as an excuse for UCLA's poor tournament appearances. He had flipped a switch and lifted the mental barrier. Instead of focusing on the things he couldn't control, he turned his attention solely to the things he could control—searching for the ideas and solutions that would take UCLA deep into the tournament again. It was no longer about the practice facility; it was about leveraging whatever tools he could find to help the team reach its potential. Wooden said, "By giving myself that crutch, I may have gotten comfortable with the way things were—not happy, but comfortable. I would never again allow myself to be satisfied that UCLA had gotten as good as we could get, improved as much as we could improve" (195).

Following this startling breakthrough in 1962, Wooden began a maniacal search for what he could do better and what would consistently take the team to the next level of competition. He went through thirteen years of notebooks and three-by-five cards to evaluate what worked and what didn't. He reorganized practice, restructured playing time, and restrained

> SUCCESS IS NEVER FINAL. RIGHT NOW SOMEONE SOMEWHERE IS TRAINING TO KICK YOUR BUTT.

BOOM!

from working players too hard before tournaments. And by reducing the number of plays he brought into a game, he kept things simple.

Coach Wooden's ability to own up to and overcome complacency is but one among many of the reasons he became indispensable to UCLA. He led the Bruins to ten NCAA national championships in twelve years, including eighty-eight straight victories and four perfect seasons. He was elected to the Basketball Hall of Fame as both a player and a coach. ESPN named him Coach of the Century.

Remember, success is never final. Right now someone somewhere is training to kick your butt. When it comes to overcoming complacency, ask yourself these questions:

- Am I happy with where I am in my career? My life?
- Will the goals I am pursuing stretch me? Do they have the potential to change me?
- What have I learned in the last *three weeks* that will expand my capabilities?
- When was the last time I seriously studied the winners in an area where I know I need to improve?
- What was the last best practice I adopted?

If you can't answer these questions quickly and substantively, then answer this question: Can you tell us, in five minutes or less, why we shouldn't outsource your job?

Tell People What They NEED to Hear vs. What They WANT to Hear

Do you want to stand out and make a difference? Tell people—your colleagues and boss(es)—what they *need* to hear versus what you think they *want* to hear. The person who will stand up to authority and say, "I think you are wrong, and here's why" is worth his or her weight in gold. Yet one of the most pervasive ways we manifest the pathology of helplessness and victimization is by not speaking up. Who says what to whom in your organization? Do you speak openly and authentically to your coworkers? Your subordinates? Your boss? The board?

In our experience many organizations give lip service to "telling it like it is," but in reality they lack the courage to live this value out loud. Why is speaking up such a problem? Why are we reticent to tell people what we really think? There are many reasons, most of which are based in fear or expediency or both.

We've been programmed to be politically correct. We've taught our children and you've probably taught yours that you just don't tell Grandma that the present she gave you for your birthday is for a five-year-old, and you are now ten. You just say thank you! You don't tell your neighbors that the hideous piece of pottery they gave you for Christmas last year has nothing to do with the décor of your house. It's just not right.

Why don't we confront people who find humor in assaulting us with sexually, racially, politically, or religiously offensive jokes? Have you ever sat across the dinner table at a restaurant with someone who talks with his mouth full and said nothing, or failed to inform a friend who whenever she asks you a question, interrupts with her own story? It's not socially or politically correct. Yet we walk away bothered and disturbed.

Just to be clear, we're not suggesting that we all become insensitive, obnoxious, hyperdriven personalities who blast people with the brutal facts of reality whenever we feel the urge. Telling it like it is ought to be done with dignity and civility. We gain a lot more ground speaking the truth in love—feedback should be a gift, not a weapon. But if we are honest, most of us err on the side of being too socially and politically correct, because that is the way we were raised.

Sometimes feedback is as difficult to give as it is to get, so we choose not to speak up because it serves us well not to. Telling it like it is can make people mad and hurt their feelings. It's messy. Who looks forward to dealing with awkwardness, confusion, and resentment? Again, feedback *is* a gift; it's just not one that is easily received. We rationalize our "going along to get along" by saying that we want to protect others from all of this emotional baggage, but if the truth be known, our lack of candor is more about avoiding risk and protecting ourselves than it is about service.

Perhaps the biggest cause driving our lack of candor at work is that we don't want to put our jobs—and our mortgages, health insurance, and children's college tuitions—on the line. Titles intimidate a lot of people, and unfortunately, they have a lot more impact on us than we care to admit. The result is that we put far too much emphasis on pleasing people with titles and not enough emphasis on taking chances and bringing our own ideas and experience to the table. Most of us believe that there are a lot of politically correct dos and don'ts that surround titles. *What can we say? What should we say? And to whom?* The devastating myth in most organizations is this: *The way to succeed around here is to tell the people in power what they want to hear.* Very few people have the courage to challenge this myth, so it continues to be perpetrated.

We've talked with CEOs and senior executives all over the globe who tell us that they want to know everything—the good, bad, and ugly. They understand that getting their fingers on the pulse of reality is critical. They know that the quality of their decision making is determined by the quality of information they receive. They don't want you to "impress" them by telling them how smart they are. Great leaders want people who care enough about the organization and its people to tell the truth, to speak candidly. Most of us like surrounding ourselves with people who agree with us. Not these leaders; they want to be surrounded with people who have the guts to debate with them, challenge the process, and make a difference. Jimmy Blanchard, chairman and former CEO of Synovus Financial, is famous for asking his people, "What are the twenty-five dumbest things we do around here, starting with me?"

> **EVERY GREAT AND GUTSY LEADER WANTS TO KNOW . . . WHO ARE THE SMARTEST PEOPLE IN THE ORGANIZATION— WHO ARE LEAST ENAMORED WITH ME OR MY TITLE— AND WHAT DO THEY THINK ABOUT MY IDEAS?**

Sometimes we forget that senior executives are real people too. They don't want to be surprised. Yet, if we are uncomfortable with the consequences of telling it like it is, their chances of being negatively surprised go up dramatically. Just like you, they want their ideas to work; they don't want to put something "out there" that will make them look foolish or be detrimental to the organization. Don't you think they'd rather scrap a bad idea before that happens? To be a contrarian, to have a healthy sense of irreverence for titles, to be brave enough to speak up is to be an MVP because there are so few people like this.

You want to know what every great and gutsy leader wants to know? He or she wants to know the answer to this question: *Who are the smartest people in the organization—who are least enamored with me or my title—and what do they think about my ideas?* Great leaders already know their own thoughts. What they want and need to know are your thoughts. If you fail to offer your thoughts, then the organization isn't getting what it paid for, and your bosses are not getting what they need. Unfortunately, there are some leaders who just don't get it.

Jackie recently helped the VPs of a large global retail chain come up with strategies to raise the level of internal and external hospitality and service. The VPs got it! As a leadership team, they were all on the same track, they were fired up, and they were ready to make some significant change happen at the store level. Unfortunately, a few EVPs (the bosses of the VPs) just didn't get it! And guess what, they weren't there. Even the

BOOM!

CEO didn't attend; he did, however, make a few painfully awkward cameo appearances. His opinions and thoughts were all off the top of his head and all off topic! Yet no one called him on it; no one tried to redirect or challenge his ideas. The team just sat there and let him drone on and on. It was tragic to watch. We fear for the brand, the engagement levels of the VPs, and the overall success of this retailer. Now, maybe you're reading this and saying to yourself, *Who are you kidding? I live in that kind of organization; we can't speak up. People—especially senior management—don't want to hear the truth. Candor kills people around here. Jobs have been lost! My life will be much safer and a lot simpler if I just avoid telling people what I really think.* Perhaps this is true, and maybe that is exactly what you should do. However, we encourage you not to put this stake in the ground permanently until you've asked yourself a couple of questions.

Question #1: What Happens to Us When We Don't Speak Up?

We check out! We become the people we *think* we need to be rather than the people we *are*. We play to the boss and feel trapped by his or her ignorance. More often than not, too much emphasis on political correctness tempers, molds, and constrains our thoughts to the point where they aren't even our thoughts anymore. The department, the organization, and the culture suffer—it becomes toxic and reactive. What a shame.

When we choose not to be candid, we compromise our authenticity; we become what Brennan Manning calls "posers." Posers bury or disguise their true feelings to avoid pain. Fear of rejection and a lust for approval make them afraid to say no, when no is the right answer. Given their inability to say no, posers are habitually overcommitted and consistently unhappy. Posers are likely to become dead people working.

In those moments when we have something to say and choose not to say it, something inside of us dies a little bit. We are forced to look in the mirror—our fakery exposed—knowing that we were afraid to "pony up" because our ideas, opinions, and feelings will not be heard. Every time we make this choice, we come a little closer to the realization that we are losing our *voice* and, along with it, our ability to make a difference.

There is another problem. When you withhold comments and criticism and only tell people what they want to hear, a great leader may see you as intellectually lazy, and your peers may see you as a suck-up. You might think you are playing it safe, but in reality you may be putting yourself at greater risk.

Question #2: What Happens to the Organization When You Don't Speak Up?

When you give up your voice, you not only disempower and dehumanize yourself, but you weaken the organization. We learned from the events of 9/11 and Hurricane Katrina how devastating it can be when critical information does not flow freely between people. Meetings drone on, decisions take longer, the best ideas never surface, frustration grows, and morale takes a major hit. When we choose not to speak frankly, the vacuum is filled with backroom politicking and manipulation.

Have you ever attended the meeting "after the meeting"—the one where the real issues get discussed and you tell people what you really think? The official meeting is the one where nobody talks candidly *to* one another. The meeting *after* the meeting is the one where people talk candidly *about* one another. It's subversive. It distracts people. And it is a complete and utter waste of time, talent, and resources. If we only had the intestinal fortitude to speak freely, think about how many meetings could be eliminated from our lives! Every time you bypass the truth and skirt the real issues, you lose.

The most formidable enemy your organization faces right now may be your lack of candor. Every organization is flawed, and every leader has blind spots—both need your insight to help them see what they can't see. Speaking candidly is your contribution to building a stronger enterprise.

If the *Cluetrain Manifesto* authors taught us anything, it is that the Internet has democratized the spread of information and demands authen-

BOOM!

ticity—both inside and outside your organization. The walls between employees and other employees, employees and customers, and customers and customers are coming down. Authentic conversations where people tell it like it is are springing up everywhere. With a couple of clicks, disgruntled former employees can air your company's dirty laundry—literally around the world—in a matter of hours. If I really want to know about the culture of your organization, or if you are going to make that critical product launch on time, I can pull up a blog and learn it all. If these kinds of conversations are happening online, why shouldn't we be making them happen face-to-face? Wouldn't we rather be identifying these issues and solving these problems *before* they make it into cyberspace?

There is a compelling business case to be made for finding the courage to speak up. Consider the following benefits to you and your organization:

Speaking Up Builds Confidence

You will stop operating from a position of helplessness. You will start to assume ownership for your ideas. You will have more confidence in your beliefs and opinions and solutions. You will be more trusted with good news, because people will know that you aren't afraid to levy the bad news.

One of the premier breeding grounds for entrepreneurs in the world today is Elanco Animal Health, a division of Eli Lilly. If we were in the explosively growing field of biotechnology, looking to place a new product idea, Elanco would be one of the first companies we would consider. Not only is Elanco's mission noble—helping the food industry produce an abundant supply of safe and affordable food by enhancing animal health, wellness, welfare, and performance—but the company is pushing the edge of the envelope in terms of unleashing talent and finding better, smarter, faster ways to develop pharmaceuticals.

In the business of bringing a new drug to market, a pharmaceutical company must satisfy stringent regulatory requirements necessary to demonstrate the safety and efficacy of the product. Satisfying these requirements for an approved animal drug can take from six to ten years and cost between $60 and $120 million.

At the end of 2002, two Elanco research associates, Genefer Douglass and Joan Buck, were coordinating two complex research studies necessary to demonstrate the safety of a new Elanco product. The outside firm conducting the actual research informed Elanco that it was going out of business, so Elanco executives carefully considered canceling the program. If they continued, the company's credibility was on the line. If they quit, years of hard work would go down the drain, because the studies would have to be rerun. The costs associated with doing this would be astronomical, and at least another two years would be added to the cycle time of bringing the product to market.

In the final meeting and after much debate, it was pretty much decided that Elanco would pull the plug on the studies. Then, in a moment of courage, Genefer Douglass spoke up and said, "Wait a minute, time out! This thing is going down the wrong track." She made a compelling argument for moving forward with the studies and put her own credibility on the line by indicating that under regulatory scrutiny there would be no issues that she and the team could not address.

The timing of Genefer's boldness completely changed the direction and momentum of the meeting. BOOM—her passion, conviction, and grasp of the details gave the executives confidence and persuaded them to press on. In the end, the studies were pivotal in receiving regulatory approval for Elanco's new product.

What could have happened if the story had gone the opposite direction? Elanco's customers would not have benefited from the therapy that this new, innovative drug provided, and Elanco would have lost millions of dollars in lost productivity.

Speaking Out Inspires Creativity

Think about how much untapped knowledge there is in most organizations. When you choose authenticity, you give others the liberty to say what they think, which in turn creates a culture of candor and authenticity. By doing this you draw more people into the conversation. The richness and diversity of ideas these players bring to the game strengthens the team and gives it a significant advantage.

Our friend Tonda Montague is the director of Employee Communications at Southwest Airlines. Tonda is extremely creative and has a gift for boiling a message down to its simplest form. A number of years ago, Tonda went to Gary Kelly, then Southwest's chief financial officer and currently the company's CEO, to discuss a new idea she had for communicating Southwest's annual profit and loss statement. Tonda wanted to make the P&L fun so people would, in fact, read it, internalize it, and use the information in it to run the business better. Her idea was to simplify the P&L using cartoonlike icons and writing it in language that an eighth grader could understand.

Initially, Gary didn't like the idea. He thought it would insult the intelligence of Southwest employees. Tonda said, "Gary, not everyone understands the numbers and speaks 'CFO-ese' like you do." Gary, who has the utmost respect for the people and the culture of Southwest, still didn't like it.

Still convinced it was the right thing to do, Tonda got Gary to agree to an experiment. She assembled a focus group of Southwest employees to provide feedback on how they would like to receive financial information. Gary shared the financials his way in traditional form while Tonda shared her off-the-wall, cartoonlike version. Which version was better understood? Which rendering did people identify with more? Which rendition had the best chance of stimulating a dialogue about revenue generation and cost containment? Tonda's version won hands down.

We've shared this fun P&L format with companies all over the world, and it's amazing how people identify with it—it's a very creative and powerful way to raise the level of business literacy in an organization. We are absolutely convinced that it has contributed to the entrepreneurial spirit for which Southwest Airlines is so well-known. But this idea would never have come to fruition had it not been for Tonda's willingness to challenge her boss. It's also a tribute to Gary Kelly's ability to admit that he was wrong and that someone—with a nonfinancial background, no less—had a better idea. Both of these players demonstrated great leadership.

Who knows how many cost-cutting innovations have been stimulated because Southwest employees better understand what happens to a dollar when it comes into the business. It's difficult to measure the cause and effect of this. What we do know is that Southwest continues to be the only major airline in the industry with thirty-four consecutive years of profitability. Are we audacious enough to think that Tonda Montague has a little something to do with this unprecedented record? Yes!

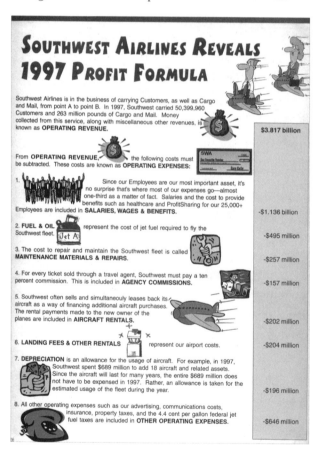

BOOM!

Speaking Out Increases Speed

Being honest and direct unclutters things. The more you speak your mind, the faster things get out on the table for people to react to. You can "shake out" ideas faster, debate their validity quicker, and act on them sooner. This not only helps the organization capitalize on windows of opportunity that open and close rapidly, but it also keeps the waters of progress within the organization from getting stagnant. You've probably heard the saying: "In the future there will be two types of organizations: the QUICK and the DEAD."

Speaking Out Eliminates Waste

How much money is saved when we eliminate the utter waste created by a lack of candor? Think about the waste of time and talent in meetings alone. How many hours of additional meeting time could you have back if you or someone else had chosen to speak up? Think about how many thick, convoluted planning manuals or slide decks could be avoided if people had the intestinal fortitude to just tell it like it is. Jack Welch, who incidentally has to be the icon for candor, said to Kevin in a meeting, "If an engineer or head of a business unit can't communicate their idea on one slide, I ask them to go back and rework it until they know their pitch better." Remember that Welch is the guy who said that one of his regrets at GE was that he didn't move fast enough.

Speaking up comes naturally for very few people. However, if we believe that we are defined by our choices, not our conditions, this can change. Like many of the principles in this book, it's a discipline. The more you do it, the easier it becomes. What can you do to contribute to a culture of candor?

1. Keep the big picture in mind. This means keeping an eye on the strategic direction of the organization as well as the personal legacy for which you want to be remembered. With these things firmly in mind, you will be in a better position to know when and how to speak up. When you ask, "How does this support our vision and strategic direction?" people get a sense that it's not about you, but rather that you have the organization's best interest in mind.

2. *Appoint yourself the devil's advocate.* Look at every side of the issue and ask yourself, "What are we missing here? What aren't we talking about? Where are the holes in what we are thinking?" Reaffirm that you are passionate about and committed to the organization's success; then purposely step on the other side of the issue and try to get others to temporarily empathize with your position. Insist that your audience look at the weaknesses of what they are advocating. You become extremely valuable to anyone, anywhere when you can constructively get others to see things from multiple points of view.

3. *Go with your gut, versus what's popular.* If you've done your homework, you will have a sense about what's right and what's wrong, about what will work and what won't. Trust your gut instinct, face your fear about speaking up, and go with it. Take a stand for what's right, not just what's popular. You will sleep better at night and be able to look yourself in the mirror in the morning. Just because you tell it like you see it doesn't mean people won't like you. Our friend General Bill Cooney, the former deputy chief executive officer of USAA, has a very simple but powerful litmus test for making decisions. See if it works for you. He told us, "The litmus test for every decision must be, 'Will it earn the respect, love, and admiration of family and friends?' because at the end of the journey, that is all that really matters!"

Christopher Locke points out in the *Cluetrain Manifesto* (New York: Perseus Books Group, 2001), "Life is too short . . . too short for office politics, for busywork and pointless paper chases, for jumping though hoops and covering [ourselves], for trying to please, to not offend, for constantly struggling to achieve some ever-receding definition of success" (1). We agree! To be able to speak the truth in love and say what we mean is liberating.

If, many years from now, you want to look back over your life and know that your work mattered, maybe it's time to call the poser out of hiding. Maybe it's time to stop playing to titles and recognize that being politically correct is no substitute for doing the right thing—even if it means questioning authority. When was the last time you were with a large group of your coworkers or your boss and really spoke your mind— refusing to beat around the bush or to sugarcoat the truth? Maybe it's time to quit rationalizing your silence in the name of safety and ask yourself, *How much of me am I losing by sucking up, and what could I gain by speaking up?*

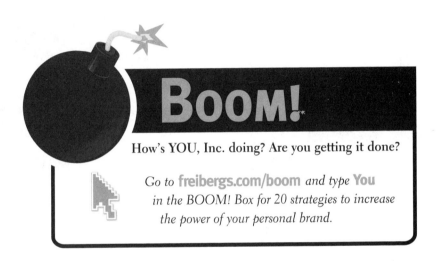

BOOM!

How's YOU, Inc. doing? Are you getting it done?

Go to **freibergs.com/boom** *and type* **You** *in the BOOM! Box for 20 strategies to increase the power of your personal brand.*

Many people tip-toe through life
just so they can arrive at death safely . . .
playing it safe is actually quite risky!

CHOICE #7

RISK MORE—GAIN MORE

The World Isn't Changed by
Those Who Are Unwilling
to Take Risks

07

"Dream big, not to escape life, but to keep life from escaping you!"

If you discover at breakfast that tomorrow will be your last day on earth, would that news have some effect on how you lived your day? You know it would. So here's the question: If life is the *only game in town*, then why aren't you playing like there's no tomorrow?

It doesn't matter where we are in the world; when we talk with CEOs and senior executives, they rarely gripe about people who take too many risks. We have yet to hear them complain about folks pursuing new initiatives, new products and services, and new revenue streams that stretch the organization and challenge the core business. As we said, most of the executives we've met in the last twenty years don't whine about employees who stand on their convictions and fight for things they deeply believe in—people who are bold and uncompromising when presenting their ideas. They do, however, talk about people who lack initiative or play it too safe and avoid taking risks.

Think about it. No one ever makes it into the innovator's hall of fame by coming up with a better imitation. It is the "game changers" who ultimately get our attention. Think Jobs at Apple, Branson at

Virgin, Whitman at eBay, Shultz at Starbucks, and Brin and Page at Google. Does "mimic" come to mind? Hardly. What *does* come to mind is *risk taker, pioneer, trailblazer, innovator,* and *market creator.*

> ## YOU CAN'T ESCAPE RISK. THERE IS ALWAYS SOMETHING AT STAKE.

Whether it is a product innovation, business systems advance, or an improvement in strategic partnerships, your ability to change the rules of the game makes you extremely valuable. The challenge here is that you can't innovate without experimenting, you can't experiment without making mistakes, and you can't make mistakes unless you are willing to risk failure and rejection. Do you have the courage to try new things, test new ideas, and challenge the status quo, particularly if your boss is the one promoting the status quo? Do you have the guts to circumvent the bureaucracy and step out beyond the boundaries of just doing your job?

Safe Is Risky!

The problem for many of us is that we think playing it safe (doing nothing) *is* safe, when in reality safe is often risky. A deer instinctively knows that if it freezes its movement in the wild, a predator will have a harder time finding it. This works in the deer's familiar environment. Yet in the unfamiliar environment of facing an oncoming car, it is a deadly strategy. You can't escape risk. There is always something at stake. You can take a leap of faith into the unknown, or you can protect the status quo. In either case you are risking something. You can't steal second base without a big lead at first, but a big lead at first could get you tagged out. One thing is certain: you can't be a great base runner unless you are willing to risk failure.

It was on November 14, 2006, that Jeff Simmons, executive director, North America, Elanco Animal Health, asked Kevin to participate in an off-site meeting with 150 members of Jeff's research and development team. Elanco realized that for continued growth and contribution to the industry, it was absolutely essential to create a "player" versus "bystander" culture. These aren't just words to the people of Elanco; the company has actually come up with a system to evaluate attitude, energy, outcomes, and the overall influence each person has on the culture and its customers. This meeting was a "call to arms" to establish a critical mass of players who were willing to jettison command-and-control leadership, eliminate tribalism and competing priorities, and radically rethink the way the organization brings a drug to market.

We've both attended a lot of these types of meetings. Everyone comes in for the big rally, the executives pontificate about change, people shake their heads in agreement, and then everyone goes back home to business-as-usual. There is no accountability, and little, if anything, changes. This meeting was different. It was obvious that people were serious about making something happen. Tension filled the room, because the players were tired of talking and ready to do something far-reaching, while the spectators could sense an impending decision—step out of the comfort zone and grow with the organization or leave.

After Kevin and a number of the executives presented their thoughts about creating a culture of commitment and accountability, the afternoon was devoted to candid discussion and action planning. Breakout groups were charged with pushing the envelope and coming up with strategies for changing the business. A lot of great ideas flowed out of group after group, but the tipping point came when Dr. Scott Holmstrom stood up and BOOM—revealed the thousand-pound gorilla in the room—Elanco's sacrosanct hierarchical management structure.

For years Elanco has been organized around a hierarchy, like every other pharmaceutical company. The structure is built around core competencies, such as chemistry, biology, or toxicology. Each expert owes his or her allegiance to his or her area of expertise and not to the team focused on delivering the outcomes.

The problem with this structure is that teams and individuals are not empowered to establish priorities and accountabilities. For example, a problem may occur in a team that requires the team members to go back to their functional group and negotiate a solution instead of moving forward fast and getting things done.

The players get extremely frustrated, and the victims make excuses and conveniently hide in the bureaucracy of the system. People's hope and morale for getting through the drug development process gets torpedoed, and productivity sinks. Of course, everyone understands the root problem because it has existed for years, but no one thinks such a radical change is possible because the organization and the industry have been doing it this way forever. It is a classic "sacred cow" situation: *no one touches the system.* That is, until Scott Holmstrom came along.

In a potentially career-breaking, wild-card move, Holmstrom, a mid-level associate ranking in the bottom half of the people in the room, grabbed the microphone and said, "I want to say what over half of the people in this room want to say. This is ridiculous; the system is not right! The problem has existed forever; we know what needs to be done; if we are going to be the best in industry research and development, then let's quit playing around. Let's fix it!" Holmstrom had come to that point where your heart starts pounding and your anxiety starts to rise as you contemplate getting up in front of 150 peers and saying what no one else has the guts to say. He proposed that teams, not management, have accountability and be empowered to deliver their projects, including the science, the people, and the budget. This included doing away with many of the command-and-control committees that had been set up to govern the process.

At the end of his discussion, Scott Holmstrom's candor grew—he did perhaps the most important thing he could've done: he looked at Jeff Simmons and the rest of the executive team and said, "I want an

BOOM!

answer to why we shouldn't do this. I want a strong, strong, thorough assessment done by you leaders, and I want you to come back and tell us, 'Why not! Why can't it be done this way?'" Everyone in the room looked to see how Jeff Simmons would handle Holmstrom. Simmons said, "We believe the way we are currently doing it is the way to go, but we will study it, and in sixty days I will get back to you with a response."

Simmons is a gutsy leader who has surrounded himself with a courageous research leadership team that is not afraid of stepping way out of the comfort zone. But even Simmons admitted that he got trapped in the status quo. He later told us, "In the weeks that followed I lost control. And in doing what's right, the organization took control."

Holmstrom began a campaign to build not a coup but a coalition of very credible players who had a lot of history with the organization. He essentially said, "Come on, join this cause. We can change this organization for the better!" Holmstrom's passion paid off. On September 28, 2006, Elanco moved out of its structure and into focused teams that drive new product development—a radical change that impacts the entire company.

Scott Holmstrom gave political correctness a shove and took a huge risk with candor. Not only did he challenge the old, established way of doing things, but he scared the people who were comfortable hiding in the old system. Will the new structure work? Only time will tell. But as the old saying goes, "If you keep doing what you've always been doing, you will keep getting what you've always been getting." What we *can* tell you is that as of this publication, product development is booming at Elanco.

The other part of this story is that Scott Holmstrom is leading one of the four teams. He took a quantum leap in terms of upward mobility because of his passion, courage, and conviction. In recognizing this young PhD, the leadership team sent a signal to the rest of the organization that essentially said, "This is the kind of player we are looking for. Speak with heartfelt passion and stand on your convictions, and you will succeed in this company. This is the kind of behavior that will make us best in class!"

BOOM!*

Do you want to create a culture where the passion for innovation is bigger than the fear of making mistakes?

Go to **freibergs.com/boom** *and type the word* **Culture** *in the BOOM! box.*

Are you building a brand within your organization that stands out like Scott Holmstrom's, or do you reside in a sea of sameness? In their book *Funky Business*, Kjell Nordström and Jonas Ridderstråle suggest that we live in a "surplus society." Here's how they describe it: "The

'surplus society' has a surplus of similar companies, employing similar people, with similar educational backgrounds, coming up with similar ideas, producing similar things, with similar prices and similar quality." This begs the question:

What makes YOU unforgettable?

What makes you stand out in the eyes of your coworkers, your boss, your customers? You become unforgettable when you leverage your unique gifts, perspectives, and voice to make a difference. Of course, this assumes that you have the courage to risk; to step through the door of uncertainty to seize an opportunity. Tom Peters asks, "How many of your top strategic initiatives would score an eight or higher on the 'game-changer' scale?" Great question. Think iPod, iTunes, and iPhone (Apple). Think digital video recorders (TiVo). Think point-to-point airlines (Southwest). Think 24/7 news (CNN). Think reality TV (*American Idol*). Think DVDs by mail (Netflix). You get the point.

Step into the Breach

Stepping into the breach is about stepping into a moment in time that you recognize is filled with an opportunity to make a difference. It is the courageous act of facing your fear and moving into what is in front of you instead of wishing you were somewhere else. In his book *Seizing Your Divine Moment*, Erwin Raphael McManus says, "Within a moment there is monumental potential. That's the mystery of a moment. It is small enough to ignore and big enough to change your life forever" (18). Your life is the sum total of what you did with the moments you had. We create our lives and our legacies in the moment. On the same page McManus says, "Each moment's personal, historic, and eternal value is directly related to the choices we make within it." Sound familiar?

Lamenting the past, living in the "good old days," or worrying about the future robs you from living in the moment. Have you ever missed a Scott Holmstrom moment—a moment you could never regain—in which you knew you could make a difference but failed to because you were either living in the past or worrying about the future? Unfortunately, moments don't often present themselves when it's convenient for us. Have you ever loaded up your calendar with trivial or mundane activities that seem important, only to miss a moment of tremendous significance? It hurts us to say this, but we've done it with our children on countless occasions.

We all miss appointments with destiny, disguised as ordinary moments. Yet players tend to be more conscious of the potential power of a moment. They give themselves the freedom to step into the moment, sensing that something is there but not knowing what they will encounter on the other side. Their radar detectors for defining a divine moment are more finely tuned simply because they look for these kinds of opportunities.

We talked with Mike Snyder, the former CEO of Red Robin International, a chain of family restaurants that serves as many types of exotic hamburgers as you can imagine. Mike told us about a general manager in one of Red Robin's restaurants who had decorated his store during the holiday season. In the hustle and bustle of greeting guests, the manager noticed three little boys who were admiring the store's Christmas tree. He knelt down on one knee in front of the children and asked them if they liked the Christmas tree.

The children were very polite and expressed an obvious excitement about the tree. When the restaurant manager asked, "Well, what does your tree at home look like?" everyone became uncomfortably silent, until finally the oldest boy looked up with embarrassment and said, "Well, we don't have one. Our daddy couldn't afford to buy a tree this year."

Without missing a beat, the store manager grabbed a couple of servers and said, "Hey, guys, you want to do something cool? Follow me." The team packaged up the tree—ornaments and all—took it out, and tied it down on top of this family's car. Once the father realized what had happened, he went back into the restaurant, found the store manager, and said, "You have no idea what you have just done to make this a special Christmas for my children."

Unbridled acts of service like this have become legendary at Red Robin International. Think of the employees and coworkers who witnessed the generosity of this restaurant manager who stepped into a moment and made history for that family. BOOM—one little act sends a ripple effect through the restaurant that says, "This is what we're about; this is the reality we're trying to create; this is the culture we're trying to build." People witness it, they're touched by it, and then they go out and try to re-create it. And when you get a handful of employees within a restaurant who try to create that kind of reality, you also create a spirit of service that defines the persona of your business.

Do you remember exactly where you were midmorning on September 11, 2001? In Dallas the key officers of Southwest Airlines gathered in the War Room at the company's General Offices. Intent on doing everything they could to ensure their employees and customers were safe, the executive team sprang into action. Greg Wells, vice president, Safety, Security and Flight Dispatch, began counting down airplanes for the executive team as the planes landed safely. It got very stressful, because Wells and his team got down to one airplane, and they didn't know where it was.

It's midmorning on 9/11, and you can't find an airplane—what are you thinking? Jim Wimberly, Southwest's former executive vice president and chief of operations, captured the intensity of the drama: "Greg Wells looked at me, and I will never forget it. I remember what he had on. I can remember exactly where he was standing. I remember that look in his eye when he said, 'We're missing one airplane.' I remember walking into the kitchen area next to the boardroom and I said one of those quick prayers: 'God help us all!'"

Fortunately, the plane had diverted to Grand Rapids, Michigan. While there was an immense sense of relief that every airplane was accounted for, the people of Southwest Airlines knew the country's nightmare had just begun. They were extremely grateful, but this was not a time to celebrate. The pilot in charge of the diverted flight, Captain Terry Taylor, said, "We landed at Grand Rapids. It's a fairly small airport and there were about forty airplanes on the tarmac. It was pure chaos." Southwest didn't have a station in Grand Rapids. This meant there were no Southwest ground crews to take care of the aircraft and, more important, the company's diverted customers.

A ground crew member from another airline came up to the pilot's window and said, "It's going to be three to four hours before we can take your passengers off this plane." At that point Captain Taylor looked out the cockpit window and saw a belt loader that wasn't being used. He said, "Could you guys at least get that belt loader up to our front door?" The operations crew brought the belt loader to the door, the flight attendants carefully escorted all 137 passengers down the belt loader, and within fifteen minutes every customer was off the plane. What this pilot did next was bold and courageous.

Captain Taylor then asked for help from several rental car compa-

BOOM!

nies to shuttle the passengers to the Amtrak station. Taylor took out a credit card and swiped it to buy train tickets for each one of the customers. Within twenty hours of landing, every one of Southwest's customers was taken care of and on their way home. No matter where you were and no matter what you were doing that horrific day, we all share one thing in common. We wanted to be close to our loved ones. By stepping into the breach and seizing a divine moment, Captain Terry Taylor made that possible for his customers.

Kathy Stahl, Director of Customer Service, Advocate Christ Medical Center from Christ Advocate Hospital in Oak Lawn, Illinois, told us about an elderly woman with acute nonlymphocyte leukemia (terminal cancer) who only had weeks to live. The woman was going through a Doppler study of her leg after developing severe pain. When she showed up at radiology with her pregnant daughter, the technician, Jennifer Hogan, overheard the daughter say, "My mother's one hope is that she will live long enough to see her granddaughter." So the tech said to the patient's daughter, "Would your mom like to see the baby today?" and took the daughter in for an ultrasound. The mother passed away four days later. The daughter, said, "It gives me great peace to know that although they never met, my mom was able to see her granddaughter at least once before she died." What Jennifer Hogan did had eternal significance. She recognized the historic potential in the moment, stepped into the breach, and owned the customer's experience.

Now, could the Red Robin manager do anything about the fact that three little boys came from a family with low income? No. Could Captain Taylor do anything about the fact that Al-Qaeda attacked the United States and that the tarmac in Grand Rapids was a parking lot? No. Could Jennifer Hogan control the fact that her patient had terminal cancer? No. But in each case the MVP involved—ordinary people like you and me—recognized the historic potential in the moment, stepped into the breach, and turned a hopeless situation into something miraculous and unforgettable.

Many of the people with whom you work are sleeping on the job. Refuse to join the sleepover and wake up! All you have is *now*, that place where the past intersects with the future. *Now* is here, but only for a moment. If you want your life and work to matter, then seize this moment in time—for it will be gone in a flash.

Step into the Adventure!

The overwhelming sense of boredom and disengagement that character-izes most organizations today can be explained, in part, by a lack of adventure. There is just not a lot to get excited about. If you are bored, if work is mundane, and you feel like a dead person working, ask yourself, *Have I risked enough?* If you are bored, maybe it's because you've never really "gotten in over your head" or given yourself permission to live dan-gerously. We are absolutely convinced that you were intended for a life of adventure. For what reason have you been given your gifts and talents and dreams if not for an adventure?

Unfortunately, many of us have chosen to surrender the adventure. We prefer the mild, bland, and predictable over the hot, spicy, and uncer-tain. Have you ever heard that voice in your head that calls you out of boredom and into the adventure? You know the one. It tempts you to say, "Dish it up, baby! And don't be stingy with the chili peppers." Fear keeps you from following it, because adventures by definition are dangerous. They are full of uncertainty. Adventures require tremendous flexibility and a willingness to "move out" on a moment's notice. This is what made the Red Robin manager's gesture so unforgettable; he not only seized the moment, but he turned the evening into an adventure for his employees as well as the family who received the unexpected Christmas tree.

Playing it safe—ignoring this voice—will keep you out of harm's way. If you are reluctant to take risks, you will probably never die on Mount Everest or in the shark-infested waters off Australia. You will probably not upset your boss for blowing $100,000 on a failed project or make your coworkers uncomfortable for revealing the thousand-pound elephant in the room. But you will miss the adventure.

Are you tired of trading courage, freedom, and autonomy for safety, control, and dependence?

As Garth Brooks sings in his song "Standing Outside the Fire," many of us like to stay close enough to the fire to stay warm, but we are afraid to jump in; we're afraid of getting burned. What we often fail to recognize is that we can also be incandescently transformed, like the glow of a log when it reaches a certain temperature. If we are honest, most of us are disappointed with and dissatisfied by our lukewarm commitments. We've successfully mitigated risk in our lives only to end up suffocating in a cocoon of solitary confinement. Deep within we yearn to throw caution to the wind, step out, and do something special with our lives. We're tired of trading courage, freedom, and autonomy for safety, control, and dependence.

Elisângela Silva Dos Santos from Brazil, a young woman who works for McDonald's, didn't trade—she threw caution to the wind. When Elisângela first applied for a crew-person job back in May 2005 in São Paulo, a friend introduced her to the hiring manager and added, "Ah, and she can sing too!" So naturally the manager asked her to sing. Hired! From that point on, every day before the restaurant opened, Elisângela would sing something for the entire crew.

To celebrate its fiftieth anniversary in 2005, McDonald's created its very own pop star contest—think American Idol—to recognize the most talented singers under the Golden Arches and reward their "I'm lovin' it" spirit. The first-ever global singing contest, called the Voice of McDonald's, was promoted to its 1.6 million employees. With over twenty-five hundred entries from around the world, McDonald's narrowed the entrants to three who would compete for the grand prize of ten thousand dollars by singing in front of more than fifteen thousand screaming and cheering convention attendees. What an opportunity!

Well, it's really only an opportunity if you are willing to take a risk, step into the adventure, and put yourself out there. And quite the risk it was for eighteen-year-old Elisângela, the oldest in a family of three girls all living in a very unsafe, low-income area of São Paulo. She had never been outside of her community and never been formally trained to sing. She actually learned to sing in church.

The thought of winning ten thousand dollars was extremely attractive, but it came with some pretty big challenges. Leaving home, going to a foreign country without knowing the language, competing with other formally trained singers, performing before thousands, and learning to sing nongospel songs was all pretty daunting to this young crew person. Yet Elisângela is a player; when fear felt bigger than opportunity, she stepped out in faith, stepped into the flame, and joined the adventure.

To leave Brazil and enter the United States, Elisângela needed a visa. When she arrived at the consulate to request it, she was denied. The authorities mocked her: "You need a visa to get to a singing contest in Orlando?" The officers thought it was a joke. For a moment she was crushed, an opportunity lost. Then, as she was leaving, another officer asked her to sing to see if she was "for real." The visa was approved! With the proper documentation in hand, Elisângela was on her way to the United States, by herself, to meet people she didn't know. Scary? Yes, but that's the nature of an adventure.

Jackie was a speaker at the World Convention and witnessed Elisângela's big debut. Even though the lyrics were Portuguese, and Jackie couldn't understand a word, when Elisângela opened her mouth, the experience was breathtaking! Apparently the judges thought so as well, because she won! Elisângela pushed through her fear, and now she is touring the world as the "voice of McDonald's." Elisângela was *not* content to "stand outside the fire" and play it safe. Instead she chose to live dangerously, to step into the unknown. The adventure has changed her life — not to mention the lives of her family and crew members. Here is what she said:

"My life has changed A LOT. First, it [winning the contest] has allowed me to fulfill a dream: to buy my family a house and move away from the slums. I've always wanted to help my family. Second, I can expand my ministry in church—I'm now being called to sing at bigger churches and communities. And finally, my whole professional life has changed. McDonald's is investing in my musical career and my development. I'm taking English and Spanish classes, I'm taking music classes, and I'm probably going to complete high school."

Imagine the opportunity Elisângela would have missed and the ambassador McDonald's wouldn't have if, when coaxed by her coworkers to try out for the competition, she had said, "It's too risky; it's too scary." Elisângela isn't alive and engaged today because she is the "voice of McDonald's"; she is the "voice of McDonald's" because she is alive, engaged, and willing to risk. She chose to be a player and *live* her life, when it could've been safer to *watch* the competition unfold from the safety of Brazil.

At McDonald's we provide opportunities for every employee's personal development. Voice of McDonald's was just such an opportunity, and Elisângela Silva Dos Santos embraced the moment. She also knew it would involve some intelligent risk-taking. Overcoming the obstacles of language, travel and performing before 15,000 McDonald's convention attendees, Elisângela sang her way to both financial and emotional life-changing rewards.

Rich Floersch
Executive Vice President,
Worldwide Human Resource, McDonald's Corporation

While Elisângela's story is inspiring, it would be a mistake to simply leave it at that—another entertaining example of a life well lived. It would be a blunder to live vicariously through Elisângela's life or the lives of others like her. You were not created to watch from the sidelines or the back of the theater.

What are your gifts? How deeply have you pushed your dreams and desires away from the daily grind of work? There is an adventure with your name on it, waiting for you to step in and assume your role. It will take you to places you've never been, places that will give you an opportunity to accomplish things you never dreamed are possible. If you step into it, you will most assuredly get in touch with some of your deepest fears. You will also get in touch with what really makes you come alive. What hangs in the balance is the quality of your life.

Your life is now; what are you waiting for?

Step Through Your Fear!

It's not the absence of fear that makes players successful; it is their ability to step through fear that makes the difference. No one is exempt from fear; it is deeply rooted in the human condition. Fear deadens our spirits and draws us into smaller lives. In fear we hesitate, procrastinate, ration-

Fear always confronts us with a choice.

alize, make excuses, and ultimately end up living smaller, less-fulfilling lives. Yet fear always confronts us with a choice, and how we handle it is *our* choice. We can do the thing we fear, or we can give in to it by not taking the risk. If we choose to face it and step through it, fear loses its stronghold. If we repress or run from fear, it gains strength and enslaves us. Each time we give in to fear, it weakens our courage.

> THERE IS AN ADVENTURE WITH YOUR NAME ON IT, WAITING FOR YOU TO STEP IN AND ASSUME YOUR ROLE.

Don Greene, a former Green Beret and member of the U.S. Army's Special Forces, said in his book *Fight Your Fear and Win*:

> If you are caught in an ambush in the jungle, fear will make you take note of where the fire is coming from and then turn and run like hell. It's a powerful instinct, but it's one that will get you shot in the back. As commandos we were taught, through repetition, how to face the fire and advance. Only by facing the source of fear and bearing down on it did we learn how to live to see another day. (91)

In the movie *Days of Thunder*, Robert Duvall plays the NASCAR pit crew chief, Harry Hogge, who does his best to mentor and periodically rein in his cocky young driver, Cole Trickle, played by Tom Cruise. At one point in the movie, Trickle comes up on a high-speed crash in a big race, and all he can see is a cloud of smoke in front of him. He has no idea what is on the other side of the smoke—cars and debris or clear track. Hogge, who can see from the pits that there is clear track, gets on the radio and tells Trickle to accelerate through the smoke. Trickle had entered the race with his confidence severely shaken. Now he had a choice—trust Hogge's information and his own skills, or become paralyzed by his fear of broadsiding another driver at maximum velocity. Trickle downshifts, steps on the gas, and blasts through the smoke, finding clear track on the other side. The burden of fear gives way to the power of freedom, and Trickle is on his way to another victory.

Is fear holding you back from taking a risk?

Go to **freibergs.com/boom** *and type the word* **Stuck** *in the BOOM! box for some more thoughts that could inspire you to step through fear.*

Like a cloud of smoke disabling us from seeing what's on the other side, fear can paralyze us. There is an interesting dichotomy illustrated in *Days of Thunder*. Courage is most needed *not* when the going is easy and the track is clear, but rather when things are extremely difficult or scary. Yet when things *are* really scary, fear makes courage more difficult to access. This is true in business as well. When the business is challenged and you are faced with a significant risk to get it back on track, fear is ignited, threatening to hold you back. This usually happens at the very point when courage is most needed to move you forward. When business is thriving and you are operating at the pinnacle of success, courage dominates. This usually happens when a little bit of healthy fear could keep you humble and hungry. In either case it just makes sense to learn how to deal with fear constructively.

In this book we've challenged you to exercise your freedom by choosing to dismantle your reverence for titles and authority; to take the initiative and lead instead of waiting for direction from above; to jettison tribalism by reaching across functional boundaries instead of building silos to protect yourself and your turf; to choose service over self-interest; to honor your responsibilities as fervently as you fight for your rights; to focus forward on what you *can* do versus looking backward and complaining about what you *can't* do; to forgive and move on when you've been hurt; to engage in work that matters, even if it means finding a new job or reframing your current one; and to stand up and speak the truth, regardless of who is in the room. Essentially, we've challenged you to be accountable for your life at work. Truth be told, this is a heroic charge. If these things frighten you, join the crowd. If they don't, are you all that in touch with reality? Stepping through fear requires a gutsy, visceral decision of the will.

In these seven choices we've also challenged you to face a fundamental truth about your existence: you are free. Embracing this truth means acknowledging the irrefutable fact that you can choose to live out of fear or courage no matter what circumstances you encounter in life. To believe otherwise is to be unwilling to admit that you are where you are in life because of the choices you made. The beauty is, when you choose to exercise courage in the face of fear, your courage muscle grows.

Courage takes practice. Practice comes from putting yourself in challenging situations that activate fear. That is, in order to exercise courage, you must be afraid. Like snake charmers who inoculate themselves—a little bit at a time—from the deadly effects of poison, courageous people develop self-confidence by taking risks, a little at a time. When speaking up here, taking on a new assignment there, and showing up in life more audaciously forces you to risk embarrassment, be afraid, and act anyway. Put yourself in enough of these challenging or dangerous situations, and the strength of your character—through winning, losing, and recovering—will grow over time. Only by coming directly into contact with fear over and over again, not by escaping it, will you learn to step through it.

Senator John McCain said, "Fear is the opportunity for courage, not proof of cowardice." When was the last time you really challenged yourself, where you went on a hunting trip in search of something that made you nervous or uncomfortable? If you never learn to step through fear, you will never be able to determine how much capacity you have and what you can do. Unless you test the limits of what you can achieve by facing fear, you'll never really know where your boundaries are. When we step through fear—BOOM—we are changed, irrevocably stretched into people we didn't know we could be.

> If you never had to stand up to something, to get up, to be knocked down, to get up again, life can walk over you wearing football cleats. But each time you get up, you're bigger, taller, finer, and more beautiful, more kind, more understanding, more loving. Each time you get up, you're more inclusive. More people can stand under your umbrella. (Maya Angelou, as cited in Katherine Martin, *Those Who Dare: Real People, Real Courage and What We Learn from Them* [Novato, California: New World Library, 2004], 212.)

So, what does it look like to step through fear and not let it control or consume you? There are no quick-fix, banish-it-forever formulas, but here are six powerful—but by no means easy—approaches that work:

1. Choose to accept your heritage. As we said earlier, you have been created in the image of God, who is fearless, sovereign, and omnipotent. You can choose to live in this heritage or you can choose to ignore or deny it. Will fear often confront you? Is it natural to feel scared? Yes. But, you don't have to live in fear, because that is not how you were created. Fear is like swallowing a foreign object. It gets inside of you, but it is *not* a part of you. Fear and anxiety do not belong to you. What *does* belong to you and what *is* a part of your heritage is freedom. Since you can't experience the freedom that is rightfully yours and feel fear at the same time, what do you do? Claim the resources that God has given you to step through fear and get moving—*you were designed to choose*!

2. **Find the bigger YES.** Make your passion bigger than your fears. It is a lot easier to say no to anything, especially fear, when you have a bigger YES to live for. When you are seized by the power of your deep-seated belief in an idea or outraged by a wrong you want to make right, you are empowered with the courage to risk. Few enemies, including fear, can stand in your way.

> WHEN WE FIGHT FOR WHAT WE BELIEVE IS TRUE, THE PILOT LIGHT OF PASSION IS LIT, A SENSE OF DUTY AND HONOR FLOW, AND THE FLAMES OF COURAGE ARE UNLEASHED.

The French mountain village of Le Chambon-sur-Lignon is famous for villagers who risked their lives during World War II to house Jewish refugees, many of whom were children, for more than four years. Their courage came from a bigger YES. Being drawn to a cause that had great significance unleashed a courageous spirit that enabled the Chambonnais to step through fear and into the eye of the hurricane. The Nazis could've leveled their village in a heartbeat. But the villagers' passion for saving the lives of innocent children was bigger than their fear of being exposed.

Stepping through fear is about looking beyond the danger you face to the significance of the outcome you could achieve. Is it weighty? Is it right? Will it make a difference? If the answer is YES, then go for it!

3. **Let truth strengthen your resolve.** What the villagers of Le Chambon-sur-Lignon had in common was a sense of the truth, of what's right. Think about Red Robin's restaurant manager and Southwest

Airline's Captain Taylor. What did they have in common? A deep-seated conviction about the "rightness" of what they were doing. Truth has the power to obliterate fear. When truth is on your side, you develop the confidence to take a direct path straight through fear.

Truth is about selling products that truly are world-class and making a difference in people's lives. Truth is about building these products in a way that doesn't objectify or dehumanize people in other countries by taking unfair advantage of them. Truth is about freeing incredibly smart people from really dumb processes that limit their potential and demoralize them. Truth is about speaking out against substandards that jeopardize the future of the organization. When we fight for what we believe is true, when we stand for what we believe is right, the pilot light of passion is lit, a sense of duty and honor flow, and the flames of courage and resolve are unleashed.

4. Take charge of your thoughts. Fear can be activated so quickly that it hits us before we even know it. In one sense fear can be a gift, a split-second survival tool designed to save our lives. Like the red lights on the dashboard of your car, fear signals impending danger. It keeps us—most of us—from jumping off tall buildings, driving down icy mountain roads too fast, and petting poisonous snakes. But fear is also irrational; it short-circuits common sense and our ability to think logically. Fear prevents us from seeing any possibilities or forming any explanations other than the ones with which we are immediately confronted. Fear robs us of life.

Taking charge of your thoughts is about stepping back and buying yourself time to question your automatic fear response *before* fear is fully activated. It's about forcing yourself to face the facts *before* fear gets out of control. Fear happens naturally, but your ability to pause long enough to think through your response to fear is not natural. That is why you must learn to argue with yourself. Let's say something bad happens that triggers a fear response in you. For example, you take an unpopular or

BOOM!

politically incorrect position in a meeting, and your boss reacts negatively. Your company outsources a major piece of work to India, leaving your job in jeopardy. You are offered a huge promotion, but it means moving overseas. Here are a few questions that will help you take charge of your thoughts and step through fear:

- *What am I telling myself about this event? What do I fear?* Sometimes the best way to tackle fear is to call it into the light. Where did this fear come from? What function does it serve? Simply exposing it can dismantle it and dilute its power. You can't step through fear if you don't know or aren't willing to admit that it exists.

- *Is it really true? Is everything I believe about this situation accurate? How much valid evidence is there to support what I fear?* Fear frequently ignores the facts. It's not always based on reality but rather our perceptions of reality. Just because you believe it doesn't necessarily make it true. Think about it— if someone else said some of the things to you that you say to yourself, you would never put up with it. So why take it from yourself?

- *What are the alternative ways to explain or interpret the cause of my fear?* It's easy to conjure up more than one cause to a bad event. Choosing the most catastrophic explanation triggers fear. Also, there are usually many possible outcomes or consequences to a bad event. Again, immediately going to "worst-case scenario" activates our fear response. If there *is* more than one way to explain an event, find out which one is most reasonable and least catastrophic. Then go with that explanation rather than jumping to an immediate conclusion. For example, if your boss doesn't respond enthusiastically to your proposal, is it because

A. you have a terrible idea;

B. you have a great idea, but you didn't do enough homework to support it; or

C. your boss had a very stressful week and didn't have time to thoroughly read it?

All are plausible explanations, but having a terrible idea is more catastrophic to you than your boss not finding the time to consider the proposal carefully.

- ***What do I really want from this situation?*** This is where you essentially ask yourself, "How bad do I want it? Is my passion for making the organization better bigger than my fear of challenging an outdated way of doing things? Is my fervor for creating a great working relationship with my coworker greater than my fear of seeking forgiveness for saying something stupid? Is my passion for being alive and fully engaged at work weightier than my fear of taking a new job?"

- ***Based on what I want to happen, what can I control? What can't I control?*** Fear is essentially about feeling out of control. The future is filled with many uncertainties and many unknowns; that's why it scares people. The more you focus on the things you can influence, the more control and less fear you will have.

- ***What initial steps can I take to gain what I want?*** By simply taking action in a positive direction, you can turn fear away, or at least reduce the intensity of its grip. As you will see later in this chapter, being on the move can be stimulating and motivating. Taking action also forces you to concentrate on what you are moving toward. This leaves less mental space for fear to occupy. By giving it mental space, we invite it to come in and set up camp. Conversely, if all the space you could give it is taken up with something else—focusing forward toward your dreams, goals, and desires—fear has no place to reside.

Developing the discipline to recognize your response to fear, and then pausing long enough to think rationally, to argue with yourself, is a key to stepping through fear.

5. *Jettison the voice of condemnation.* Inside all of us is what many have labeled the "inner critic." The inner critic is a voice that we think is ours, but it is not ours. Just as we believe in God, we also believe in a spirit of evil that wants to destroy the things that make you come alive. This enemy would like nothing more than for you to believe he doesn't exist. His assault often comes in the disguise of your own thoughts, your inner critic.

Whatever the words, the message is always the same—guilt, shame, criticism, hopelessness, and condemnation. This voice comes with a very different tone and a very different motive than the voice of constructive criticism that embraces accountability and seeks constant improvement. Its motive is to shut you down and hold you back, to throw a wet blanket over your aspirations, and to prevent you from taking action.

Anytime your thoughts show up in the form of condemnation, see it as a warning—see it as the bad wolf we exposed in Choice #4, and do not nourish it. Those thoughts are not your own; they come from an enemy that wants you to be a dead person working. You may choose to participate with and expand upon them by ruminating, but originally they were not your thoughts. Stepping through fear is about recognizing the voice of condemnation and not making agreements with it. This voice is crafty and persistent, so you have to be stern. Give it no time and no room to attach itself to you. That means you must call it out and speak to it with authority.

If it says, *Put this idea in front of the board or the senior executives and you will get nailed*, then respond, *No, I've done my homework. There are credible people within the organization who agree with my interpretation of the problem and the potential solution. I've built a solid, well-thought-out business case for what I'm proposing.*

If it says, *You're going to fail. You will look like an idiot,* think, *Yep, that's a possibility. But my greater failure would be acting like a coward and doing nothing when I thoroughly believe in this. I won't look like an idiot to those who understand that failure is a part of attempting great things.*

If it says, *You've made a lot of mistakes already,* recognize that, of course, change is a messy process. No one figures it out completely or implements it perfectly. That's part of the game. Just because you've hit a few speed bumps doesn't mean it's not the right thing to do.

If it says, *This could be the biggest embarrassment of your career,* respond, *Go away! It could also be a great success story. This isn't about me; it's about doing what is right for the organization. My worth as a person does not depend on my success or failure.*

If it says, *You're not good enough; you don't have what it takes. Others could do it better,* understand that, yes, you are good enough. But it doesn't matter. No one else is stepping up to the plate, and something needs to be done. So we are going to find out, because you're stepping into the breach.

You may not be able to control when an attack from your inner critic / the bad wolf is launched, but you can control how you will handle that attack. You can choose to destroy the judgments and criticisms that come your way by identifying them, immediately escorting them out of your mind, and focusing on the resources you *do* have to move toward your goals and engage in work that matters.

6. Expect no guarantees. Wouldn't it be nice if we could be guaranteed success or at least freedom from harm when undertaking a major risk? Unfortunately, we all know the world doesn't work that way. If you wait for a guarantee before stepping through fear, the only thing you will be guaranteed is missing a window of opportunity. Success demands that you stare down the possibility of failure and all of its consequences and "let 'er rip!"

Aspire to little and you will fail little. But that is not the way of players who make their marks in the world. Erik Weihenmayer said, "If you think you are going to do something big and exciting without fear and doubt, and without worrying that you're making the wrong decision about a hundred times a day, you're being unrealistic."

Weihenmayer, the first blind mountain climber to summit Mount Everest, didn't play it safe—because nothing worth doing is risk-free. There is no escape route from personal pain, suffering, and sacrifice. But with a big YES also comes big thrill—*and* the potential to make a big difference. With

THE MORE THINGS YOU TRY, THE MORE YOU WILL FAIL. IF FAILURE IS ESSENTIALLY REJECTION, THE SOLUTION TO THE PROBLEM IS EITHER TO QUIT TAKING RISKS OR TO REDEFINE WHAT IT MEANS TO FAIL.

a big YES there is a powerful, magnetic force that draws you through fear toward that thing you must do. The simple lesson is this: we don't get to live big, full, interesting lives—we don't get to be alive at work and make a difference—without risking something. To live without risk is to risk not living. To play it safe is to already have lost the game no matter what the score is, because you are leaving something on the table.

One of the best ways of finding the courage to step through fear is by conducting an audit of how you have done this successfully in the past. Here's another exercise for you to try. Look back over your life and your career. Identify five times when you were confronted with fear and stepped through it before taking a major risk. For each scenario ask yourself these questions:

- What made the situation/event/decision risky?

- What was the source of the fear?

- What was the tipping point or moment of truth when I decided to step through it?

- Where did my courage come from?

- What was the outcome?

Sometimes we forget that we've already created a legacy of stepping through fear. Or, if we haven't forgotten, we don't attach enough value to it. Knowing that you have stepped through fear in the past and made it out alive might be the single biggest motivator for doing it again. Quite frankly, we all have selective memories, and sometimes it is convenient to forget and give in to fear when we would rather escape responsibility. The audit could be the first stride toward stepping though fear and being accountable. By reminding yourself of past success, you don't easily let yourself off the hook in a current situation.

Another tool that could be helpful is this same exercise done from a different perspective. Identify five times when you were confronted with fear, caved in, and chose to avoid the risk. For each scenario ask yourself these questions:

- What was I afraid of?

- How do I feel about the way I handled fear?

- Am I proud of what I did?

- How would I handle the same situation again?

The point of this exercise is *not* to make you feel bad, but sometimes a deep sense of regret over the way we handled fear in the past motivates us to handle it differently in the future. We've both made choices when

BOOM!

confronted by fear, only to wish we could have "do-overs." Remembering these times might be just the incentive you need to step through fear.

Rethink Failure

The greatest need of human existence is to be loved and accepted. Is it any wonder, then, that the greatest fear we face is the fear of rejection? Since our work is a statement about who we are, a lot of our self-worth/significance is wrapped up in what we do and how we perform. Many people consider themselves a success or a failure depending on how the world accepts what they bring to it.

If the world rejects our work, we consider it a personal failure. Consequently, failure is often seen as personal rejection instead of an opportunity to do something a different way. If you offer up a wild-card idea in a meeting, and the group shoots it down, you could easily tell yourself, "I've just been rejected." If you take a well-thought-out risk that doesn't succeed, and it costs your company a lot of money, your interpretation of what it all means might be, "I'm not cut out for this. The rejection is too much to handle."

WE SIMPLY CANNOT HAVE THE VITALITY WE DESPERATELY LONG FOR AT WORK IF WE ARE UNWILLING TO FAIL.

Equating failure with personal rejection is very dangerous, because it sets you up for a lethal ride. Innovation and creativity require that you experiment and take risks. The more things you try, the more you will fail. If

The more things you try, the more you will fail.
Risk more, fail faster!

failure is essentially rejection, the solution to the problem is either to quit taking risks or to redefine what it means to fail. Avoiding the risk is certainly a lot easier and may offer temporary peace, but in the long run it will agitate you. At some point you have to wake up and admit that you quit—on yourself, your loved ones, and the people with whom you work.

Since we all aspire to greater things, quitting is not an option. We've already established that those who risk little, live little. We simply cannot have the vitality we desperately long for at work if we are unwilling to fail. Our organizations cannot succeed if we continue to insist on playing it safe.

The better strategy is to *rethink* failure. Let's be realistic: if you take us up on the challenges of this book, if you step into the breach, if you step into the adventure, and particularly if you step through fear, you *will* periodically find failure on the other side. Maybe that is not such a bad thing. We've been taught to fear failure, but maybe a critical link to risking more is to see failure as an essential ingredient to getting what we want and what our organizations need. We ask audiences all over the globe, "How many of you have rewarded someone for an intelligent or gutsy failure in the last six months?" Once in a while a hand will go up, but not very often. Yet failure has often been called "the back door to success."

Failure can permanently disable or strengthen us, depending on how we look at it. If we redefine failure as a prerequisite to greater things, perhaps we would embrace it more freely. For example:

- *Failure builds resilience.* As Maya Angelou believes, the more times you get knocked down and get back up, the stronger you become. Thick skin, inner strength, and the ability to bounce back are character strengths essential to people who step though fear.

- *Failure exposes blind spots.* We see the difference between the impact we *think* we have on people—customers, coworkers, bosses—and the *real* impact we have on them.

- *Failure broadens our perspective.* Sometimes failure forces us to see the world through the eyes of others. Failure often shows us where we went wrong, what we didn't consider, and who we didn't involve in making something happen.

- *Failure makes us humble.* It makes us more open to learning and the influence of others.

- *Failure promotes creativity.* When we fail, we become more resourceful; we learn how *not* to do something, which brings us closer to doing something else more successfully.

Max Planck, the German professor and father of quantum physics who won the Nobel Prize in Physics in 1918, said, "Looking back . . . over the long and labyrinthine path which finally led to the discovery [of quantum theory], I am vividly reminded of Goethe's saying that men will always be making mistakes as long as they are striving for something" (as cited in John W. Gardner, *Self-Renewal: The Individual and the Innovative Society* [New York: Norton, 1981], 15). The fact is, players fail more because they risk more. They give themselves the freedom to risk because they understand that failure is a stepping-stone to success. We are not only asking you to *rethink* failure, but we are also challenging you to embrace it as a positive force in your life, an absolute necessity.

> WE ARE NOT ONLY ASKING YOU TO RETHINK FAILURE, BUT WE ARE ALSO CHALLENGING YOU TO EMBRACE IT AS A POSITIVE FORCE IN YOUR LIFE, AN ABSOLUTE NECESSITY.

Ask Hank Aaron, Barry Bonds, Mark McGwire, and Sammy Sosa how many times they miss the ball (failure) relative to the number of home runs they hit. Can you imagine striking out 2,597 times in your career? That's Reggie Jackson. He also hit 563 home runs!

What Happens When We Fail to Rethink Failure?

Most organizations start down the road to stagnation when the fear of failure causes people to forfeit their dreams and their willingness to risk defeat. The longer the organization has been around, the more it has to lose—boldness and daring give way to caution. Open-mindedness, flexibility, and experimentation are strangled by rigidity and dogmatism. Creativity slumbers under the shadow of fear. People aren't willing to make mistakes. Ultimately, the organization's capacity to adapt is lost. In a competitive business environment, this is very dangerous. But let's remind ourselves: organizations are creations of our own choosing. They become this way because of the decisions *we* make.

The same thing happens to us as individuals. When we are young, we are restless, idealistic, and bulletproof. Our minds are open. We're willing to go for it. We'll try anything once. Then somewhere along the line, we surrender our youthfulness and spontaneity. By the time we reach middle age, we create an ever-expanding list in our heads of things we have no intention of trying again, because we remember the pain of trying them once and failing. As we become more staid and set in our ways, our capacity to learn and grow, to change and adapt, diminishes. The older we get, the smarter and more experienced we become at rationalizing our behavior, but behind all the justification for doing nothing, we secretly know that we are afraid. This fear of failure extracts a heavy price, because it prevents the kind of exploration that enables us to live bigger, richer, fuller lives.

Stop Getting Ready—Do Something Now!

In the late 1990s, Kevin took on a consulting assignment to work with a large firm based in Japan. A U.S. division of the firm had been faltering, and management just seemed to be stuck, paralyzed in the downward spiral. The president was removed, and headquarters in Japan had asked Dick Rosen, chairman and former CEO of AVX Corporation, to step in for a couple of months to help get the company back on track. Rosen is a stellar leader and a get-it-done kind of guy. The organization had suffered from what business writer Patrick Lencioni calls "death by meeting." Shortly after his arrival, in an off-site retreat, Rosen had seen enough. In a fit of frustration he stood up in the middle of an executive's planning presentation and barked, "Look, you've got to stop planning and do something!" Obviously thrown by the interruption, the executive looked back and said, "Do what?" Rosen yelled, "SOMETHING INSTEAD OF NOTHING!"

It was an instructive moment for Kevin, and we are sure it was an epiphany for the fifty executives in the room. Rosen's passion for execution and candor jolted the organization out of its slumber.

You cannot make a difference in neutral. The MVPs we've introduced you to in this book have many things in common; chief among them is DSN—their willingness to *do something now*. The difference between living life intentionally and watching life just happen is DSN. Not tomorrow, not next week or next month, but *now*. Quite frankly, your spouse, your children, your boss, your coworkers, and your customers don't care about what you *intend* to do. They care about what you *do*. No one can read your mind and see your intentions. At the end of the journey, what ultimately determines the quality of your life is what you do.

In August 1990, Richard Branson, the eccentric founder of the Virgin brand, was struggling to keep Virgin Atlantic alive. Iraq had just invaded Kuwait, and the news reported that 150,000 refugees had crossed into Jordan. Branson had become friends with King Hussein and Queen Noor of Jordan and called them to see how he could help. The queen said they could use blankets, because the desert was very hot during the day and very cold at night. The blankets could be used for shade during the day and to keep people warm after dark. When Branson asked how many blankets were needed, the queen said one hundred thousand. "A few young children have already died," she replied. "We've got only two or three days before hundreds start to die. It's urgent, Richard."

> YOUR SPOUSE, YOUR CHILDREN, YOUR BOSS, YOUR COWORKERS, AND YOUR CUSTOMERS DON'T CARE ABOUT WHAT YOU INTEND TO DO. THEY CARE ABOUT WHAT YOU DO.

Within two days Virgin Atlantic staff had loaded one of its 747s with forty thousand blankets, tons of rice, and medical supplies, and it was on its way to Jordan. Making the most of the trip, the plane also returned to London with British people who had been stranded in Jordan. Branson's initiative had a chain-reaction effect. Shortly after, British Airways followed suit with its own relief effort to Jordan.

A few days later, Branson was watching Saddam Hussein on television and learned that Saddam was using British hostages as a human shield. Branson was one of the few Westerners who had direct access to King Hussein of Jordan, and the king, wanting to remain neutral in the Gulf conflict, was one of the few people Saddam trusted. Branson came up with an idea and asked if the king would take a proposal to Saddam: perhaps Saddam would trade hostages for medical supplies. Branson ended up handwriting a personal letter to Saddam, asking him to release all foreigners trapped in Iraq in exchange for medical supplies.

King Hussein personally translated Branson's letter into Arabic, wrote his own cover letter to accompany it, and had it sent by special courier to Iraq. Two days later Saddam agreed to release sick hostages, women, and children with one catch: he wanted Branson and a dignitary to fly to Iraq and personally ask him on television. Branson got the former prime minister, Sir Edward Heath, to agree. With a war about to unfold, it was a courageous decision.

Even in lieu of the promise that they would have safe passage in and out of Iraq, many believed that Branson was foolish, if not crazy. Surely Saddam would take Heath and Branson hostage and impound the plane. This was scary for Branson on a personal level, but it also had a potential effect on the people of Virgin Atlantic. Given the risk, Virgin had no insurance on the plane. If Saddam *did* take it, Virgin Atlantic would be financially devastated.

There was a tremendous sigh of relief when the plane left Iraq with the hostages and both Heath and Branson on board. Mission accomplished! Every great adventure is filled with peril. In this case the risk was worth it. Look over the life and career of Richard Branson. Again and again you will see that DSN has been the key to his success and to his living life with passion.

As we said earlier, players are results oriented. They measure success by making things happen and getting things done. Our intent herein is not to burden you with a try-harder–do-more philosophy, but rather to lift the burden and create more freedom and aliveness in your life. We certainly hope the book has given you the insight and tools to do this. But we can assure you that the insight and tools on these pages have no intrinsic value. You *must* act on them. The land of intent is littered with "wannabes," "could bes," and "should've beens" who pondered, planned, and pontificated, but failed to act. They love the line, "Let me think about it." And they frequently get caught in the trap of planning to plan. Players, on the other hand, move—often with a sense of urgency—on things that matter.

Like everything we've talked about, DSN is a choice. Who feels like getting out of bed at 5:30 every morning to go work out? Who feels like calling the disappointed customer to get to the bottom of what went wrong? Who feels like digging in and changing the whole distribution channel because the existing market has matured? Waiting for the motivation to come *before* you act is a big mistake. Life, energy, passion, and motivation often follow action. Acting creates momentum, momentum creates energy, and energy stimulates further action. Get moving, and the creative juices begin to flow, potential partners cross your path, and —BOOM—exciting new opportunities present themselves. Stay put and you will inevitably feel stuck.

What Keeps Us from Acting?

Some of us don't act because, honestly, we are not in enough pain. You may have heard the story about the farmer sitting on his front porch with an old bloodhound that was moaning. A visitor came by to chat and noticed the hound groaning. The visitor asked the farmer, "What's wrong with the hound?"

The farmer responded, "He's sittin' on a nail." When the visitor asked why the dog didn't move, the farmer replied, "Because it doesn't hurt bad enough." We would rather live with the comfort of the status quo—however boring or dysfunctional it may be—and complain about it rather than do something risky and change. DSN is scary because it almost always disrupts your life.

Some of us don't act because we don't think we have enough information. Roy Spence, president of GSD&M, one of the most successful advertising agencies in the world, said, "We look for *dreamers* and *doers*, but no *inbetweeners*." If you have a propensity to study and overanalyze issues, you may be more right than everyone else. You might have the very best report loaded with unbelievable research and all the latest facts. You may be lauded for knowing more about the subject than anyone. Your proposal may be flawless. You may also be the last player to the table!

General George Patton said, "A good battle plan that you can act on today can be better than a perfect one tomorrow." Being right and being late won't help your organization achieve competitive advantage. What we are talking about here is the kind of preparation people hide behind because they are afraid to act. We're talking about making the cost-benefit analysis a way of life. "We need to study it further" often becomes an excuse for doing nothing. Waiting until you have all the answers is a deadly strategy, because in this information-exploding world, it will never happen. Knowledge isn't power until you DSN.

Some of us don't act because we are paralyzed by chaos and uncertainty. Many of us live in a fog that dominates our work lives. We lack clarity. When it comes to making decisions or capitalizing on opportunities, this lack of clarity often paralyzes us. Shoot, if the truth be known, we're all confused. Nobody knows exactly what he or she is doing all the time. And nobody knows everything he needs to know completely. As former Intel CEO Andy Grove put it, "None of us has a real understanding of where we are heading. But decisions don't wait for the picture to be clarified. So you take your shots and clean up the bad ones later."

When you're going 90 miles per hour with your hair on fire in conditions that change constantly, you won't always have a complete picture. If the answers were clear and the data definitive, it would be easy to draw conclusions, make decisions, and lead. If the windows of opportunity stayed open just a little bit longer, and the schedule wasn't so tight, you could plan a more thorough approach. If the landscape of business wasn't so complex and politically charged, you could navigate more accurately and freely. "If, if, if, if only . . ."

The world is full of people waiting for the chaos to clear—but it never happens. Just because you don't completely understand what's going on within your organization or in the market, that doesn't give you a license to take a seat on the sidelines. Make yourself valuable. Stop looking higher up the organizational chart for clarity and security. Don't wait for your boss or your boss's boss to step out of her office to slow everything down and explain your place in the crazy world of work. Don't play dumb, and never act like you don't know what needs to be done—most of the time you *do*. Rally the people you need, go get the information you want, and give yourself permission to act.

In the face of uncertainty, get involved, improvise, and DSN! If you make some mistakes along the way, use them as an opportunity to practice redefining failure, and move on. Keep going until you get it right. Show your boss and your coworkers that you are interested in doing something more than just staying busy. In the face of uncertainty, the world rewards action.

> THE PROBLEM FOR MOST OF US IS WE ARE MORE AFRAID OF FAILURE THAN WE ARE OF REGRET. TOO OFTEN, BY THE TIME WE WISE UP, IT'S TOO LATE.

We are more alive, hopeful, and engaged when we are in motion. Life comes from movement. That's why physicians want people up and moving after surgery. Movement stimulates the flow of blood; it facilitates healing. The same is true in organizations. This is why we are big fans of Richard Branson. He has built a $4 billion enterprise structured around two hundred small companies. With very little hierarchy and no centralized Virgin headquarters, Branson has created an organization characterized by perpetual motion. He rarely says no. People don't get stagnant because new ideas don't get lost; they get acted upon.

Action is contagious. When you act, you have the potential to stimulate action in others. This is what happened when British Airways took blankets into Jordan after watching Virgin do it. It's happened to many of us even at a more local level. You pull up to an intersection behind a car that is stalled. Embarrassed because he or she is holding up traffic, the driver doesn't quite know what to do. All of a sudden another driver pulls over, jumps out of the car, and begins to push the stalled car. Then another driver does the same thing. Pretty soon the car is out of the way and traffic is moving again. The action of one person primed the pump for others to join in.

Fear is challenged through action. One person with the courage to speak up in a meeting often gives several others the courage to do the same. Action has the potential to impassion others. The courageous step you take today might be a gift to someone who is inspired to take bold action tomorrow. People want leadership. You might be surprised at how many people would follow you if you would just lead the way and DSN.

Throw Deep!

Risking more and failing faster requires you to let go, to step out of your comfort zone. If you aren't prepared to let go of something comfortable, you'll never be able to move forward and grow because you will forever be under the control of the thing you can't give up. A child never expands her capacity to walk without letting go of the railing. A trapeze artist never experiences the joy of flying or learns to trust the net without letting go of the bar. And you will never experience the full weight of your potential to make a mark in this world until you are willing to face the fear that holds you in its grip. So, what would you do today if you knew you were good enough? What would you do if you weren't afraid of:

. . . being wrong?
. . . losing control?
. . . making a mistake?
. . . looking foolish?
. . . feeling rejected?
. . . being alone?

BOOM!

Studies show that when you ask elderly people what they would do differently if they had their lives to live over again, most will respond with descriptions of what they *didn't* do—risks they didn't take, words they never spoke, time they didn't spend.

The problem for most of us is we are more afraid of failure than we are of regret. Too often, by the time we wise up, it's too late. The next time you are tempted to "pull a punch" or play it safe, ask yourself these questions:

- *What am I risking by playing it safe?*

- *What do I stand to gain by taking this risk?*

- *What do I stand to lose by NOT taking this risk?*

- *What would I do today if I were going to be really brave?*

In the 1980s a sportswriter asked Kenny Stabler, the legendary left-handed quarterback for the Oakland Raiders, to comment on the meaning of novelist Jack London's famous credo. The reporter read,

> "I would rather be ashes than dust. I would rather that my spark should burn out in a brilliant blaze than it should be stifled by dry rot. I would rather be a superb meteor, every atom in me a magnificent glow, than a sleepy, permanent planet. For the proper function of a man is to live, not to exist. I shall not waste my days trying to prolong them. I shall use my time."

When the writer asked, "What does that mean to you, Kenny?" Stabler didn't hesitate. He said . . .

"THROW DEEP!"

Not bad advice for those who want to blow the doors off business-as-usual!

Your Choices Shape Your Life
and Your Life Is in Your Hands

INVITATION

Blow the Doors Off
Business-as-Usual

*"Your life is not a dress rehearsal.
Your life is now."*

Throughout these pages we have invited you to be a player, to step out of the crowd, to step off the sideline and onto the field. We've challenged you to stop pretending that you are in the game and actually get in the game. We've encouraged you to speak the truth and challenge the people, policies, and practices that jeopardize your organization's future. We've tried to convince you that leadership is a choice, not a title, and that doing nothing will lead you to failure more often than it will success. But you already know this. Like us, you can point to a number of times in your life when a window of opportunity to make a difference opened, you hesitated, you ignored the call, you failed to act, and then it closed. Had you stepped through fear and into the adventure, your life and the lives of others would look very different today. You can't do anything about the moments you've lost, but you *can* learn from them. You can let them inspire you and give you the courage to get up and do something now.

There is a revolution under way; it's a revolution of men and women who refuse to be victims and who choose to take charge of their lives at work—a revolution that will blow the doors off business-as-usual. Those of us involved in this revolution—from executives to the front line—are absolutely convinced that the culture and the success of the organization is the *will of the people* as much as it is the will of the CEO. We are also convinced that this is our moment—a moment when the world is ready to reach beyond the mediocrity of dead people working and grab hold of something new. On our watch we want to do something extraordinary with our gifts and talents. History will be the judge, but the script is up to us. We invite you to join this movement by embracing the seven choices presented in this book, the seven choices you *must* make if you are going to blow the doors off business-as-usual!

If you accept our call to arms and join this revolution, at least three things will happen: you *will* expand your influence, you *will* become a positive force for change, and you *will* live with fewer regrets. Now, you can say, "Revolution is a frighteningly strong word. Slaying dragons and storming castles isn't for the faint at heart." You can procrastinate and rationalize: "I'll do it tomorrow or next week." Or you can refuse to let the potential for failure hold you back. You can close this book and take a significant step toward making your mark in the world right *now* by

reading The Manifesto on the next page, signing it, making it your own, and then committing yourself to living it out loud!

Whichever way you decide to go, keep in mind: time is a tyrant. It takes no prisoners, and it never stands still. The moments of opportunity you miss at work and in life can never be regained. Your life is not a dress rehearsal. Your life is now. Time is ticking. Guess what? IT'S YOUR MOVE!

THE MANIFESTO

We Are Designed to Choose . . .

and Defined by Choice!

The freedom to choose may be the most powerful attribute and precious resource I have in my life.

It shapes who I become, the success I achieve, and my influence in the world. I am a product of my choices, not my conditions. Therefore, I have made following decisions:

CHOICE #1

In the game of life, there are players and there are those who shrink from their God-given abilities. Players charge onto the field with passion, energy, and a desire to win—sometimes they get their hands dirty, their faces sweaty, and their bodies bloody and bruised by giving their all to the game.

I Choose to Be a Player

CHOICE #2

Using "I don't have authority" is an excuse for doing nothing. Leadership is neither a title nor a position; it's a choice. I will lead where I am planted. My happiness, job satisfaction, sense of accomplishment, and ultimate success depend upon ME, not THEM. When I refuse to shift the responsibility for these things to someone else, I stop being a victim! I recognize that the REAL OPPONENT is out there among our competitors, not in here among my teammates. I will collaborate.

People can be foolish, stupid, abrasive, insensitive, self-centered, and dishonest, but I will not be held hostage by anger and resentment. I will forgive. By doing this . . .

I Choose to Be Accountable

CHOICE #3

The world is not here to make me happy. My happiness comes from using my gifts to serve the world. To give unselfishly is to gain immeasurably.

I Choose Service over Self-Interest

CHOICE #4

I can focus on what isn't working, why it can't be done, and who's to blame, or I can focus on what is working, how it can be done, and what I want to achieve. I can be part of the solution or part of the problem.

I will move from "Yeah, but . . ." to "Yes, and . . ." and "What if . . . ?"

I Choose to Focus Forward

CHOICE #5

My work is my signature—a statement about me; it determines my reputation.

I will make it a masterpiece. To know that my work counts is to know that I count. If I engage in work that makes me come alive, the world will beat a path to my door.

I Choose to Play to My Genius

CHOICE #6

No one is paying me today for what I did yesterday. When I stop bringing something of value to the game, the game is over. I am dedicated to results over rhetoric and red tape.

I Choose to Get It Done

CHOICE #7

Life without risk and adventure is a life not fully lived. I will never discover my true capabilities unless I explore the boundaries and test the limits of what I can achieve. How I handle fear is my choice. If I choose to face it and step through it, fear loses its stronghold, giving creativity and innovation a chance to flourish. If I repress or run from fear, it gains strength and enslaves me. Life is not a dress rehearsal.

I Choose to Risk More and Gain More

Albrecht, Karl. *The Only Thing That Matters: Bringing the Power of the Customer into the Center of Your Business.* New York: HarperBusiness, 1992.

Campolo, Tony. *Let Me Tell You a Story: Life Lessons from Unexpected Places and Unlikely People.* Nashville: Word Publishing, 2000.

Cross, Rob, and Andrew Parker. *The Hidden Power of Social Networks: Understanding How Work Really Gets Done in Organizations.* Boston: Harvard Business School Press, 2004.

Frankl, Victor. *Man's Search for Meaning.* Boston: Beacon Press, 2006.

Freiberg, Kevin and Jackie. *GUTS!: Companies That Blow the Doors Off Business-as-Usual.* New York: Currency, 2004.

———. *NUTS!: Southwest Airlines' Crazy Recipe for Business and Personal Success.* Austin: Bard Books, 1996.

Gates, Bill. *Business @ the Speed of Thought.* New York: Warner Books, 1999.

Greene, Don. *Fight Your Fear and Win.* New York: Broadway Books, 2001.

Hansel, Tim. *You Gotta Keep Dancing.* Illinois: D.C. Cook, 1985.

Lee, Harper. *To Kill a Mockingbird.* Philadelphia: Lippincott, 1960.

Locke, Christopher. *Cluetrain Manifesto: The End of Business as Usual.* Cambridge: Perseus Books, 2000.

Marine, Katherine. *Those Who Dare: Real People, Real Courage and What We Learn from Them.* Novato: New World Library, 2004.

McManus, Erwin Raphael. *Seizing Your Divine Moment.* Nashville: Thomas Nelson, 2002.

Peterson, Christopher, and Martin Seligman. *Character Strengths and Virtues.* Oxford: Oxford University Press, 2004.

Reeve, Christopher. *Nothing Is Impossible: Reflections on a New Life.* New York: Random House, 2002.

Reeve, Christopher. *Still Me.* New York: Ballantine, 1999.

Ridderstråle, Jonas, and Kjell Nordström. *Funky Business.* London: BookHouse Publishing, 2000.

Seligman Martin. *Authentic Happiness: Using the New Positive Psychology to Realize Your Potential for Lasting Fulfillment.* New York: The Free Press, 2002.

Vannoy, Steven. *The 10 Greatest Gifts I Give My Children.* New York: Fireside, 1994.

Warren, Rick. *The Purpose Driven Life.* Grand Rapids: Zondervan, 2002.

Williamson, Marianne. *A Return to Love.* New York: Harper Collins, 1992.

Wooden, John. *Wooden on Leadership.* New York: McGraw-Hill, 2005.

BIBLIOGRAPHY

INDEX

Drs. Kevin and Jackie Freiberg are on a mission to create corporate cultures where impassioned people wake up every day and come to work fully engaged, knowing they're going to be part of something special—places where people have the freedom to make a difference and change the world!

Among the busiest professional speakers on the circuit today, Kevin and Jackie bring their genuine, edgy, in-your-face, fun, and entertaining style to corporations and associations all over the world. They have a global practice working with organizations in Europe, Japan, India, Central and South America, as well as companies throughout the United States and Canada. Their firm, the San Diego Consulting Group, Inc. and its public speaking arm, is a premier resource for business leaders who are looking for ways to lead more effectively, differentiate more radically, and win more decisively—leaders who want to be on the forefront of a revolution driving the new economy.

The Freibergs have been interviewed by CBS's *60 Minutes* and appeared on CNBC and the CBS Morning News for their views on the critical link between happy employees and turned-on, passionate customers. Their writing has been featured in the *Wall Street Journal* and *USA Today*, and they have contributed to articles for *Business Week*, *Investor's Business Daily*, *The Washington Post*, *Leader to Leader*, and the *San Diego Business Journal*.

Kevin and Jackie live in San Diego. They have three children—Taylor-Grace, Aubrey, and Dylan. The Freibergs are doing their best to raise these kids in such a way that they will not have to be fixed as adults.

The Freiberg family is actively involved in a first-of-its-kind high school for homeless children, called the Monarch High School Project in downtown San Diego. They hope this school will be a model for other cities across the nation.

ABOUT THE AUTHORS

Writing is often a lonely pursuit. You start with a passion for saying something you deem vital, only to face the demons of doubt that cause you to periodically (OK, often) question the value of your contribution. And throughout the journey you steal time from the ones who love you most. So, that is where we start:

Thank you, Taylor-Grace, Aubrey, and Dylan.

You are absolutely God's gifts to us. Thank you for forgiving the time we have lost. Thank you for making us so proud of who you are becoming. We love you more than you could possibly imagine and promise to embrace these seven choices as we guide you through life's adventure.

Thank you, Team.

Coordinating the lives of two busy people who want to WOW their clients and "be there" for their kids in the midst of a writing year is no walk in the park. Travel arrangements, publishing deadlines, and countless administrative details make our wonderful team heroes. Wherever we are in the world, the feedback is always the same: "Your staff is terrific. They are a great team to work with!" Thank you for being such incredible ambassadors.

Trish Derho, Chief Freiberg Fanatic, celebrating her tenthth year with us, does an amazing job of building and managing client relationships. Trish is our rock star with a servant's heart. Jennifer DiCenzo, Mistress of Logistics, thank you for not only running our office but doing it (and everything else) with a "whatever it takes" mentality. In the midst of all our chaos, you both bring calm.

Paige Ryan, Chief Numbers Nerd, thank you for monitoring the cash flow, bringing order to the books, and having the smallest of details always available. We sleep at night because you don't!

Adam Richardson, our design aficionado and go-to guy for anything technical and everything creative. Adam is responsible for creating many of the images that make this book look and feel different. We value your skills and treasure your friendship.

Bob and Peg Eddy, our financial advisors. Thank you for your wise counsel and unwavering support—and for turning us on to the "good wolf / bad wolf" story. May the Good Wolf live strong!

Ken Blue is our chief spiritual strategist and one of the most gifted thinkers we know. Ken brings insight to every project and every relationship we engage in and he keeps all of us focused on what's truly important and what ultimately matters.

Thank you Kevin Small.

Kevin is a strategic genius who understands the business of writing and speaking and makes things happen. When it comes to marketing, positioning, and giving a project visibility, he is way ahead of his time. Kevin found this project a home with a publisher who not only got excited about the manuscript, but had the ability to look beyond one book and embrace our brand and our body of work as well.

Thank you to the extraordinary crew at Thomas Nelson.

Our publisher, Joel Miller, assembled an extremely talented team to make this project a reality. Joel, one of the greatest gifts you can give someone is to put your faith in their work. Thanks for believing in us—even when we pushed the envelope and broke the rules. Victor Oliver, acquisitions editor, saw the potential in this manuscript from the very beginning and shared his wisdom unselfishly. Vic's convictions are bold, and his passion for clarity is a gift to you, our readers! A huge thanks to Kristen Parrish, our senior editor and the queen of details; you quickly, patiently, insightfully, and diplomatically pored through the manuscript and made it far more polished. For that we are extremely grateful. And to Heather Skelton, associate editor, who cheerfully and ever so competently managed a myriad of details and changes in the layout of the book—particularly in the eleventh hour. The interior layout of the book was done by Debbie Eicholtz and Kay Meadows—thanks for upping up with us and for working so hard to get it done. After completing a manuscript, few things are more critical to authors than the design of a book jacket. Thank you Belinda Bass, packaging director, and Kristen Vasgaard, packaging manager, for listening to our ideas and creating a cover design that supports the central message of the book. Of course, producing a book is one thing; successfully bringing it to market is another. Thanks to the Nelson marketing team of Brian Mitchell, Dave Schroeder, Rachel Osteen, and Curt Harding for giving the book visibility and creating pull with the retailers. The whole crew at Nelson could not have been better to work with!

Thank you, Peter Economy and Dain Dunston.

Peter, thanks for making critical connections, writing with us, and hanging in there! Dain, thanks for some excellent stories, for helping us see the forest through the trees, and for making early drafts so much more readable.

Thank you Craig McCann, Guy Martin and Team Blueprints in South Africa.

Two of the most creative and energizing people we know, Craig and Guy came to us with an innovative follow-up process for helping companies and individuals measure and more fully embrace the choices conveyed in the book. These two guys BOOM! out loud!

Thank you, Levine Greenberg Literary Agency.

Jim Levine, thanks for bringing focus to the original proposal, smoothing over the rough edges, and connecting us to interested publishers.

You are well connected and responsible for the initial momentum behind this book.

Thank you to the people who have shaped our perspectives.

A huge thank-you to the intellectual giants whose lives and work have stimulated our thoughts and contributed to many of the ideas in this book: Herb Kelleher, Coach Wooden, the late Victor Frankl, Peter Block, Peter Koestenbaum, Seth Godin, Gary Hamel, John Eldredge, Erwin Raphael McManus, Ken Blue, Brennan Manning, Alex Pattakos, John Miller, Doug Hall, Marty Seligman, Tom Peters, John Gardner, and Tony Campolo. You all have inspired our lives!

Thanks to those of you who shared your stories with us.

There are many in the body of this text who have chosen well! You have shown us—through vivid, living, personal example—what it means to be fully alive at work, and you deserve the biggest kudos. We regret that we have not the space to thank each one of you individually. But rest assured, by the way you live your lives, you have challenged us to examine our own. By making your mark in the world, you have inspired us to risk more and fear less. Thank you for blessing us with the choices you've made!

Thank you to the Giver of life.

Words simply can't do justice to the gratitude we have for the God who created us in His image. He designed us to choose and desires that our choices will create a better world than the one we inherited. To follow Him is to LIVE—dangerously and fully alive. And what a ride it can be!

Two Best-Selling Authors

The Freibergs are enemies of the ordinary. They have a blatant disregard for conventional thinking and business-as-usual. Why? Because the world is not changed by those who are unwilling to take risks. Yet, most businesses are trapped in a sea of sameness. **Standing out** requires courage, imagination, ingenuity and the freedom to push the envelope. It also requires people who refuse to be victims and who choose to take charge of their lives at work—people who are willing to reach beyond the mediocrity of *Dead People Working*™ and do something extraordinary with their gifts and talents.

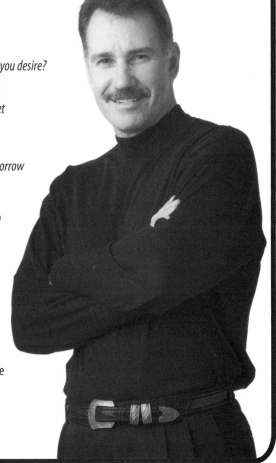

What makes you unforgettable?

Are you worthy of the customer loyalty you desire?

Is your culture an extraordinary magnet
for world-class talent?

If you or your company were gone tomorrow
would you be missed?

How many people in your organization
are working on things that matter?

Is your company changing faster than
the market? Are you changing faster
than your company?

With questions like these, Kevin or Jackie will inspire you to defy mediocrity, assume personal responsibility for the success of your organization and create a business that is **BOOMING!**

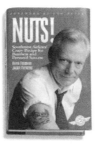

The BOOM! Formula

The choices outlined in BOOM! can have a dramatic impact on improving your organization—but only if they become part of your cultural DNA, only if they become a way of life and a way of doing business.

So the question becomes: *How do you inspire people in your organization to internalize these seven choices and then live them out loud every day?*

We think we have found a way.

We have partnered with BluePrints—a creative team from South Africa—to translate the BOOM! principles into a formula for success, a formula for defying mediocrity and Blowing the Doors Off Business-as-Usual.

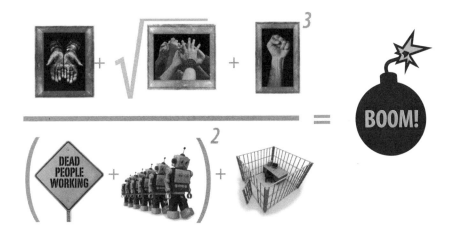

This unique formula—measured through an online survey—evaluates the degree to which the organization and individuals within the organization are living the BOOM principles at work.

A unique feedback mechanism that reminds people to consciously think about the choices they make at work, the BOOM! formula can be a powerful tool for culture change.

freibergs.com

To discover more about this remarkable tool, visit
www.freibergs.com/boomformula